THE CATH(
In Accordance wi

Volume 3A: Administrative Marriage Nullity
Process Acts

Reverend Peter O. Akpoghiran, J.C.D.

The Catholic Formulary in Accordance with the Code of Canon Law, Volume 3A: Administrative Marriage Nullity Process Acts

Copyright © 2020 by Reverend Peter O. Akpoghiran, J.C.D.
Publisher: Guadalupe Book Publishers, New Orleans, Louisiana
Email: guadalupebookpublishers@gmail.com

Printed and bound in the United States of America.

ISBN: 9781658622639

Nihil Obstat:	Reverend Vinh D. Luu, J.C.L.
	Judge
	Metropolitan Tribunal
	Archdiocese of New Orleans
	March 19, 2020,
	Solemnity of Saint Joseph, husband of the Blessed Virgin Mary
Imprimatur:	Most Reverend Gregory M. Aymond
	Archbishop of New Orleans, Louisiana
	March 25, 2020,
	Solemnity of the Annunciation of the Lord

The *Nihil Obstat* and *Imprimatur* are official declarations that a book or a pamphlet is free of doctrinal error. No implication is contained therein that those who have granted the *Nihil Obstat* and Imprimatur agree with the contents, opinions, or statements expressed.

Canons cited in this text are used with permission and taken from the Code of Canon Law Latin-English New English Edition, Washington, Canon Law Society of America, 2012 and from *Mitis Iudex Dominus Iesus, Libreria Editrice Vaticana*.

Some Canon Law Books by the Author:

1. Proofs in Marriage Nullity Process.
2. *Mitis Iudex*: Text and Commentary.
3. The Catholic Formulary in Accordance with the Code of Canon Law, Vol. 1A: Ecclesiastical Offices and Ministries Acts.
4. The Catholic Formulary in Accordance with the Code of Canon Law, Vol. 2A: Sacraments and Parish Administration Acts.
5. The Catholic Formulary in Accordance with the Code of Canon Law, Vol. 3A: Administrative Marriage Nullity Process Acts.
6. The Catholic Formulary in Accordance with the Code of Canon Law, Vol. 4A: Judicial Marriage Nullity Process Acts.
7. The Catholic Formulary in Accordance with the Code of Canon Law, Vol. 5A: Marriage Nullity Appeal Process Acts.
8. The Catholic Formulary in Accordance with the Code of Canon Law, Vol. 6A: Canonical Institutes and Societies Acts.
9. The Catholic Formulary in Accordance with the Code of Canon Law, Vol. 7A: Eremitical and Order of Virgins Acts.
10. The Catholic Formulary in Accordance with the Code of Canon Law, Vol. 8A: Penal Process Acts.
11. The Catholic Formulary in Accordance with the Code of Canon Law, Vol. 9A: Clerical Dispensations and Readmission Acts.
12. Canon Law of Evidence in Penal Cases: A Commentary on Canons 1526-1586 of the Code of Canon Law.
13. *Delicta Graviora* Manual, Second Edition, Volume 1: A Commentary on Articles 1-7 of the *Normae de Gravioribus Delictis Congregationi pro Doctrina Fidei Reservatis*.
14. *Delicta Graviora* Manual, Second Edition, Volume 2: A Commentary on Articles 8-20 of the *Normae de Gravioribus Delictis Congregationi pro Doctrina Fidei Reservatis*.
15. *Delicta Graviora* Manual, Second Edition, Volume 3: A Commentary on Articles 21-31 of the *Normae de Gravioribus Delictis Congregationi pro Doctrina Fidei Reservatis*.

ABBREVIATIONS

1. §   Paragraph
2. °   Number
3. art.   Article
4. artt.   Articles
5. *CIC/17*   1917 Code of Canon Law
6. *AAS*   *Acta Apostolicae Sedis*
7. c.   Canon
8. cc.   Canons
9. CC: Carbon Copy
10. Can.   Canon
11. Cann.   Canons
12. *CCEO*   *Codex of Canonum
             Ecclesiarum Orientalium*
13. CDF   Congregation for the
             Doctrine of the Faith
14. cf.   Confer
15. *CIC*   *Codex Iuris Canonici*
16. *DC*   *Dignitas connubii*
17. N.   Name
18. NABRE   New American Bible Revised
             Edition

TABLE OF CONTENT

SECTION 3:   HOW TO DETERMINE THE CORRECT
TYPE OF MARRIAGE NULLITY CASE........................... 218

FOREWORD

The Code of Canon Law and other canonical legislation serve to fulfill that renewal of the laws of the church, which was mandated by the Second Vatican Council and to order and organize the hierarchical and organic structure of the Church. Legislative texts also serve to order and organize the exercise of the functions divinely entrusted to the Church, especially that of sacred power and of the administration of the sacraments.

The revised code also allows for a reasonable amount of discretionary power and authority at the level of the particular church so that pastors and those entrusted with the care of souls should strike the happy medium between the legal observations of the law and the pastoral conditions and circumstances of each particular church. Thus, the code is imbued with both a legal and a pastoral character.

The revised code also defines and safeguards the rights and obligations of persons. It seems important that in the exercise of one's rights and obligations in the church and in the exercise of sacred power, certain ecclesiastical legislation should be set forth as public ecclesiastical documents. It is also equally important that a collection of samples of public ecclesiastical documents should be made available, even by means of a book to serve as a guide to those who would be putting into practical application the various legislations of the Church.

With a confident spirit I am pleased to present this edition of *The Catholic Formulary* by Father Peter O. Akpoghiran, J.C.D.

I am grateful to Father Peter Akpoghiran for his research and for presenting this material in a very understandable, practical, and helpful way. This book will be helpful to those who are in church ministry and to all who wish to grow in an understanding of Canon Law.

The Code of Canon Law and other ecclesiastical legislative texts demand that some acts be drawn up as public ecclesiastical documents. This demand has been met by the publication of this book. There is a plethora of sample documents in this book that most church officials will find useful in the exercise of their ministry. Those of us who exercise some form of leadership in the

Church will also find this book indispensable in the practical application of church laws and doctrines to real life situations, especially in tribunal ministry.

I endorse and approve this book and recommend it to all bishops, ordinaries, clerics, religious, and the laity for the faithful observance of their ecclesiastical ministry.

Most Reverend Gregory M. Aymond
Archbishop of New Orleans, Louisiana
September 14, 2019,
Feast of the Exaltation of the Holy Cross.

INTRODUCTION

On September 8, 2015, Pope Francis promulgated the *motu proprio, Mitis Iudex Dominus Iesus* which reformed canons 1671 to 1691 of the Code of Canon Law and the *motu proprio, Mitis et Misericors Iesus* which reformed canons 1357 to 1377 of the Code of Canons of the Eastern Churches pertaining to the declaration of the nullity of marriage. Both *motu proprii* took effect December 8, 2015. Given the new procedures for the declaration of marriage nullity, ordinaries, hierarchs, and Catholic tribunals across the world have had to revise and update both their process and documents for the declaration of marriage nullity.

This volume of *The Catholic Formulary* has been revised and updated pursuant to the promulgations of *Mitis Iudex* and *Mitis et Misericors* and in light of the re-arrangement of the other volumes of *The Catholic Formulary*. This volume contains the various causes pertaining to marriage dissolution and marriage nullity, which a first instance tribunal is competent to process. It also contains explanation of frequently used terms and frequently asked questions regarding the nullity and dissolution of marriages.

The citations of any of the canons between canons 1671 to 1691 of the *CIC* and between canons 1357 to 1377 of the *CCEO* refer to the revised canons of *Mitis Iudex* and *Mitis et Misericors* respectively. For example, when canon 1672 is cited in this book, it refers to the canon 1672 which has been promulgated by means of *Mitis Iudex*. The same applies to all the other canons promulgated by means of *Mitis Iudex* and *Mitis Iudex et Misericors*.

A later law abrogates, or derogates from, an earlier law if it states so expressly. (c. 20). "In a case of doubt, the revocation of a pre-existing law is not presumed, but later laws must be related to the earlier ones and, insofar as possible, must be harmonized with them."[1] Thus, with regards to the Instruction, *Dignitas connubii,* issued on January 25, 2005, by the Pontifical Council for Legislative Texts, the normative articles of *Dignitas connubii* which have not been revoked by *Mitis Iudex* remain in force. And some of these articles which still retain the force of law or *ius vigens* have been cited and referenced in this book. The articles of

---

[1] C. 21.

the Instruction *Dignitas connubii* that have been revoked by *Mitis Iudex* and *Mitis et Misericors* are articles 10 §1, 13, 22 §2, 24 §1, 30 §3, 43 §2, 46 §2, 7°-10°, 47 §2, 65, 69 §2, 118, 119, 126 §1, 127, 135 §1, 140, 1°-2°, 180, 202, 264-265 and some parts of articles 290 and 301 §1. All the other articles of *Dignitas connubii* "retain their force and must be observed outside of the legitimate use of the abbreviated process before the diocesan bishop."[2]

Therefore, the Instruction *Dignitas connubii* "continues to be in force, except for the articles of the aforementioned Instruction that explained canons of the former legislation, now modified and no longer present in the new canons, and also those articles that do not conform with the procedural rules attached to the *motu proprio*. In the interpretation of *Dignitas connubii*, one should moreover take into account the fundamental criteria of the reform."[3]

The Code of Canon Law and other ecclesiastical legislative texts are the primary sources of law in the Church. Canonical legislations demand the drawing up of certain acts as public ecclesiastical documents in the observance of the law. With particular reference to the documents required for the observance of the declaration of marriage nullity or the dissolution of marriage, it is hoped that the publication of this book will meet that demand also in order to fulfill the requirements of the law. There is a plethora of sample documents in this book which tribunal officials will find useful in the exercise of their ministry. Others who exercise some form of leadership in the Church will also find this book indispensable in the practical application of church laws and doctrines to real life situations.

This volume discusses the administrative matrimonial nullity process, and provides the requirements, procedures, and sample documents for each administrative process. In addition, the volumes of *The Catholic Formulary* have been re-arranged in order to preserve some of the volumes within certain sizes.

---

[2] William L. Daniel, "An Analysis of Pope Francis' 2015 Reform of the General Legislation Governing Causes of Nullity of Marriage," in *The Jurist* 75 (2015) p. 463.

[3] Frans Daneels, "A First Approach to the Reform of the Process for the Declaration of Nullity of Marriage, in *The Jurist* 76 (2016) p. 120.

Every effort has been made to ensure that the commentaries on the law and the sample documents provided in this book are in conformity the requirements of canon law. The author disclaims any loss or liability that may be incurred as a result of using this book. The Code of Canon Law and other legislative documents of the Church are the definitive sources of canonical legislations and for the drawing up of ecclesiastical documents. Use this book as a reference guide, a resource material, a handbook, a manual, a *vademecum* in drawing up the official document of yours.

In conclusion, my gratitude goes first of all to God not only for the publication of this book, but also for his many blessings, mercies, and graces in my life. Special thanks to Archbishop Gregory M. Aymond, Archbishop of New Orleans, Louisiana, USA, for his support. I am also grateful to Reverend Vinh D. Luu, J.C.L., Judge, Metropolitan Tribunal of New Orleans, for his review of this book.

Very Reverend Peter O. Akpoghiran, J.C.D.
Judicial Vicar and Chancellor
Archdiocese of New Orleans, Louisiana
March 19, 2020,
Solemnity of Saint Joseph,
Spouse of the Blessed Virgin Mary.

SECTION 1:   DECREES ESTABLISHING TRIBUNALS

CHAPTER 1: DECREE OF THE BISHOP ERECTING A DIOCE-SAN TRIBUNAL OF FIRST INSTANCE

1. "The bishop is to establish a diocesan tribunal for his diocese to handle cases of nullity of marriage without prejudice to the faculty of the same bishop to approach another nearby diocesan or interdiocesan tribunal."[1]
2. "In dioceses which lack their own tribunals, the bishop should take care that, as soon as possible, persons are formed who can zealously assist in setting up marriage tribunals, even by means of courses in well-established and continuous institutions sponsored by the diocese or in cooperation with groupings of dioceses and with the assistance of the Apostolic See."[2]
3. If a diocesan bishop has withdrawn from a diocesan or interdiocesan tribunal and is to establish his own diocesan tribunal, he is to issue a decree to that effect. The bishop, however, is to notify the Apostolic Signatura of his decision.
4. The following sample decree of the constitution of a diocesan tribunal of first instance has been provided by the Apostolic Tribunal of the Roman Rota.[3]

On the bishop's letterhead

DECREE OF CONSTITUTION OF THE TRIBUNAL OF FIRST INSANCE OF THE DIOCESE OF N. (*NAME OF THE DIOCESE*)

Prot. N. ....

I, N., (*name of the diocesan bishop*)

---

[1] C.1673 §2.

[2] Procedural Rules, art. 8 §1.

[3] Apostolic Tribunal of the Roman Rota, *Subsidium* for the Application of the M.p. *Mitis Iudex Dominus Iesus* (Vatican City, January 2016) pp. 59-60.

Bishop of the Arch/Diocese of N. (*name of the diocese*)

In fulfillment of the reform of the procedures for matrimonial nullity approved by Pope Francis in his *Motu proprio "Mitis Iudex"* of 15 August 2015, which has entirely substituted the procedure for the declaration of the nullity of marriage (cann. 1671-1691) provided by the Code of Canon Law of 1983, and has been established "to provide openly that the bishop himself, in the church over which he has been appointed shepherd and head, is by that very fact the judge of those faithful entrusted to his care," (M.p. *Mitis Iudex, preface,* III) and that "due to his duty as pastor, has the greatest care for catholic unity with Peter in faith and discipline" (M.p. *Mitis Iudex, preface,* IV);

Having considered that

- The preoccupation for the salvation of souls remains the ultimate purpose of the Church,
- The great number of the faithful who – while desiring to provide for their own consciences, too often are discouraged by the juridical structures of the Church because of physical and moral distances – demand that the Church "like a good mother, be near her children,"
- Can. 1673 §2 of CIC directs that: "The Bishop is to establish for his own diocese a diocesan tribunal for cases of nullity of marriages,"
- The constitution of the Diocesan Tribunal for the cases of nullity of marriage for our Arch/Diocese, up to this time entrusted to the Inter-diocesan Ecclesiastical Tribunal of N., guarantees better the 'speeding up of proceedings, called by the Synod of Bishops and established by Pope Francis, both in the more agile "ordinary process," as well as in the 'briefer process,"

BY THIS PRESENT DECREE
CONSTITUTE

The Arch/Diocesan Tribunal of N., with its seat in ... at the diocesan Chancery in ..., effective as of ... (*date*), which is to be considered competent for all legal effects for the adjudication and definition in first instance also of causes of marriage nullity which up to this time were entrusted to the Inter-diocesan Ecclesiastical Tribunal of N. and the Tribunal of Appeal of N.

Future challenges to the sentences issued by Our Tribunal are regulated by canons 1619-1640 and can be proposed either to the Metropolitan Tribunal of N. of second instance or to the Apostolic Tribunal of the Roman Rota, according to the norms of can. 1673 §6.

And therefore, following Article 8 §2 of the *Motu proprio "Mitis Iudex,"*

I WITHDRAW

Formally from the Inter-diocesan Ecclesiastical Tribunal of N., constituted according to the norms of canon 1423 CIC.

Furthermore, those matrimonial nullity cases whose competence, by virtue of can. 1672 of the *Motu proprio, "Mitis Iudex,"* belongs to our Tribunal, and which are now in course of adjudication in first instance before the Inter-diocesan Ecclesiastical Tribunal of N., are to be transferred to our Diocesan Tribunal, if by ... (*date*) the concordance of the doubt has not yet been formulated, according to the norms of law.

With this present Decree the mandate is given to all the competent Offices of our Curia to prepare the most of every aspect, also of economic and operational nature, so that our Arch/Diocesan Tribunal will adequately be operational from ... (*date*), with the purpose of adequately exercising its activity and responding to the needs of the faithful requiring the verification of the truth about the existence of the bond of their failed marriage.
Given on ..., at ....
Signed by the diocesan bishop and by the chancellor.

CHAPTER 2:   DECREE OF THE BISHOP GRANTING COMPE-
TENCE FOR MARRIAGE NULLITY CASES TO HIS DIOCE-
SAN TRIBUNAL

1. "The bishop is to establish a diocesan tribunal for his diocese to handle cases of nullity of marriage without prejudice to the faculty of the same bishop to approach another
nearby diocesan or interdiocesan tribunal."[4]
2. "If a diocesan tribunal already exists, but does not have
competence for cases of matrimonial nullity, the Bishop
will issue a decree by which he confers such competence
to his tribunal to deal with matrimonial cases."[5]
3. The following sample decree entrusting the competence
for marriage nullity cases to an already existing diocesan
tribunal has been provided by the Apostolic Tribunal of
the Roman Rota.[6]

DECREE ENTRUSTING THE COMPETENCE FOR MARRIAGE
NULLITY CASES TO TRIBUNAL OF THE DIOCESE OF N.
(NAME OF THE DIOCESE)

Prot. N. ....

I, N., (name of the diocesan bishop)

Bishop of the Arch/Diocese of N. (name of the diocese)

In fulfillment of the reform of the procedures for matrimonial
nullity approved by Pope Francis in his Motu proprio "Mitis Iudex"
of 15 August 2015, which has entirely substituted the procedure

---

[4] C. 1673 §2

[5] Apostolic Tribunal of the Roman Rota, Subsidium for the Application of the M.p. Mitis Iudex Dominus Iesus (Vatican City, January 2016)
p. 17.

[6] Apostolic Tribunal of the Roman Rota, Subsidium for the Application of the M.p. Mitis Iudex Dominus Iesus (Vatican City, January 2016)
pp. 61-61.

for the declaration of the nullity of marriage (cann. 1671-1691) provided by the Code of Canon Law of 1983, and has been established "to provide openly that the bishop himself, in the church over which he has been appointed shepherd and head, is by that very fact the judge of those faithful entrusted to his care, (M.p. *Mitis Iudex, preface,* III) and that 'due to his duty as pastor, has the greatest care for catholic unity with Peter in faith and discipline (M.p. *Mitis Iudex, preface,* IV);

Having considered that

-   The preoccupation for the salvation of souls remains the ultimate purpose of the Church,
-   The great number of the faithful who – while desiring to provide for their own consciences, too often are discouraged by the juridical structures of the Church because of physical and moral distances – demand that the Church "like a good mother, be near her children,"
-   Can. 1673 §2 of CIC directs that: "The Bishop is to establish for his own diocese a diocesan tribunal for cases of nullity of marriages,"
-   For decades in our Arch/Diocesan the diocesan Tribunal has been functioning, but incompetent to adjudicate cases of matrimonial nullity;
-   The conferring of the competence to our Diocesan Tribunal to treat and define also marriage nullity cases in the first grade of judgment guarantees better the "speeding up of proceedings, called for by the Synod of Bishops and established by Pope Francis, both in the more agile "ordinary process," as well as in the "briefer process;"

BY THIS PRESENT DECREE
CONSTITUTE

The Arch/Diocesan Tribunal of N., with its seat in ... at the diocesan Chancery in ..., effective as of ... (*date*),

THE NECESSARY COMPETENCE TO ADJUDICATE AND DEFINE MARRIAGE NULLITY CASES IN FIRST INSTANCE

which to date have been entrusted to the Inter-diocesan Ecclesiastical Tribunal of....

Future challenges to the sentences issued by Our Tribunal are regulated by canons 1619-1640 and can be proposed either to the Metropolitan Tribunal of N. of second instance or to the Apostolic Tribunal of the Roman Rota, according to the norms of can. 1673 §6.

And therefore, following Article 8 §2 of the *Motu proprio "Mitis Iudex,"*

I WITHDRAW

Formally from the Inter-diocesan Ecclesiastical Tribunal of N., constituted according to the norms of canon 1423 CIC.

Furthermore, those matrimonial nullity cases whose competence, by virtue of can. 1672 of the *Motu proprio "Mitis Iudex,"* belongs to our Tribunal, and which are now in course of adjudication in first instance before the Inter-diocesan Ecclesiastical Tribunal of N., are to be transferred to our Diocesan Tribunal, if by ... (*date*) the concordance of the doubt has not yet been formulated, according to the norms of law.

With this present Decree the mandate is given to all the competent Offices of our Curia to prepare the most of every aspect, also of economic and operational nature, so that our Arch/Diocesan Tribunal will adequately be operational from ... (*date*), with the purpose of adequately exercising its activity and responding to the needs of the faithful requiring the verification of the truth about the existence of the bond of their failed marriage.

Given on ..., at ....
Signed by the diocesan bishop and by the chancellor.

CHAPTER 3: THE DECREE OF THE BISHOP WITHDRAW- ING FROM AN INTERDIOCESAN TRIBUNAL TO A NEARER TRIBUNAL

1. "The bishop is to establish a diocesan tribunal for his dio- cese to handle cases of nullity of marriage without preju- dice to the faculty of the same bishop to approach another nearby diocesan or interdiocesan tribunal."[7]
2. "The law now promulgated and clarified by the intention (*mens*) of the Pontiff gives free and immediate right to the Bishop to withdraw from an existing structure of an inter- diocesan tribunal, if he decides to form his own tribunal or if he chooses a nearer one."[8]
3. If a diocesan bishop who is part of an already existing in- terdiocesan tribunal decides to withdraw from that inter- diocesan structure and become part of another diocesan tribunal that is closer or more proximate to his diocese, he is to issue a decree to that effect. However, before he with- draws from the interdiocesan structure and issues the de- cree thereof, he is to notify the other bishops who are part of the interdiocesan tribunal, especially the bishop mod- erator of the interdiocesan tribunal. In addition, he is also to obtain the approval of the diocesan bishop of the tribu- nal with which he wishes to associate. He is also to notify the Apostolic Signatura of the withdrawal and of new ar- rangement.
4. The following sample decree has been provided by the Apostolic Tribunal of the Roman Rota.[9]

---

[7] C.1673 §2

[8] Apostolic Tribunal of the Roman Rota, *Subsidium* for the Applica- tion of the M.p. *Mitis Iudex Dominus Iesus* (Vatican City, January 2016) p. 17.

[9] Apostolic Tribunal of the Roman Rota, *Subsidium* for the Applica- tion of the M.p. *Mitis Iudex Dominus Iesus* (Vatican City, January 2016) pp. 63-64.

DECREE WITHDRAWING FROM AN INTERDIOCESAN TRI-
BUNAL OF THE ARCH/DIOCESE OF N. TO THE TRIBUNAL
OF THE DIOCESE OF N. (*NAME OF THAT DIOCESE*)

Prot. N. ....

I, N., (*name of the diocesan bishop*)
Bishop of the Arch/Diocese of N. (*name of the diocese*)

In fulfillment of the reform of the procedures for matrimonial nullity approved by Pope Francis in his *Motu proprio "Mitis Iudex"* of 15 August 2015, which has entirely substituted the procedure for the declaration of the nullity of marriage (cann. 1671-1691) provided by the Code of Canon Law of 1983, and has been established "to provide openly that the bishop himself, in the church over which he has been appointed shepherd and head, is by that very fact the judge of those faithful entrusted to his care, (M.p. *Mitis Iudex, preface,* III) and that 'due to his duty as pastor, has the greatest care for catholic unity with Peter in faith and discipline (M.p. *Mitis Iudex, preface,* IV);

Having considered that

-      The preoccupation for the salvation of souls remains the ultimate purpose of the Church,
-      The great number of the faithful who – while desiring to provide for their own consciences, too often are discouraged by the juridical structures of the Church because of physical and moral distances – demand that the Church "like a good mother, be near her children,"
-      Can. 1673 §2 of CIC directs that: "The Bishop is to establish for his own diocese a diocesan tribunal for cases of nullity of marriages,"
-      For now it is not yet possible to constitute our own Diocesan Tribunal for matrimonial nullity cases of our diocese;
-      It will be my personal responsibility to prepare as quickly as possible persons who will be able to work in the Tribunal on matrimonial nullity cases, so as to be able eventually to constitute

in our own Arch/Diocese a tribunal, as legislated in the M.p. *Mitis Iudex*, art. 8 §1 of the *Procedural Rules*,

-       The conferring of competence to adjudicate and define matrimonial nullity cases in first instance to the Ecclesiastical Tribunal of N., guarantees better the 'speeding up of proceedings, called by the Synod of Bishops and established by Pope Francis,

BY THIS PRESENT DECREE
I ESTABLISH

That marriage nullity cases which can be defined with the briefer process according to the norm of canon 1683 will be treated and defined by me as determined by the canons 1683-1687.

I RECEDE

According to the norm of Art. 8 §2 of the *Motu proprio, Mitis Iudex,* from the Inter-diocesan Ecclesiastical Tribunal of N. constituted according to the provisions of can. 1423 CIC.

I ACCEDE

ad triennium, in conformity with canon 1673 §2 of the CIC, to the Ecclesiastical Tribunal of the Arch/Diocese N., with its seat in ... at the diocesan Chancery in ..., effective as of ... (*date*), which is to be considered, for all legal effects, competent for the adjudication and the definition in first instance of marriage nullity cases from our Arch/Diocese, which until now were entrusted to the Inter-diocesan Ecclesiastical Tribunal of N.

Furthermore, the matrimonial nullity cases whose competence, by virtue of can. 1672 of the *Motu proprio "Mitis Iudex,"* is of Our Tribunal, and which are now in course of adjudication in first instance before the Inter-diocesan Ecclesiastical Tribunal of N., are to be transferred to the Ecclesiastical Tribunal of the Arch/Diocese of ..., if by ... (*date*) the doubt has not yet been formulated, according to the norms of law.

Given on ..., at ....
Signed by the diocesan bishop and by the chancellor.

CHAPTER 4: THE PETITION TO THE HOLY SEE FOR THE ESTABLISHMENT OF AN INTERDIOCESAN TRIBUNAL OF FIRST AND SECOND INSTANCE

1. If the diocesan bishops, including the metropolitans of more than one ecclesiastical provinces wish to constitute an interdiocesan tribunal, they are to petition for its authorization from the Supreme Tribunal of the Apostolic Signatura.
2. The following sample petition requesting for the authorization of the Holy See for the constitution of an interdiocesan tribunal of first and second instance for more ecclesiastical provinces has been provided by the Apostolic Tribunal of the Roman Rota.[10] It can be adapted if the petition pertains to one ecclesiastical province only.

On the letterhead of the archbishop who is expected to be the episcopal moderator of the proposed interdiocesan tribunal.

Date

To His Eminence
N. Cardinal N.
The Cardinal Prefect
Supreme Tribunal of the Apostolic Signatura

Your Eminence

The undersigned Metropolitan Archbishops of N. and of N.; following the entry into force of the two *motu proprios "Mitis Iudex Dominus Iesus"* and *"Mitis et Misericors Iesus"* on 8 December 2015;

---

[10] Apostolic Tribunal of the Roman Rota, *Subsidium* for the Application of the M.p. *Mitis Iudex Dominus Iesus* (Vatican City, January 2016) pp. 65-66.

Considering that for the moment it is not yet possible to constitute Diocesan Tribunals for the marriage nullity cases of Our Dioceses;

Having established by common agreement to constitute an inter-diocesan tribunal of first and second instance, as is shown in the attached memorandum of the meeting of the two Metropolitans held on ...;

In conformity with the provisions of the M.p. *Mitis Iudex,* canon 1673 §§2 and 6, and in accordance with the *mens* of the Supreme Legislator of the Church, clearly expressed through the Dean of the Roman Rota on 4 November 2015, according to which is upheld "the ability, according to the norms of law, that is, with the approval of the Holy See, that Metropolitans of two or more Ecclesiastical Provinces can come together to create an inter-diocesan tribunal both of first and of second instances (*"Mens"* of the Pontiff, in *Oss. Rom.,* 8 November 2015, n. 2);

REQUEST

From the Supreme Tribunal of the Apostolic Signatura the aforementioned authorization for the constitution of the Inter-diocesan Tribunal of First and Second Instance for the Metropolitan Provinces of ... and of ....

Awaiting Your Kind Response to Our Request
We remain
Fraternally Yours in Christ

Date and Place

† _____
Archbishop of N.

† _____
Archbishop of N.

SECTION 2:   THE ADMINISTRATIVE MARRIAGE NULLITY PROCESS

CHAPTER 5: LACK OF CANONICAL FORM

1. The Notion of Lack of Canonical Form

According to canon 1108 §§1-2, only those marriages are valid which are contracted before the local ordinary, pastor, or a priest or deacon delegated by either of them, who assist, and before two witnesses according to the rules expressed in the following canons and without prejudice to the exceptions mentioned in canons 144, 1112, §1, 1116, and 1127, §§1-2. The person who assists at a marriage is understood to be only that person who is present, asks for the manifestation of the consent of the contracting parties, and receives it in the name of the Church.

Thus, a lack of form or lack of canonical form is a marriage in which a Catholic married civilly or married in a non-Catholic ceremony without dispensation from canonical form and the marriage was not subsequently validated in the Church. When the canonical form has not been observed and the marriage was not later validated in the Church, the administrative process of canons 1066-1067 is used to declare such marriages invalid.

2. How to Determine a Lack of Form Case

HOW TO DETERMINE A LACK OF CANONICAL FORM
CASE

The following questions will help you determine whether you have a lack of form case:

1. □ YES □ NO Was one of the contracting parties a Catholic at the time of the wedding?
2. □ YES □ NO Did the marriage take place before a Catholic bishop, priest, or deacon and before two lay witnesses?
3. □ YES □ NO Did the Catholic party obtain a dispensation to be married in a ceremony other than a Catholic one?
4. □ YES □ NO Was the marriage ever subsequently witnessed or validated by a Catholic bishop, priest, or deacon?

5. ☐ YES ☐ NO Was the marriage ever subsequently sanated by a Catholic bishop or his delegate.

If the answer to question 1 is YES and the answers to questions 2, 3, 4, and 5 are NO, it may be a lack of form case. The tribunal, however, will provide a definitive answer, based on the totality of the facts and circumstances of the case. For more information.

3. The Requirements for Granting Lack of Form Petition

i.   At least one of the contracting parties must be a baptized Catholic or must have been received into full communion with the Catholic Church at the time of the wedding.
ii. The marriage did not take place before a Catholic bishop, priest, or deacon and before two lay witnesses.
iii. The Catholic party did not obtain a dispensation from canonical form.
iv. The marriage was never subsequently witnessed, validated, or sanated by a Catholic bishop, priest, or deacon.

4. The Procedures for Granting Lack of Form Petition

I. *The Gathering of the Documents*

The documents to be gathered include:

☐ A copy of Baptismal Certificate/Profession of Faith for Catholic party/parties issued within last 6 months.
☐ A copy of the Marriage Certificate.
☐ A copy of the Divorce Decree.

II. *The Submission of the Petition and other Forms to the Tribunal*

After the documents have been gathered, the lack of form petition is completed. The completed petition and the other documents gathered and sent to the tribunal.

A sample of a lack of form petition is provided below.

III. *The Checking of the Documents and Records by the Tribunal*

When the documents including the petition have been received by the tribunal, they are checked for completeness and that all is in order with the documents. Before the decree of lack of canonical form is issued and if the marriage took place within the diocesan jurisdiction, a tribunal official is to check the diocesan record of dispensation and its record of sanation to verify that no dispensation was granted from canonical form for the marriage. If the marriage took place in another diocese, a letter is usually sent to the competent ecclesiastical authority in that diocese so that they may check their records to verify that no dispensation was granted and that the marriage was not subsequently sanated. If the diocese *ad quem* does not respond within the time stipulated for them, the tribunal *a quo* can proceed and issue the decree of the lack of form.

If the marriage took place in another diocese, especially in a different country and if the mailing of a letter to that diocese for them to check their records would unduly delay the granting of the petition, the tribunal handling the petition can ask the petitioner to swear an affidavit that to the best of his or her knowledge no dispensation from canonical form was obtained and that the marriage was not sanated.

For a sample form of the affidavit of the petitioner, see the sample of the lack of form petition provided in this chapter below.

IV. *The Citation of the Respondent*

In most lack of form cases, the respondent is not cited, especially if the fact of the Catholic baptism or reception into the Catholic Church of the Catholic party and the lack of dispensation from canonical form and the non-sanation of the marriage can be established by means of documentary proofs. However, in some lack of form cases, the respondent is the Catholic party and the precise information regarding the church and date of the Catholic baptism or reception into the Catholic Church of the respondent is not known. If this is the case, the respondent can be cited to provide the required information. To establish the conferral of baptism, if prejudicial to no one, the declaration of one witness beyond all exception is sufficient or the oath of the one baptized is sufficient if the person received baptism as an adult. (c. 876). While some respondents cooperate with the tribunal, others do not. If the respondent refuses to provide the information, the tribunal can ask the petitioner to provide a witness who knows the respondent and who can complete and sign the witness character affidavit form, a sample of which has been provided below.

For a sample form of the citation letter to the respondent, see this chapter below.

For a sample form of the respondent questionnaire, see this chapter below.

V. *Character Witness Affidavit*

A witness affidavit may be needed if, for example, the marriage took place in another diocese and to send correspondence to that diocese in order for them to check their records whether a dispensation from canonical form or a radical sanation was granted for the marriage would unduly delay the resolution of the case. A witness affidavit may also be needed if the proof of the Catholic baptism or reception into full communion with the Catholic Church cannot be obtained.

A sample form of the character witness affidavit is provided below.

VI. *The Issuance of the Decree of Lack of Form*

When the tribunal has received the petition and the other documents, the tribunal checks to ensure that it has all the required documents, that they have been completed, and that no dispensation from canonical form or a radical sanation of the marriage was granted. When all is in order with the documents, the tribunal is then to issue the decree of lack of form.

A sample form of the decree of lack of form is provided under this chapter below.

VII. *The Notification of the Decree of Lack of Form to the Priest or Deacon and to the Parties*

After the decree has been issued, it is then mailed to the priest or deacon preparing the petitioner for marriage. A copy of the decree and the letter is preserved in the tribunal archives.

5. The Sample Documents for Granting Lack of Form Petition

5.1. *The Lack of Form Petition*

PETITION FOR A DECLARATION OF NULLITY OF MARRIAGE BASED ON LACK OF CANONICAL FORM

Diocesan Logo Address. Phone: __ Fax: __	Tribunal Use Only
	_____ Petitioner
	_____ Respondent
	Protocol No.: _____

TYPE OR PRINT ALL INFORMATION
E-mailed documents will not be accepted

1. PARTIES' INFORMATION

PETITIONER'S NAME: _____
First Middle Last (Maiden) Names
ADDRESS: _____
Street/P.O. Box City   State   Zip
DATE OF BIRTH: _____
TELEPHONE: (Home): _____ (Cell): _____
RELIGION AT THE TIME OF THE MARRIAGE: _____

RESPONDENT'S NAME: _____
First Middle (Maiden) Last Names

ADDRESS: _____
Street/P.O. Box City   State   Zip

DATE OF BIRTH: _____

TELEPHONE: (Home): _____ (Cell): _____

RELIGION AT THE TIME OF THE MARRIAGE: _____

2. CHURCH OF BAPTISM OR PROFESSION OF FAITH OF THE CATHOLIC PARTY (If both parties are Catholics, provide information for the Petitioner only)

Name of Church_____

Address_____
Street/P.O. Box City, State, Zip code

Date of Baptism or Profession of Faith _____.
       Rite: __Latin __ Eastern

Has the Catholic party ever officially joined a non-Catholic Church? __Yes   __No

If Yes, state denomination _____ and date of membership _____

3. THE MARRIAGE AND DIVORCE

Place of Marriage _____
                                  City   State

Date of Marriage: _____

Name of Diocese: _____

Name of Officiant: _____

Civil Official/Religious Affiliation: (*check one*)
☐ Civil Official ☐ Civil Judge ☐ Justice of the Peace ☐ Rabbi
☐ Orthodox Priest ☐ Minister ☐ Other _____

Date of Divorce: _____

Place of Divorce: _____

Are the obligations of justice to former spouse and any children born of this marriage (e.g., provision for support and the upbringing of children) being met or have they been met (c.1071)? ☐ Yes ☐ No

4. PRIOR MARRIAGES

Were you or your former spouse married prior to this marriage (civil or ecclesial): ☐ Yes ☐ No

If yes, list marriages providing the following information. If there are more than two previous marriages, please provide the information on a different sheet of paper.

NAME OF SPOUSE: _____
                            First, Middle, Last (maiden, if woman)
RELIGION: _____

DATE OF MARRIAGE: _____
PLACE OF MARRIAGE_____
                          Venue   City   State
CIVIL DIVORCE: _____
                      Month   Date   Year
NAME OF SPOUSE: _____
                         First, Middle, Last (maiden, if woman)
RELIGION: _____
DATE OF MARRIAGE: _____
PLACE OF MARRIAGE: _____
                         Venue City   State
CIVIL DIVORCE: _____

5. AFFIDAVIT OF THE PETITIONER

I, the undersigned Petitioner, do hereby declare that at the time of my marriage to the above named Respondent: (*check all that apply*)

☐ The Catholic party named above was a baptized Catholic or was received into full communion with the Catholic Church prior to the marriage.

☐ The Catholic party named above had the obligation to observe the Catholic form of marriage. (cc. 1108; 1117).

☐ The marriage did not take place before a Catholic priest or deacon.

☐ The marriage was not ever subsequently witnessed, validated, or blessed by an official representative of the Catholic Church.

☐ The Catholic party neither requested nor obtained dispensation to be married in a non-Catholic marriage ceremony.

☐ If this is a marriage that occurred after March 25, 1967 between a Catholic and a baptized Eastern Rite non-Catholic, the marriage ceremony was performed without the intervention of a Sacred Minister of the Eastern Church (c. 1127 §1).

I hereby declare also that the obligations of justice to former spouse and any children born of this marriage (e.g., provision for support and the upbringing of children) are being met or have been fulfilled. (c. 1071).

I have enclosed the following documents and a freewill donation: (*Please check documents enclosed*)

☐ A copy of Baptismal Certificate/Profession of Faith for Catholic party/parties issued within last 6 months.

☐ A copy of the Marriage Certificate.

☐ A copy of the Divorce Decree.

☐ Freewill donation $____

_____ (*signature*)   _____

Name of the Petitioner   Date

6. AFFIDAVIT OF THE PROCURATOR

I, the undersigned Procurator, attests that to the best of my knowledge the above statements are true. I have no reason to doubt the veracity of the statement.

_____ (*signature*)   _____

Name of Cleric   Date

_____

Church Name

_____

Address, City, State, Zip Code

```
┌─────────────────────────────────────────────────────┐
│                  TRIBUNAL USE ONLY                    │
│                                                       │
│    1.  Diocesan Record of Dispensation checked: YES __ (Prot. │
│        No. __ Year __) NO__                           │
│    2.  Diocesan Record of Sanation checked: YES __ (Prot. No. │
│        __ Year __) NO__                               │
│    3.  Letter sent on … (date) to the Diocese of ____, where the │
│        marriage took place to check their record for dispensa- │
│        tion and sanation: YES __ (Prot. No. __ Year ___) NO__ │
│                                                       │
│    Information checked by _____, on     _____   │
│                            Notary            Date     │
│    Petition Granted: _____YES _____NO                 │
│                                                       │
│                                                       │
│    _____           _____        │
│    Judicial Vicar or Delegate       Date              │
│                                                       │
└─────────────────────────────────────────────────────┘
```

5.2. *The Character Witness Attestation Form*

It sometimes happen that the fact of the baptism of the Catholic party or of reception into full communion with the Catholic Church cannot be proven by means of the certificate of baptism or the certificate of reception into full communion with the Catholic Church. In such cases, a person who knows the Catholic party can swear an affidavit marriage that the Catholic party was baptized or received into the Catholic Church prior to the marriage. "To prove the conferral of baptism, if prejudicial to no one, the declaration of one witness beyond all exception is sufficient or the oath of the one baptized if the person received baptism as an adult." (c. 876).

Cover Letter to the Petitioner

Case

Date

Name
Address

Dear N.:

Be advised that this Tribunal has received your petition for a declaration of the nullity of your marriage to N.

You have requested the nullity of the marriage based on the ground of lack of dispensation from canonical form. The Tribunal is need of more information regarding the case. Kindly give the enclosed "Character Witness Affidavit" Form to a trustworthy person who knows you well to complete, sign, and date. The completed Form is to be returned to the Tribunal at your earliest convenience so that we can proceed with your case.

In keeping with the canons of Church law, the decision of the Tribunal has no civil effects and does not alter in any way the obligations of the final divorce action.

Sincerely Yours in Christ,
Signed by the judicial vicar or his delegate

Enclosure: Character Witness Attestation
CC:
=================================
On separate tribunal letterhead

LACK OF CANONICAL FORM: CHARACTER WITNESS AFFIDAVIT REGARDING THE MARRIAGE OF N. AND N.

CASE

Thank you for taking the time to complete this form. Kindly answer truthfully the questions provided below. The completed form is to be returned to the Tribunal as soon as possible.

1. State your relationship to the Parties

   _____

2. Upon information and belief, the Catholic party received Catholic baptism or full communion into the Catholic Church prior to the marriage.

3. I, _____, solemnly declare, affirm, and state that I know that the marriage between _____ and _____

                     Petitioner   *Respondent*

   was performed before a civil official or a non-Catholic minister on _____ in _____

                  Date   *City, State, Country*

4. I know this to be true because

   _____
       (provide the reason, e.g., I attended the wedding, etc.).

5. To the best of my knowledge, this marriage was never subsequently celebrated or validated in the Catholic Church.

6. I declare that the information the Petitioner has provided to the Tribunal is the truth.

7. This information has been provided solely for the purpose of the ecclesiastical declaration of the nullity of marriage according to the laws of the Catholic Church.

I affirm the truth of these statements.

_____   _____
Signature   Date

5.3. *The Citation Letter to the Respondent*

Case

Date

Name
Address

Dear N.:

Please be advised that your former spouse, N., has petitioned for a decree of the nullity of his/her marriage to you on the grounds that, at the time of the marriage, you were a baptized Catholic but you did not marry him/her before a Roman Catholic bishop, priest, or deacon and two witnesses.

We shall like to obtain some information from you concerning the marriage.

Kindly fill, sign, and date the enclosed questionnaire along with the Tribunal Policy of Confidentiality and return them to us by ... (*date*).

If we do not hear from you by this date, the Tribunal will consider your silence as consent that you were a baptized Catholic or was received into the Catholic Church prior to the marriage and a decision will be made in the case.

If I can be of any assistance to you throughout this process, please call me at the telephone number during business hours.

With appreciation for your assistance.

Sincerely Yours in Christ,

Reverend N.
Judicial Vicar

Enclosure: The Respondent Questionnaire

5.4. *The Respondent Questionnaire*

On separate tribunal letterhead

LACK OF CANONICAL FORM:
RESPONDENT QUESTIONNAIRE
Regarding the Marriage of
N. and N.

Case

Please complete and return this form to the tribunal in the envelope provided. Thank you!

1. Were you a baptized Catholic at the time of the marriage or had you been received into full communion with the Catholic Church prior to the marriage?

   If yes, please provide us with a copy of your baptismal certificate or certificate of full communion into the Catholic Church, if available.

2. Did the marriage take place before a Catholic priest or deacon?

3. What is the name and title of the person who conducted the wedding and received the vows?

4. What is the date of the marriage? The city, state, and country?

5. Was the marriage ever subsequently validated or blessed by a Catholic priest or deacon?

6. Did he/you obtain a dispensation to be married in a ceremony other than a Catholic one? If so provide documentation.

I swear or affirm the truth of these answers.

Signature: _____   Date: _____

5.5. The Decree of Lack of Form

5.5.1. Option 1

DECREE OF NULLITY OF MARRIAGE
BASED ON LACK OF CANONICAL FORM

CASE

By the special delegation of his Excellency, Most Reverend N, Bishop of N., the Tribunal of the Diocese of N., using the administrative procedures of canons 1066-1067 of the 1983 Code of Canon Law in the case of the attempted marriage between N. and N., hereby issues this decree.

THE FACTS

1. On __ (*date*), N., __ years of age, Petitioner, a Catholic, married N., Respondent, … (*religion*), __ years of age, before a civil official (or, non-Catholic minister) in __ (*county/civil parish/local govt. area, city, state*). The length of the marital co-habitation was __ years and __ months. A civil divorce was obtained on __ (*date*).
2. On __ (*date*), this Tribunal received the petition of N. (*name of the petitioner*) for a declaration of the invalidity of his/her marriage to N. (*name of the respondent*) based on lack of canonical form.
3. After having gathered all the pertinent documents in the case and after having carefully observed all the requirements of the law, this Tribunal now renders its definitive decision in the case.

THE LAW

Can. 1108 §1. Only those marriages are valid which are contracted before the local ordinary, pastor, or a priest or deacon delegated by either of them, who assist, and before two witnesses according to the rules expressed in the following canons and without prejudice to the exceptions mentioned in cann. 144, 1112, §1, 1116, and 1127, §§1-2.

4. The canonical form consists of the following elements, all of which must be verified concurrently:

   a. The officiating cleric is the local ordinary or the pastor, or a priest or a deacon delegated by either the local ordinary or the pastor;
   b. The cleric is present at the wedding and asks for the manifestation of the consent of the contracting parties, and receives it in the name of the Church; and
   c. The two witnesses are present at the celebration of the marriage.

5. The absence or lack of all the elements that define the canonical form would render a marriage in which at least one of the parties is Catholic invalid on grounds of lack of canonical form. Therefore, "should a Catholic party attempt marriage before civil authority or before a minister of some other religion (i.e., without a dispensation from the canonical form), such a celebration obviously lacks all element of canonical form." (*Coram* Boccafola, 12 March 1998, *Studia Canonica*, 34 (2000) p. 521).

6. The law of the Church obliges Catholics to observe the canonical form of marriage before the local ordinary, pastor, or priest or deacon delegated by them, and in the presence of two witnesses (c. 1108, §1). The Catholic minister asks for the parties' manifestation of consent and receives it in the name of the Church (c. 1108 §2). Furthermore, Canon 1117 states that the canonical form of marriage must be

observed if at least one of the parties contracting marriage was baptized in the Catholic Church or received into it.

7. So important is this form of marriage that, even when a marriage was so witnessed but is then discovered to be invalid due to a diriment impediment, a renewal of consent according to the proper form is to take place (c. 1156 §1), even if both parties furnished consent and did not later revoke it (c. 1156 §2).

8. The authentic interpretation of the Pontifical Commission for the Authentic Interpretation of the Code of Canon Law has declared that the law "at least by implication, allows the administrative procedure for the simple lack of form case." (See, Lawrence G. Wren, *Authentic Interpretations on the 1983*, CLSA, 1993, p. 14). Thus, a simple lack of form does not require a judicial process; a simple administrative procedure suffices.

THE ARGUMENT

9. An authentic certificate of baptism issued by __ (*Name of the parish, city, state, {and country}*) proves that N. (*name of the Catholic party/petitioner*) was baptized on … (*date*), at N. (*name of the parish*) Parish, …, … (*city, state*), and thus held to observe the canonical form of marriage.

10. *If applicable:* A sworn affidavit provided by N., (*name of the affiant and his/her relationship to the petitioner*), to which no exception or contradiction could be posited, proves that N. (*name of the Catholic party*) was baptized at (*Name of the Parish, City, State, {Country}*), in the Diocese of N., and thus bound to observe the canonical form of marriage.

11. Public documents and sworn declarations admitting of no reasonable contradiction provide proof that the marriage took place on __ (*date*), before a civil official/a non-Catholic minister. No dispensation was granted for the marriage to be celebrated outside of the canonical form.

12. Sworn testimonies admitting of no reasonable contradiction also provide verification that the attempted marriage

was never subsequently blessed or validated in the Catholic Church. The baptismal certificate fails to show any reference to the marriage.

13. It is, therefore, clear from all the documentations presented to the Tribunal that the Catholic party neither observed the canonical form of marriage to which the Catholic party was bound nor was the attempted marriage ever subsequently blessed or validated in the Catholic Church. A document of civil divorce was given them on __ (*date*).

WHEREFORE, having carefully considered the laws of the Catholic Church and the facts of the case, which are based on the submitted documents and verifications subject to no reasonable contradiction or exception, and mindful that the bond of marriage is to be maintained until the contrary is proven (c. 1060), I, the undersigned Ecclesiastical Judge, hereby pronounce, declare, and decree the following:

The marriage attempted by N. and N. is invalid because of lack of canonical form.

That is, the nullity of the marriage in the case has been proven on the grounds that the Catholic party neither observed the required canonical form at the time of the attempted marriage nor subsequently blessed or validated the attempted marriage in the Catholic Church. (cc. 1117; 1108 §§1-2).

This decree is for ecclesiastical purposes only, and has no civil effects whatsoever. Both parties are reminded that the decision of this ecclesiastical Tribunal does not release either party from any natural, moral, or civil obligations toward this spouse and any children born of this union. (cc. 1691 §1 and 1071 §1, 3°).

Given at the Tribunal of N., (*City, State*) on ... (*Date*).
Signed by judicial vicar and by the notary.
Official seal.

5.5.2. Option 2

DECREE OF NULLITY OF MARRIAGE
BASED ON LACK OF CANONICAL FORM

CASE

By the special delegation of his Excellency, Most Reverend N,
Bishop of N., the Tribunal of the Diocese of N., using the administrative procedures of canons 1066-1067 of the 1983 Code of Canon
Law in the case of the attempted marriage between N. and N.,
hereby issues this decree.

THE FACTS

1. On __ (*date*), N., __ years of age, Petitioner, a Catholic,
    married N., Respondent, … (*religion*), __ years of age, be-
    fore a civil official (or, non-Catholic minister) in __
    (*county/civil parish/local govt. area, city, state*). The length of
    the marital co-habitation was __ years and __ months. A
    civil divorce was obtained on __ (*date*).
2. On __ (*date*), this Tribunal received the petition of N. (*name
    of the petitioner*) for a declaration of the invalidity of
    his/her marriage to N. (*name of the respondent*) based on
    lack of canonical form.

THE LAW

Can. 1108 §1. Only those marriages are valid which are contracted before the local ordinary, pastor, or a priest or deacon delegated by either of them, who assist, and before two witnesses according to the rules expressed in the following canons and without
prejudice to the exceptions mentioned in cann. 144, 1112, §1, 1116,
and 1127, §§1-2.

THE ARGUMENT

3. An authentic certificate of baptism issued by ___ (*Name of the parish, city, state, {and country}*) proves that N. (*name of the Catholic party/petitioner*) was baptized on … (*date*), at N. (*name of the parish*) Parish, …, … (*city, state*), and thus held to observe the canonical form of marriage.

4. *If applicable:* A sworn affidavit provided by N., (*name of the affiant and his/her relationship to the petitioner*), to which no exception or contradiction could be posited, proves that N. (*name of the Catholic party*) was baptized at (*Name of the Parish, City, State, {Country}*), in the Diocese of N., and thus bound to observe the canonical form of marriage.

5. Public documents and sworn declarations admitting of no reasonable contradiction provide proof that the marriage took place on ___ (*date*), before a civil official/a non-Catholic minister. No dispensation was granted for the marriage to be celebrated outside of the canonical form.

6. Sworn testimonies admitting of no reasonable contradiction also provide verification that the attempted marriage was never subsequently blessed or validated in the Catholic Church. The baptismal certificate fails to show any reference to the marriage.

7. It is, therefore, clear from all the documentations presented to the Tribunal that the Catholic party neither observed the canonical form of marriage to which the Catholic party was bound nor was the attempted marriage ever subsequently blessed or validated in the Catholic Church. A document of civil divorce was given them on ___ (*date*).

WHEREFORE, having carefully considered the laws of the Catholic Church and the facts of the case, which are based on the submitted documents and verifications subject to no reasonable contradiction or exception, and mindful that the bond of marriage is to be maintained until the contrary is proven (c. 1060), I, the undersigned Ecclesiastical Judge, hereby pronounce, declare, and decree the following:

The marriage attempted by N. and N. is invalid because of lack of canonical form.

That is, the nullity of the marriage in the case has been proven on the grounds that the Catholic party neither observed the required canonical form at the time of the attempted marriage nor subsequently blessed or validated the attempted marriage in the Catholic Church. (cc. 1117; 1108 §§1-2).

This decree is for ecclesiastical purposes only, and has no civil effects whatsoever. Both parties are reminded that the decision of this ecclesiastical Tribunal does not release either party from any natural, moral, or civil obligations toward this spouse and any children born of this union. (cc. 1691 §1 and 1071 §1, 3°).

Given at the Tribunal of N., (*City, State*) on ... (*Date*).
Signed by judicial vicar and by the notary.
Official seal.

5.5.3. Option 3

DECREE OF NULLITY OF MARRIAGE:
LACK OF CANONICAL FORM

Case

Whereas Canon 1108 §1 of the 1983 Code of the Canon Law requires a Roman Catholic to contract marriage before a Roman Catholic bishop, priest, or deacon and two witnesses;

Whereas it is understood that the contracting of a marriage by a Roman Catholic before a Roman Catholic bishop, priest, or deacon and two witnesses is termed the canonical form of marriage;

Whereas it is evident from authentic documents and declarations that N. (*name of the catholic party*) was baptized on ... (*date*), at N. (*name of the parish*) Parish, ..., ... (*city, state*), and thus bound to observe the canonical form of marriage;

Whereas the same evidence proves that N. (*name of the catholic party*) married N. (*name of the non-Catholic party*) before the justice of the peace (or: a non-Catholic religious minister) on … (*date*), in …, … (*city, state*);

Whereas no dispensation from canonical form regarding the marriage was granted by the competent ecclesiastical authority;

Whereas the marriage was never subsequently contracted, validated, or sanated in accordance with ecclesiastical law;

Wherefore I, the undersigned Ecclesiastical Judge, hereby pronounce, declare, and decree that:

The marriage attempted by N. and N. is invalid by reason of lack of canonical form.

This decree is for ecclesiastical purposes only, and has no civil effects whatsoever. Both parties are reminded that the decision of this ecclesiastical Tribunal does not release either party from any natural, moral, or civil obligations toward this spouse and any children born of this union. (cc. 1691 §1 and 1071 §1, 3°).

Given at the Tribunal of the Diocese of N., N. (*name of the diocese, and state*), on … (*date*).

Signed by the judicial vicar or judge and by the ecclesiastical notary.

CHAPTER 6: RATIFIED AND NON-CONSUMMATED MAR-RIAGE

1. "For a just cause, the Roman Pontiff can dissolve a non-consummated marriage between baptized persons or between a baptized party and an unbaptized party at the request of both parties or of one of them, even if the other party is unwilling."[1]
2. A valid marriage between baptized persons is called a ratified marriage. If the marriage has been consummated, then it is called a ratified and consummated marriage (*ratum et consummatum*). A marriage is consummated if the spouses have performed between themselves in a human manner the conjugal act which in itself is suitable for the procreation of offspring, to which marriage is ordered by its nature and by which the spouses become one flesh. (c. 1061 §1). A marriage that is *ratum et consummatum* can be dissolved by no human power and by no cause, except death. (c. 1141).
3. If one or both parties are unbaptized prior to the marriage, they contract a natural bond of marriage. However, with the valid reception of baptism by both parties this natural bond becomes sacramental, and the marriage, which until that moment was natural, becomes ratified, that is, it becomes a sacramental marriage.[2]
4. If a marriage between a baptized man and a baptized woman was not consummated, then it is called a ratified and non-consummated marriage. (*ratum et non-consummatum*). For a just cause, a ratified and non-consummated marriage between baptized persons can be dissolved by the Roman Pontiff for a just reason, at the request of both parties or of either party, even if the other is unwilling. (c. 1142).

---

[1] C. 1142.

[2] Wojciech Kowal and William H. Woestman, *Special Marriage Cases and Procedures* (Ottawa, Canada: St. Paul University, 2008) p. 21.

5. Similarly, for a just cause, a marriage between a baptized party and an unbaptized party also can be dissolved by the Roman Pontiff at the request of both parties or of either party, even if the other is unwilling. (c. 1142).

6. The dissolution of non-consummated marriages (c. 1142) is placed under Book IV, Part 1, Title VII, Chapter IX, Article I, "Dissolution of the Bond" of the 1983 Code of Canon Law.

7. The distinction between the declaration of the nullity of a marriage and the dissolution of a marriage must be kept in mind in regard to terminology. (*DC,* art. 7 §2). While, on the one hand, the declaration of marriage nullity pertains to an invalid marriage, on the other hand, the dissolution of marriage pertains to a dispensation from the bond of a valid marriage.

1. How to Determine a Non-Consummated Marriage Case

The following questions will help you determine whether you have a non-consummated marriage case:

1. YES ☐ NO. Is there a probable doubt that the marriage was not ever consummated?
2. ☐ YES ☐ NO. Is there a just cause to dissolve the marriage bond?
3. ☐ YES ☐ NO. Is it true there is no hope of reconciliation between the parties and that conjugal living cannot be restored?
4. ☐ YES ☐ NO. Is it true there would be no scandal if the pope were to grant the dissolution?

If each of the answers to all 4 questions is "YES," you may have a ratified and non-consummated marriage case.

2. The Requirements for the Granting of the Dispensation from Non-Consummated Marriage

1. There must be a probable doubt regarding the non-consummation of the marriage.

"Whenever, during the instruction of a case, a very probable doubt arises as to whether the marriage was ever consummated, the tribunal, having heard both parties, can suspend the case of nullity, complete the instruction for a dispensation *super rato*, and then transmit the acts to the Apostolic See together with a petition for a dispensation from either one or both of the spouses and the *votum* of the tribunal and the bishop."[3]

A doubt is probable if there is a plausible cause to decide in favor of a proposition, even if there is a reason to decide the matter the opposite way. Thus, there is a probable doubt regarding whether a marriage was ever consummated if there are reasons which strongly indicate that the marriage may not have been ever consummated, even if there are some reasons to the contrary.

2. There is a just cause for the granting of the dispensation.

"For a just cause, the Roman Pontiff can dissolve a non-consummated marriage between baptized persons or between a baptized party and an unbaptized party at the request of both parties or of either party, even if the other is unwilling."[4]

A just cause is determined in each case after having taken into account all the circumstances, persons, and facts of the case. A just cause, for example, in light of the praxis of the Holy See, is serious aversion of the couple towards themselves without hope of reconciliation, successful marriages with other subsequent spouses, fear of probable future scandal, discord and quarrels among the relatives, civil separation or divorce without the danger of incontinence of the innocent party, probable impotence with danger of incontinence, contracting of an incurable disease

---

[3] *CIC,* c. 1678 §4.
[4] C. 1142.

after the marriage, or partial proof of defect of consent or of an impediment. This is not an exhaustive list. However, in all cases, the salvation of souls (*salus animarum*) is a just cause.[5]

3. There must be proof of the non-consummation of the marriage.

If the spouses have lived together after the celebration of their marriage, consummation is presumed.[6] However, the canonical presumption of the consummation of a marriage can be over-turned if non-consummation can be proven because of the lack of opportunity, or because of some physical defect of one or both parties, or because of moral argument, any of which is to be sub-stantiated by sworn testimonies and documents.

Lack of opportunity is when the consummation was not pos-sible because there was neither the time, nor the place, nor the opportunity to consummate the marriage.[7] For example, after the wedding, the couple had neither the time, nor the place, nor the opportunity subsequently to consummate the marriage because of one reason or the other. The lack of opportunity to consum-mate the marriage subsequent to the celebration of the marriage must be supported by proofs.

The non-consummation of a marriage can be also due to some psychological or physiological defect on the part of the man or on the part the woman which made it impossible for the marriage to have ever been consummated. The physiological defect is demon-strated by means of proof or by means of the physical examina-tion of the parties by medical experts that given the state of the genitalia of the man or of the woman or of some other parts of the body, which was present at the time of the exchange of marital consent, they could not have consummated the marriage.

---

[5] Kowal and Woestman, p. 36.

[6] C. 1061 §2.

[7] Sacred Congregation of the Sacraments, May 7, 1923, *Decree and Rules of Procedure for Cases on Non-consummation of Marriage,* in *AAS* 15 (1923) pp. 389-414. See also *Canon Law Digest,* vol. 1, p. 786.

The physical examination of the spouses is employed only if it is necessary to attain the juridical proof of the fact of non-consummation.[8] Thus, the physical examination of the parties is to be omitted under any one of the following conditions, namely:

a) If consummation was impossible because there was neither time, place, nor opportunity for consummating the marriage.
b) If the woman was previously married, or has subsequently lived with another man, or it is certain the woman has lost her virginity.
c) If the party declines to have such an examination.
d) If in view of the moral excellence of the parties and of the witnesses and after serious consideration have been given to the corroborative supports or arguments, full proof of the alleged non-consummation of the marriage is had in the judgment of the bishop.[9]

Non-consummation of a marriage can be also proven by moral arguments. This consists in the sworn depositions on the part of the parties and of witnesses, including character witnesses corroborated by facts, documents, and information obtained at a non-suspect time and corroborated also by juridical arguments from which full proof of the non-consummation of the marriage can be gotten in the judgment of the bishop. "If the parties disagree on the essentials, and if the petitioner lacks credibility, the moral argument cannot constitute adequate proof."[10]

---

[8] Sacred Congregation for the Sacraments, March 7, 1972, *Emended Procedure in Cases of Non-consummation of Marriage*, n. II (c), *in AAS* 64 (1972) pp. 244-252. Also in *CLD* 7: 988-997.

[9] Sacred Congregation for the Sacraments, March 7, 1972, *Emended Procedure in Cases of Non-consummation of Marriage*, n. II (c).

[10] Kowal and Woestman, p. 34.

3. The Procedures for the Instruction of Non-Consummated Marriage Cases

1. The Submission of the Petition

"Only the spouses, or one of them even if the other is unwilling, have the right to petition for the favor of a dispensation from a marriage *ratum et non consummatum*."[11]

The petition for a dispensation of a ratified and non-consummated marriage to be granted by the Roman Pontiff can arise in one of two ways. The first mode for the introduction of a petition for a dispensation from a ratified and non-consummated marriage is when one of the parties submits *ab initio* a petition for the dispensation. In this mode, the case was not first introduced as a petition for a declaration of the nullity of the marriage, but from the very beginning of the process, it was introduced as a petition for the dispensation of a ratified and non-consummated marriage. If from the instruction of the case, there seems to be solid and juridical reasons regarding the non-consummation of the marriage, the instruction of the case is to be continued to the end using the process for the dissolution of a ratified and non-consummated marriage.

However, if during the instruction of a petition for dispensation from a *ratum et non-consummatum*, a prudent and reasonable doubt arises in the mind of the instructor that the marriage may have been consummated, the bishop personally or through his delegate is to advise the petitioner to petition instead for a declaration of the nullity of the marriage rather than for the favor of a dispensation from the bond of a ratified and non-consummated marriage. "If from the petition for dispensation from a ratified and non-consummated marriage arises a prudent doubt concerning the validity of the marriage, and if one of the parties desires to have the nullity of the marriage considered, it is up to the Bishop to advise the spouses to have the case treated judicially or

---

[11] C. 1697.

to begin the process for non-consummation, provided there appears a basis for it."[12]

The ratified and non-consummation process does not accuse the marriage of nullity. Rather, the process seeks from the Roman Pontiff the favor of the dissolution of the marriage bond or the favor of a dispensation from the marriage bond due to the non-consummation of the marriage. Therefore, if during a *ratum et non-consummatum* process, there are indications which point to the consummation of the marriage and, therefore, to the possible nullity of the marriage, the petitioner can be advised to submit a formal case petition for a declaration of the nullity of the marriage based on the plausible grounds of nullity applicable to the case.

The second way a petition for a dispensation from a ratified and non-consummated marriage can arise in the tribunal is when the case was first introduced to the tribunal as a petition for a declaration of nullity of the marriage. However, either prior to or subsequent to the instruction of the case, there arises in the mind of the judge a probable doubt in favor of the argument that the marriage may not have been consummated, the judge is to notify both parties regarding the probable doubt of the non-consummation of the marriage and, after hearing both parties, suspend the marriage nullity process and complete the instruction for a dispensation *super rato*.[13] Upon the completion of the *super rato* instruction, the acts of the case, the petition submitted by one or both parties for a dispensation *super rato*, the report of the instructor, and the *votum* of the bishop are transmitted to the Apostolic See. "Whenever, during the instruction of a case, a very probable doubt arises as to whether the marriage was ever consummated, the tribunal, having heard both parties, can suspend the case of nullity, complete the instruction for a dispensation *super rato*, and then transmit the acts to the Apostolic See together with a petition

---

[12] Sacred Congregation for the Sacraments, December 20, 1986, Prot. No. 1400/86, *The Process for the Dispensation from a Ratified and Non-consummated Marriage*, n. 3.

[13] C. 1678 §4.

for a dispensation from either one or both of the spouses and the *votum* of the tribunal and the bishop."[14]

A prudent doubt can arise in the mind of the judge, if, for example, a case of nullity of marriage has been prosecuted under the ground of impotence and from the acts and proofs evidence emerges in the judgment of the tribunal that the case pertains not to impotence but of an as yet non-consummated marriage. "Insofar as there may be question of other grounds of nullity (e.g., defect of consent, force and fear, etc.) and in the judgment of the said tribunal the nullity of the marriage cannot be established but incidentally a strongly probable doubt on the non-consummation of the marriage emerges, then each or both parties have the right to present a petition to the Supreme Pontiff for an apostolic dispensation from the sacramental, non-consummated marriage. The presiding judge has the right to instruct the case in accordance with the norms [of law]. Then all the *acta*, as above, with the customary animadversions of the defender of the bond and the opinion of the tribunal and of the bishop, should be transmitted to the [Apostolic See]."[15]

If a change is made from a petition for a declaration of the nullity of the marriage to a petition for a dispensation from a ratified and non-consummated marriage, the same tribunal is to instruct the case. "If a judicial petition to declare the nullity of the same marriage has been introduced, however, the instruction is to be entrusted to the same tribunal."[16] If in the judgment of the tribunal the proofs collected so far concerning the non-consummation of the marriage are determined to be yet insufficient, the judge is to complete the instruction of the case for a dispensation *super rato*. When the instruction has been completed, the full acts of the case together with the animadversions of the defender of the bond, the report of the instructor, and the *votum* of the bishop

---

[14] *CIC*, c. 1678 §4.

[15] Sacred Congregation for the Sacraments, March 7, 1972, *Emended Procedure in Cases of Non-consummation of Marriage*, n. I (e).

[16] C. 1700 §2.

based on arguments both in law and in facts are to be forwarded to the Apostolic See.[17]

The law does not require the diocesan bishop or the tribunal to arrive at moral certainty regarding the non-consummation of the marriage or to determine whether the reason for the petition meets the threshold for a just cause. "Only the Apostolic See adjudicates the fact of the non-consummation of a marriage and the existence of a just cause to grant a dispensation."[18] What is required at the local level, in accordance with canon 1678 §4, is a probable doubt regarding non-consummation of the marriage. It is also up to the Holy See to determine whether the case meets the requirement of a just cause for the dispensation to be granted. "Only the Roman Pontiff, however, grants the dispensation."[19]

The old canon 1681 required the consent of both parties to change the petition from a declaration of nullity of the marriage to a petition for a dispensation for a ratified and non-consummated marriage. According to the old canon 1681: "Whenever, during the instruction of a case, a very probable doubt emerges that consummation of the marriage did not occur, after suspending the case of nullity with the consent of the parties (*consensu partium*), the tribunal can complete the instruction for a dispensation *super rato* and then transmit the acts to the Apostolic See together with a petition for a dispensation from either one or both of the spouses and the *votum* of the tribunal and the bishop."[20]

However, with the promulgation of *Mitis Iudex* and *Mitis et Misericors*, the consent of the parties is no longer required, but that the tribunal should consult the parties before remitting a case to one of a dispensation *super rato*. "Whenever, during the instruction of a case, a very probable doubt arises as to whether the marriage was ever consummated, the tribunal, having heard both parties (*auditis partibus*), can suspend the case of nullity, complete

---

[17] Sacred Congregation for the Sacraments, March 7, 1972, *Emended Procedure in Cases of Non-consummation of Marriage*, n. I (e). See also *Dignitas connubii*, art. 153 §3.

[18] C. 1698 §1.

[19] C. 1689 §2.

[20] CIC/83, old c. 1681.

the instruction for a dispensation *super rato*, and then transmit the acts to the Apostolic See together with a petition for a dispensation from either one or both of the spouses and the *votum* of the tribunal and the bishop."[21]

Canon 1678 §4 respects, however, the rights of the parties by requiring that both parties be heard first before a change of petition for a declaration of nullity to a petition for a dispensation from a ratified and non-consummated marriage can be effected. For the parties to make a truly informed decision, they should be informed of the differences between both procedures, and be assured of the cooperation of the tribunal personnel in carrying out their wishes.[22] Both parties have the right to be heard first before the judge can legitimately decree the suspension of the nullity process and remit the case to a dispensation from a ratified and non-consummated marriage.

The petition for a dispensation *super rato* can be submitted by one or both parties, but not by the promoter of justice. Although the petition must be always addressed to the Supreme Pontiff, the petition is presented to the competent bishop who, after having considered the law and the facts, is to ensure that the petition is instructed in accordance with the norm of law.

However, if there are special difficulties with the case, whether of a juridical or moral nature, the diocesan bishop is to consult the Apostolic See. "If the proposed case has special difficulties of the juridical or moral order, however, the diocesan bishop is to consult the Apostolic See."[23] After the bishop has heard from the Apostolic See, he is to follow its directives. Cases which present special difficulties and for which the bishop is to consult the Apostolic See before beginning the case are, for example, "contraceptive intercourse; acknowledged penetration without ejaculation; if a child is born by conception through absorption of the semen [i.e., without penetration], artificial insemination, and other procedures of contemporary medical sciences; absence of consummation because intercourse was not performed

---

[21] *CIC,* c. 1678 §4; *CCEO,* c. 1364 §4.
[22] Kowal and Woestman, p. 42.
[23] C. 1699 §2.

voluntarily (*humano modo*); danger of scandal or financial harm related to the granting of the favor and similar difficulties."[24] The purpose of this prior consultation is for the Apostolic See to share some of its experiences in these matters with the diocesan bishop to facilitate the proper instruction of the case.[25]

In conclusion, the petition of one or both of the spouses is directed to the Holy Father, with a summary of the matrimonial history, an indication of the causes that have prevented the consummation, the reasons for the dispensation being sought, the date and place of the drafting of the *libellus*, and the diocese of the domicile or quasi-domicile of one or both petitioners. The request ought to be signed by hand.[26]

Some of the important documents to be submitted along with the petition are the baptismal certificates of the parties, the marriage certificate, birth certificates of children conceived before the marriage, divorce decree, and any medical report.

For a sample form of a petition for the dissolution of a non-consummated marriage, the parties information form, the witness information form, and the agreement of understanding, see this chapter below.

For a sample form of the summary of the matrimonial history, see this chapter below.

2.   The Competent Bishop

"The person competent to accept a *libellus* seeking a dispensation is the diocesan bishop of the domicile or quasi-domicile of the petitioner, who must arrange for the instruction of the process if the petition is well founded."[27]

---

[24] Congregation for the Sacraments, December 20, 1986, Prot. No. 1400/86, *The Process for the Dispensation from a Ratified and Non-consummated Marriage*, n. 2.

[25] Kowal and Woestman, p. 41.

[26] Congregation for Divine Worship and Discipline of the Sacraments, June 13, 2009, "Instruction of a Cause for Dispensation of a *Ratum et Non-Consummatum* Marriage," in *Roman Replies* 2009) p. 29.

[27] C. 1699 §1.

The bishop competent to accept the petition for the dispensation of the marriage is the diocesan bishop of the diocese or particular church in which the petitioner has a domicile or a quasi-domicile. (c. 102 §§1-2). The same norm applies to those who are equivalent in law to a bishop. (c. 381 §2).

If the bishop either personally or through his delegate rejects the petition requesting a dispensation *super rato*, the aggrieved party has the right to take hierarchical recourse against the decision of the bishop to reject the petition. "Recourse to the Apostolic See is available against a decree by which a bishop rejects a *libellus*."[28]

3. The Decree of Acceptance, Constitution, and Citation

After the petition and other documents have been submitted, the bishop is to issue a decree of the appointment of the instructor, the defender of the bond, and the notary. "The instructing judge, which in a first instance Tribunal will be a single judge, must always be a priest, who can rely, in case of necessity, on a lay person, but as an auditor only."[29]

After the bishop has issued decree of acceptance, constitution, and citation, the instructor is to cite the parties. "As soon as the petition is received, the Bishop will see to it that the other party is informed, and, whenever there appears to be hope of success, the parties will be induced to solve their difficulties and to resume conjugal life."[30] If the respondent opposes or objects to the dissolution of the bond itself or to the claim of the non-consummation of the marriage, or to both, the reasons should be carefully evaluated as this has probative value on the claim of the peti-

---

[28] C. 1699 §3.

[29] Congregation for Divine Worship and Discipline of the Sacraments, June 13, 2009, "Instruction of a Cause for Dispensation of a *Ratum et Non-Consummatum* Marriage," in *Roman Replies* 2009) p. 30.

[30] Sacred Congregation for the Sacraments, December 20, 1986, Prot. No. 1400/86, *The Process for the Dispensation from a Ratified and Non-consummated Marriage*, n. 4.

tioner that the marriage was not consummated. However, bearing in mind canon 1592 §1 and *Dignitas connubii* 138 §3, "if the respondent, legitimately cited, does not respond to the citation, the tribunal may interpret this silence as a tacit assent to the suspension of the process and to the procedure for requesting the dispensation."[31]

The defender of the bond is likewise cited. "The defender of the bond must always intervene in these processes."[32] The role of the defender of the bond is to explain and present everything that can be reasonably argued against the granting of the petition. (cf. c. 1432).

Unless the bishop himself is the instructor, the instructor, the defender of the bond, and the notary should take an oath to carry out their office faithfully and to observe secrecy, and the document by which the oath was taken should be included in the acts.

The parties do not need advocates. However, the bishop can permit the parties to have advocates if it is a difficult case. "A legal representative is not admitted, but because of the difficulty of a case, a bishop can permit the petitioner or the respondent to have the assistance of a legal expert."[33] The roles of the legal expert are very limited. The legal expert "can only aid the parties in introducing the case, collecting the proofs, and, in case of a negative decision, in presenting the case again, observing what has to be observed."[34]

For a sample form of the decree of acceptance, constitution, and citation, see this chapter below.

For a sample form of the oath of the instructor, the defender of the bond, and the notary, see this chapter below.

---

[31] Congregation for Divine Worship and Discipline of the Sacraments, June 13, 2009, "Instruction of a Cause for Dispensation of a *Ratum et Non-Consummatum* Marriage," in *Roman Replies* 2009) p. 30.

[32] C. 1701 §1.

[33] C. 1701 §2.

[34] Sacred Congregation for the Sacraments, December 20, 1986, Prot. No. 1400/86, *The Process for the Dispensation from a Ratified and Non-consummated Marriage*, n. 6.

4. The Instruction of the Case

"Without prejudice to the prescript of can. [1678 §4], the bishop is to entrust the instruction of these processes either in a stable manner or in individual cases to his tribunal, that of another diocese, or a suitable priest."[35]

The diocesan bishop can assign the processing of petitions for dispensation from ratified and non-consummated marriage either in a stable manner or on a case-by-case basis to the diocesan tribunal, or to the tribunal of another diocese, or to a competent priest (*sacerdos*).[36] However, if the probable cause for doubting whether the marriage was ever consummated arose after a petition for a declaration of the nullity of the marriage has been already submitted to a competent tribunal, this tribunal, after having heard the parties, is to decree the suspension of the nullity of the process, complete the instruction for a dispensation *super rato,* and forward the acts of the case, including the petition, the observations of the defender of the bond, the *votum* of the judge instructor, and the *votum* of the diocesan bishop to the Apostolic See.

"In the instruction each spouse is to be heard, and the canons on the collection of proofs in the ordinary contentious trial and in cases of the nullity of marriage are to be observed insofar as possible, provided that they can be reconciled with the character of these processes."[37] Thus, in the instruction of the process, both spouses are to be heard. The citations of the parties and of the witnesses are to be made through the public postal services or by some other very secure method according to the norms established in particular law. The fact of the notification and its method must be evident in the acts.[38] "If a party or a witness refuses to give evidence before the judge, it is permitted for them to be

---

[35] C. 1700 §1.

[36] Sacred Congregation for the Sacraments, December 20, 1986, Prot. No. 1400/86, *The Process for the Dispensation from a Ratified and Non-consummated Marriage,* n. 5.

[37] C. 1702.

[38] C. 1509 §§1-2.

heard by another cleric or layperson appointed by the judge, or to make a declaration before a notary public or in any other lawful way, e.g., by letter, as long as it is clear that it is genuine and authentic."[39]

The efforts which have been made to cite the parties and the witnesses must be documented. "The absence of the parties taking part in the process is to be declared according to the legal norms and should be noted in the acts."[40]

Canons 1547-1573 regarding the admission, examination, and evaluation of witness testimony are to be observed. The parties and witnesses are also to take an oath individually to tell the truth and to observe confidentially regarding the questions and answers, since this matter is of a private nature. The bishop or his delegate must vigilantly see to it that neither of the parties in the case nor the witnesses nor the experts ever dares to make a false deposition or to withhold the truth. He knows, and through him all the interested persons should know, that the favor of a dispensation cannot be granted unless two things are proved: that the marriage was actually not consummated and that a just cause, that is, a proportionally serious reason, exists. If one or the other is lacking, the rescript of favor, inasmuch as it labors from obreption, in nowise benefits the one who receives it.[41]

"The interrogation of the parties is to be conducted by the Instructor in the presence of the Notary and the Defender of the Bond, under oath to speak the truth, with questions designed to clarify the marriage of the parties and, at the conclusion, under oath confirming the truth of what was said. In particularly delicate or complex cases involving the manner of intimate life, a

---

[39] Sacred Congregation for the Sacraments, December 20, 1986, Prot. No. 1400/86, *The Process for the Dispensation from a Ratified and Non-consummated Marriage*, n. 9.

[40] Sacred Congregation for the Sacraments, December 20, 1986, Prot. No. 1400/86, *The Process for the Dispensation from a Ratified and Non-consummated Marriage*, n. 10.

[41] Sacred Congregation for the Sacraments, March 7, 1972, *Emended Procedure in Cases of Non-consummation of Marriage*, n. I (f). See also *CIC*, c. 63 §2.

medical expert may be present to pose the question."[42]

If an expert is to be cited, canons 1574-1581 and 1678 are also to be observed. The instructor can secure the services of one or more experts, if the instructor believes it is necessary to prove the fact of the non-consummation of the marriage.[43]

The instructor also interviews the witnesses using the questions prepared beforehand. The questions and the interview are to be in accordance with the norm of law.[44] "The interrogation of witnesses, indicated by the parties or selected by the Instructor, under oath to speak the truth, is to be conducted with prepared questions, pertaining to their knowledge of the non-consummation and of the more significant aspects of the case."[45]

If necessary, character witnesses who can testify to the credibility of the parties should be presented.[46] "Insofar as possible, pastors will seek evidence of the credibility and honesty of the parties and witnesses. If this cannot be obtained, the Curia will seek other documents for judging the value of the depositions. All these will be carefully included in the acts."[47] Thus, the instructor is also to collect attestations of the credibility of the parties from their pastors or, in the absence of their pastors, from

---

[42] Congregation for Divine Worship and Discipline of the Sacraments, June 13, 2009, "Instruction of a Cause for Dispensation of a *Ratum et Non-Consummatum* Marriage," in *Roman Replies* 2009) p. 30.

[43] Sacred Congregation for the Sacraments, December 20, 1986, Prot. No. 1400/86, *The Process for the Dispensation from a Ratified and Non-consummated Marriage*, nn. 15-20.

[44] Sacred Congregation for the Sacraments, December 20, 1986, Prot. No. 1400/86, *The Process for the Dispensation from a Ratified and Non-consummated Marriage*, n. 11. See also cc. 1592; 1509.

[45] Congregation for Divine Worship and Discipline of the Sacraments, June 13, 2009, "Instruction of a Cause for Dispensation of a *Ratum et Non-Consummatum* Marriage," in *Roman Replies* 2009) p. 30.

[46] Sacred Congregation for the Sacraments, December 20, 1986, Prot. No. 1400/86, *The Process for the Dispensation from a Ratified and Non-consummated Marriage*, n. 14.

[47] Sacred Congregation for the Sacraments, December 20, 1986, Prot. No. 1400/86, *The Process for the Dispensation from a Ratified and Non-consummated Marriage*, n. 8.

other priests, religious, or laity who have particular knowledge of the parties.[48]

See this chapter below for a sample form of:

- The questionnaire for the examination of the parties.
- The questionnaire for the examination of the witnesses.
- The medical release form.
- The appointment decree of the medical examiner.
- The oath of the medical examiner.
- The appointment decree of the matron, nurse, or medical assistant.
- The oath of the medical assistant.

5. The Publication of the Acts

"Can. 1703 §1. There is no publication of the acts. If the judge perceives that the proofs brought forward seriously hinder the request of the petitioner or the exception of the respondent, however, he is prudently to inform the interested party. §2. The judge can show a document introduced or a testimony received to a party who requests it and set a time to present observations."[49]

In the instruction of *non-consumatum* cases, there is usually no publication of the acts. However, if, from the proofs that have been gathered, there is a probable cause which can make one assent that the marriage may have been consummated, the acts are to be published to the parties. Furthermore, if a party requests to review or inspect a document or a testimony that has been introduced into the process as proofs, the specific act or acts are to be published to the party. A deadline should be given to this party for the inspection of the act and another deadline for the presentation of comments and observations regarding the proof or proofs which have been reviewed.

---

[48] Congregation for Divine Worship and Discipline of the Sacraments, June 13, 2009, "Instruction of a Cause for Dispensation of a *Ratum et Non-Consummatum* Marriage," in *Roman Replies* 2009) p. 30.
[49] C. 1703 §§1-2.

6. The Decree of Conclusion and Instructor's Report

"When the instruction has been completed, the instructor is to give all the acts along with a suitable report to the bishop, who is to prepare a votum on the veracity of the fact of the non-consummation, the just cause for the dispensation, and the suitability of the favor."[50]

Subsequent to the completion of the instruction of the case, the defender of the bond is to write his or her observations regarding the case. The defender of the bond is required by his office to put forward and explain everything that can be reasonably proposed against the dispensation of the marriage.[51]

The instructor is to write a report which will include a summary of the whole process.[52]

For a sample form of the brief of the defender of the bond, see this chapter below.

For a sample form of the report of the instructor, see this chapter below.

7. The Votum of the Bishop

Subsequent to the presentation of the brief of the defender of the bond and the report of the instructor, the *votum pro rei veritate* of the bishop is also prepared for him and the acts of the case are to be sent to his office. Although the bishop himself can draw up his *votum*, he can, nonetheless, give general delegation for it to be

---

[50] C. 1704 §1.

[51] Sacred Congregation for the Sacraments, December 20, 1986, Prot. No. 1400/86, *The Process for the Dispensation from a Ratified and Non-consummated Marriage*, n. 22. See also c. 1432.

[52] Sacred Congregation for the Sacraments, December 20, 1986, Prot. No. 1400/86, *The Process for the Dispensation from a Ratified and Non-consummated Marriage*, n. 21. See also, Congregation for Divine Worship and Discipline of the Sacraments, June 13, 2009, "Instruction of a Cause for Dispensation of a *Ratum et Non-Consummatum* Marriage," in *Roman Replies* 2009) p. 29.

drawn up for him (cf. cc. 134 §2; 137 §1) for his review, approval, and signature.[53]

"If the instruction of the process has been entrusted to another tribunal according to the norm of can. 1700, the observations in favor of the bond are to be made in the same forum; the *votum* mentioned in §1, however, pertains to the entrusting bishop, to whom the instructor is to hand over a suitable report together with the acts."[54]

The *votum* of the bishop should indicate the following elements:

- The fact of the non-consummation of the marriage.
- The just cause for granting the dispensation.
- The opportuneness of the favor, especially for pastoral reasons.
- The absence of scandal, bewilderment of the faithful, and harm of any kind that could arise from the granting of the favor.
- The grant of the favor in relation to the good of souls and the restoration of peace of conscience.[55]

With regards to the processing fee or tax, the Apostolic See "is always sensitive to the inclusion of a request for a reduction in fees and, in more severe cases, even a total exemption, provided it is accompanied by documentation and a recommendation from the diocesan curia, which, in turn, declares its inability to cover the actual costs locally" for the Apostolic See.[56]

---

[53] Sacred Congregation for the Sacraments, December 20, 1986, Prot. No. 1400/86, *The Process for the Dispensation from a Ratified and Non-consummated Marriage*, n. 22a.

[54] C. 1704 §2.

[55] Sacred Congregation for the Sacraments, December 20, 1986, Prot. No. 1400/86, *The Process for the Dispensation from a Ratified and Non-consummated Marriage*, n. 23c.

[56] Congregation for Divine Worship and Discipline of the Sacraments, June 13, 2009, "Instruction of a Cause for Dispensation of a *Ratum et Non-Consummatum* Marriage," in *Roman Replies* 2009) p. 31.

For a sample form of the *votum* of the bishop, see this chapter below.

8.   The Transmittal of the Acts to the Apostolic See

"The bishop is to transmit to the Apostolic See all the acts together with his *votum* and the observations of the defender of the bond."[57]

Effective August 20, 2011, the competency for *non-consummatum* cases has been transferred from the Congregation for Divine Worship and the Discipline of the Sacraments to the Apostolic Tribunal of the Roman Rota. Pope Benedict XVI, in his the Apostolic Letter in the form of the *Motu Proprio, Quaerit Semper*, prescribed, *inter alia*, that: "An Office has been set up at this Tribunal to examine the fact of non-consummation in a marriage and the existence of a just cause for granting a dispensation. It therefore receives all the acts, together with the *votum* of the Bishop and the remarks of the Defender of the Bond, weighs them according to its own special procedure and, if the case warrants it, submits a petition to the Supreme Pontiff requesting the dispensation.[58]

To facilitate the study of the acts at the Roman Rota:

- The acts should be typed or word processed for legibility.
- Handwritten documents must be typed out.
- Documents drawn up in some less well-known language must be translated into anyone of the principal Western European languages which are widely known.
- The pages should be numbered.
- The pages should be clipped together, stapled, or bound.

---

[57] C. 1705 §1.

[58] Pope Benedict XVI, August 20, 2011, Apostolic Letter in the form of the *Motu Proprio, Quaerit Semper*, art. 2, §2.

- There should be a table of contents or index indicating the various documents and the pages where each document can be located in the acts.
- Three copies of the acts must be made and sent to the Apostolic See.
- The acts must be authenticated by an ecclesiastical notary.

When all the foregoing protocols have been observed, the complete acts of the case including the observations of the defender of the bond, the report of the instructor, and the bishop's *votum* are sent to the Roman Rota, usually via the Nunciature.[59]

In forwarding the acts of the case to the Apostolic See, include, if applicable, the acts of a canonical trial of the case for the declaration of nullity of marriage, medical records, police reports, private letters.[60]

9. The Supplementary Instruction of the Case by the Apostolic See

"If supplemental instruction is required in the judgment of the Apostolic See, this requirement will be communicated to the bishop with an indication of the points on which the instruction must be completed."[61]

If there are difficulties or if some points are not clear in the case, the Roman Rota may send the bishop a supplementary instruction of the case. Thus, if in the judgment of the Roman Rota, further instruction is required to prove the alleged non-consummation, the bishop will be informed of this along with what additional elements are needed for adequate proof. Even if the Rota

---

[59] Sacred Congregation for the Sacraments, March 7, 1972, *Emended Procedure in Cases of Non-consummation of Marriage,* n. II (g). See also, Kowal and Woestman, p. 50.

[60] Congregation for Divine Worship and Discipline of the Sacraments, June 13, 2009, "Instruction of a Cause for Dispensation of a *Ratum et Non-Consummatum* Marriage," in *Roman Replies* 2009) p. 30.

[61] C. 1705 §2.

replies that non-consummation has not been proven in the acts, the parties with the assistance of a legal expert always have the faculty of determining whether any grave reason or anything of importance can be brought forward to justify a resubmission of the petition.

"If the Apostolic See replies that non-consummation has not been established from the materials presented, then the legal expert mentioned in can. 1701, §2 can inspect the acts of the process, though not the votum of the bishop, at the tribunal to consider whether any grave reason can be brought forth in order to resubmit the petition."[62] In the case of a negative decision rendered by the Roman Rota in the case, the legal expert can, after studying the acts, with the exception of the bishop's *votum*, request further instruction of the case, write observations to clarify difficulties, place other required legal acts, and help the petitioner present the case again.[63]

In conclusion, except more information has been requested from the diocese or the local level has delayed in sending back the further instruction to Rome, the goal of the Apostolic See is to complete the process between two to three months.

10. The Apostolic Rescript of Dispensation

"The Apostolic See transmits the rescript of the dispensation to the bishop who will notify the parties about the rescript and also as soon as possible will order the pastor both of the place where the marriage was contracted and of the place of baptism to note the granting of the dispensation in the marriage and baptismal registers." [64]

After the acts have been carefully examined by the Roman Rota if an affirmative vote is rendered in the case, the case is then presented to the Supreme Pontiff with the recommendation that the dissolution be granted. It is the Pontiff who makes the decision to grant a dispensation *super rato*. Over ninety-seven percent

---

[62] C.1705 §3.
[63] Kowal and Woestman, p. 51.
[64] C. 1706.

of cases receive an affirmative decision. The rescript is issued by the Roman Rota, and sent to the bishop. It is his responsibility to notify the parties and the pastors of the place(s) where the marriage was contracted and where the parties were baptized. This is done so that the proper notices can be placed in the parish registers. [65]

The apostolic rescript of the dispensation is granted based on two elements, namely: that the marriage was actually not consummated and that a just cause, that is, a proportionally serious reason, exists in the case. If one or the other is lacking, the rescript of favor, inasmuch as it labors from obreption, does not benefit the one who receives it. It is evident, therefore, that "if a new marriage is perchance entered into after the dispensation, it can always be declared null if it later becomes known that the first marriage was actually sacramental and consummated."[66]

"After a papal grant of dispensation has been given regarding the bond of a non-consummated marriage, the spouses have the right to enter into other marriages provided that such entrance is not prohibited. Such prohibition can be expressed in two ways: by the phrase 'according to intent,' (and in this case the 'intent' can vary and is appropriately explained) or by the phrase 'forbidden.'"[67]

"a) The phrase expressed in the words 'according to intent,' which is a prohibitory phrase, is wont to be appended as often as the fact of non-consummation hinges on causes of lesser moment, its removal is entrusted to the bishop in such wise that he may more expeditiously provide for the pastoral needs of the faithful. However, the bishop should not allow the party requesting the removal of the phrase to enter a new marriage unless, after the prescribed regulations have been observed, the party is found to

---

[65] Kowal and Woestman, p. 52.

[66] Sacred Congregation for the Sacraments, March 7, 1972, *Emended Procedure in Cases of Non-consummation of Marriage*, n. I (f).

[67] Sacred Congregation for the Sacraments, March 7, 1972, *Emended Procedure in Cases of Non-consummation of Marriage*, n. III.

be truly suited to sustaining the marriage obligations and promises to discharge the conjugal duties in the future in an upright and Christian manner."[68]

"b) On the other hand, in special cases, namely, when the reason for the non-consummation is a physical or psychic defect of greater moment and seriousness, 'forbidden' in relation to other marriages may be appended. Unless it is expressly stated in the rescript, this addendum is not a diriment [impediment] but only prohibitive and its removal is reserved to the Apostolic See. Permissions, however, to enter a new marriage is granted if the petitioner, after having addressed a petition to the [Apostolic See] and after having fulfilled the prescribed conditions, is judged qualified for the proper exercise of the conjugal acts."[69]

"It is left to the judgment of the bishop and to his pastoral consideration to inform the party with whom it is intended to enter a new marriage, about the one or other phrase appended in the rescript of dispensation and later removed from it." [70]

---

[68] Sacred Congregation for the Sacraments, March 7, 1972, *Emended Procedure in Cases of Non-consummation of Marriage,* n. III (a). See also, Sacred Congregation for the Sacraments, December 20, 1986, Prot. No. 1400/86, *The Process for the Dispensation from a Ratified and Non-consummated Marriage,* n. 25.

[69] Sacred Congregation for the Sacraments, March 7, 1972, *Emended Procedure in Cases of Non-consummation of Marriage,* n. III (b). See also, Sacred Congregation for the Sacraments, December 20, 1986, Prot. No. 1400/86, *The Process for the Dispensation from a Ratified and Non-consummated Marriage,* n. 25.

[70] Sacred Congregation for the Sacraments, March 7, 1972, *Emended Procedure in Cases of Non-consummation of Marriage,* n. III.

4. The Sample Documents for the Instruction of Non-Consummated Marriage Cases

4.1. *The Petition*

TRIBUNAL NAME, ADDRESS, & LOGO

PETITION FOR THE FAVOR OF THE DISSOLUTION NON-CONSUMMATED MARRIAGE
(Please fill in all the blanks and answer all questions as completely as possible).

HOLY FATHER:

I, _____, humbly present this petition for the dissolution of the bond of my marriage to _____ on the ground of the non-consummation of the marriage. I contracted this marriage on ___ day of ___ in the year of our Lord ____ at _____. We obtained a decree of civil divorce on ___ at _____. There is no possibility of restoring the partnership of conjugal life. There will be no public scandal should this dissolution be granted. I sincerely request that you as the Vicar of Christ dissolve my marriage for the good of souls and for peace of conscience so that I may enter a new marriage validly and licitly according to the laws of God and of the Holy Catholic Church.

☐ I am a Catholic and my former spouse is also a Catholic.
☐ I am a Catholic and my former spouse is a baptized non-Catholic of _____ Denomination.
☐ I am a baptized non-Catholic of _____ Denomination and my former spouse is a Catholic.
☐ I am a baptized non-Catholic of _____ Denomination and my former spouse is a baptized non-Catholic of _____ Denomination.
☐ I am unbaptized and my former spouse is a Catholic.
☐ I am unbaptized and my former spouse is a baptized non-Catholic of _____ Denomination.

I have attached a full and accurate presentation of all the facts and the reasons for petitioning for the rescript of dispensation. I attest that the information presented is true to the best of my knowledge.

_____   _____

Signature of Petitioner   Date

4.2. *The Summary of the Matrimonial History*

SUMMARY OF THE MATRIMONIAL HISTORY
(Please, answer the following questions and submit it along with the petition)

1. Please, give a summary of the history of the marriage. For example, where and when did you first meet each other? What was the date of the marriage? What venue and city did it take place? What marriage preparation classes or programs were done towards the marriage? Give any other important information that occurred prior to the marriage.
2. What are the causes that prevented the consummation of the marriage?
3. What are the reasons for requesting the dispensation from the pope?

Please, sign and date your response and send it to the tribunal. Thank you.

4.3. *The Parties Information Form*
In a separate sheet of paper

PARTIES INFORMATION

PETITIONER:

Name: _____
          First, Middle, Maiden & Current Last Name

Address: _____
Street, City, State, Zip Code
Phone: Work: (___) _____ Home: (___) _____ Cell: (___) _____
E-mail: _____
Religion: _____ Date of Birth: _____ Age _____
Church of Baptism: _____ Date of Baptism: _____
Church Address: _____
Street, City, State, Zip Code
RESPONDENT:

Name: _____
First, Middle, Maiden & Current Last Name
Address: _____
Street, City, State, Zip Code
Phone: Work: (___) _____ Home: (___) _____ Cell: (___) _____
E-mail: _____
Religion: _____ Date of Birth: _____ Age _____
Church of Baptism: _____ Date of Baptism: _____
Church Address: _____
Street, City, State, Zip Code
MARRIAGE:

Place/Church: _____ Date: _____
Address: _____County:_____
Street, City, State, Zip Code
DIVORCE:
Date: _____County:_____ State: _____

4.4. *The Witness Information Form*

WITNESS INFORMATION

On a separate sheet of paper

Please identify witnesses who knew you and the other party prior to and subsequent to the marriage. Please include at least two names for witnesses. Contact them first to ensure that they are willing to testify.

Witness 1:

Name: _____
Address: _____
Tel.: Home (___) _____ Work (___) _____ Cell (___) _____
Email: _____
Relationship: _____ How long acquainted? _____

Witness 2:

Name: _____
Address: _____
Tel.: Home (___) _____ Work (___) _____ Cell (___) _____
Email: _____
Relationship: _____ How long acquainted? _____

Witness 3:

Name: _____
Address: _____
Tel.: Home (___) _____ Work (___) _____ Cell (___) _____
Email: _____
Relationship: _____ How long acquainted? _____

Witness 4:

Name: _____
Address: _____
Tel.: Home (___) _____ Work (___) _____ Cell (___) _____
Email: _____
Relationship: _____ How long acquainted? _____

4.5. *The Agreement of Understanding Form*

AGREEMENT OF UNDERSTANDING

On separate sheets of paper

I, the undersigned Petitioner, understand that:

1. A dispensation cannot be granted until I have provided sufficient evidence that my marriage was not consummated.
2. The submission of this petition does not guarantee that a dispensation will be granted.
3. I am obliged to provide the Tribunal with a current address and phone number of my former spouse. I agree to document what attempts I made to locate my former spouse.
4. I may not set a date for marriage in the Catholic Church until I have received a definitive response from the Tribunal.
5. I understand that the Tribunal, in the investigation of the case, may employ the services of a psychological professional or other expert witness and I hereby authorize the Tribunal to disclose complete information concerning my case to such a professional for case review.
6. The dispensation of a marriage is an ecclesiastical matter and has no effects in civil law.
7. I voluntarily waive now and in the future any right under law to the subpoena or judicial discovery of the testimonies and acts of this case. This is to provide for candor and openness in testimony, in recognition of the purely spiritual and religious nature of these proceedings, and to allow the Tribunal to process this case free from undue entanglements or hindrances. This waiver is given without reservation and condition.
8. Only the Petitioner and the Respondent may seek information regarding this case.
9. I agree to keep confidential and secret any information that I shall learn in the course of the proceeding because all testimony in this case is given for the possible apostolic rescript of dispensation regarding my marriage; and, because my interest is solely to present my case to the Tribunal, I promise not to use information that I may learn

through the case in any other forum or for any other purpose.

10. I swear that all information contained in and accompanying my petition, as well as in future statements written and oral provided during this process, is and will be the whole truth and nothing but the truth, so help me God.

_____   _____

Signature of Petitioner   Date

_____

Name of the Petitioner

4.6. *The Checklist*

On separate sheets of paper

DOCUMENTS ENCLOSED
The following have been submitted with the Petition:

- ☐ The marriage license of the marriage between the Petitioner and the Respondent.
- ☐ The marriage certificate of the marriage between the Petitioner and the Respondent.
- ☐ Final divorce decree.
- ☐ Baptismal certificate or proof of Baptism of the baptized party or parties.

4.7. *The Decree of Acceptance, Constitution, and Citation*

Case

Decree:
Commission of the Tribunal

Re: Dispensation from the bond of the non-consummated marriage between:

N., Petitioner, and N., Respondent

Having received the petition of N., Petitioner, in which he/she is requesting the Holy Father to dissolve the marriage between the Petitioner and the Respondent on the grounds of the non-consummation of the marriage, and

Having determined that the Petitioner is domiciled in this Diocese, I, as the Bishop of N., is competent to accept the petition by virtue of canon 1699 §1.

There exists some basis as well as a just cause for the petition. There is no hope of reconciliation between the spouses. I hereby accept the Petition. I nominate and delegate the instruction of the case to the following persons:

Judge Instructor:	Reverend N.
Auditor:	N.
Defender of the Bond:	N.
Notary:	N.

I grant to the Judge Instructor the authority to sub-delegate others to assist him in the instruction of the process and to appoint substitutes for the defender of the bond and the notary for a just cause.

Furthermore, I hereby cite the Parties and the Defender of the Bond to the process. This Decree is to be communicated to the Parties, the Defender of the Bond, and they are to respond within fifteen (15) days of the notification of this Decree.

The instruction of the process is to be conducted and completed in accordance with the norms of the Code of Canon Law, especially canon 1678 §4 and canons 1697-1706 and the supplementary norms issued by the Apostolic See for the processing of *super rato et non consummatum* marriages.

Given at ... (*Place*), on ... (*date*).

Signed by the Ordinary.

Signed by the Notary.

4.8. *The Oath of the Judge Instructor*

Case

The Oath of the Judge Instructor

Having been named and appointed by the Most Reverend N., Bishop of N., as the Judge Instructor for the instruction and completion of the petition for the dispensation of the marriage bond between N., Petitioner, and N., Respondent, which has been submitted on the grounds of the non-consummation of the marriage,

I hereby swear that I will properly and faithfully observe the duties of this office and comply with the norms of the Code of Canon Law and the supplementary norms issued by the Apostolic See for processing of non-consummated marriages. I also promise to observe secrecy. So help me God.

_____   _____

Name   Date
Judge Instructor

4.9. *The Oath of the Defender of the Bond*

Case

The Oath of the Defender of the Bond

Having been named and appointed by the Most Reverend N., Bishop of N., as the Defender of the Bond for the instruction and completion of the petition for the dispensation of the marriage bond between N., Petitioner, and N., Respondent, which has been submitted on the grounds of the non-consummation of the marriage,

I hereby swear that I will properly and faithfully observe the duties of this office and comply with the norms of the Code of Canon Law and the supplementary norms issued by the Apostolic See for processing of non-consummated marriages. I also promise to observe secrecy. So help me God.

_____   _____
Name   Date
Defender of the Bond

4.10. *The Oath of the Notary*

Case

The Oath of the Notary

Having been named and appointed by the Most Reverend N., Bishop of N., as the Notary for the instruction and completion of the petition for the dispensation of the marriage bond between N., Petitioner, and N., Respondent, which has been submitted on the grounds of the non-consummation of the marriage,

I hereby swear that I will properly and faithfully observe the duties of this office and comply with the norms of the Code of Canon Law and the supplementary norms issued by the Apostolic See for processing of non-consummated marriages. I also promise to observe secrecy. So help me God.

_____   _____
Name   Date
Defender of the Bond

4.11. *The Questionnaire for the Examination of the Parties*

PARTIES' QUESTIONNAIRE FOR THE DISSOLUTION OF A NON-CONSUMMATED MARRIAGE

I. General Questions

1. Do you solemnly swear to tell the truth, the whole truth, and nothing but the truth, so help you God?
2. What are your full names (including maiden name)?
3. What is your address and telephone number?
4. When and where were you born?
5. When and where was your former spouse born?

6. By what means do you have to establish your identity (e.g., driver's license)? A copy of the proof of your identity is to be made and included in the documents of the case.
7. When and from whom did you learn that a non-consummated marriage can be dispensed by the Roman Pontiff?
8. Does your former spouse agree that the marriage should be dissolved? Please, provide reasons for your answer.

II. Your Life Before Marriage

A. *Family Background*

1. Describe the life of your parents together and the way they got along.
2. Describe the way in which you got along with each of your parents.
3. Describe your relationship with your siblings while growing-up.
4. Describe how your relationship with family members and the marriage of your parents might have impacted your views on marriage.
5. Were there issues in your family that may have affected your ability to establish a stable marriage? For example, abuse, addictions, repeated infidelity, multiple divorces, remarriage, extreme strictness, serious illness, etc.?
6. Did you experience any physical or psychological problems or traumas during your childhood, adolescence, or young adulthood? If so, how did these issues affect your readiness to take on the obligations of marriage life?

B. *Personality and Character*

1. Describe your behavior toward alcohol and drugs;

specifically any addictive or abusive behavior.
2. Describe your relationship with the opposite sex, dating habits, and/or any addictive behavior(s); e.g., gambling, internet, cybersex, pornography.
3. Write a brief sketch of your personality; comment on your weak and strong points at the time of the wedding and now.

III. Your Former Spouse's Life Before Marriage

Kindly answer the following questions regarding your former spouse to the best of your knowledge.

A. *Family Background*

1. Describe the life of his/her parents together and the way they got along.
2. Describe the way in which he/she got along with each of his/her parents.
3. Describe his/her relationship with siblings.
4. Describe how his/her relationship with family members and the marriage of his/her parents might have impacted his/her views on marriage.
5. Were there issues in his/her family that may have affected his/her ability to establish a stable marriage? For example, abuse, addictions, repeated infidelity, multiple divorces, remarriage, extreme strictness, serious illness, etc.?
6. Did you experience any physical or psychological problems or traumas during your childhood, adolescence, or young adulthood? If so, how did these issues affect your readiness to take on the obligations of marriage life?

B. *Personality and Character*

1. Describe his/her behavior toward alcohol and

drugs; specifically any addictive or abusive behavior.

2. Describe his/her relationship with the opposite sex, dating habits, and/or any addictive behavior(s); e.g., gambling, internet, cybersex, pornography.

3. Write a brief sketch of his/her personality; comment on his/her weak and strong points at the time of the wedding and now.

IV. Courtship and Engagement

1. When did you meet? When did you begin dating? Were there problems during the dating period?

2. When did you get engaged? Describe how the decision to marry was reached. How long was the engagement?

3. Describe what discussion you had about the rights and obligations of marriage.

4. Describe your attitudes and intentions about having children. Did you agree to not have children? If so, why? If you agreed to wait to have children, was this essential to your agreement to marry? Why? Did you tell anyone of this before the wedding? Who?

5. If your relationship with each other was a sexually active one prior to marriage, when did this begin? How did this influence your decision to marry?

6. What were the attitude of families and friends toward the proposed marriage?

7. Indicate the church preparations you had for this marriage.

8. Did you feel pressured to marry? If so, who or what was pressuring you and how? Please explain.

9. Were there other factors that had a major influence on you/your former at the time? Please explain.

10. Did either of you hide anything about yourselves

from each other to make sure the wedding would take place? If so, what was hidden? Did it become a problem during the marriage? Please explain.

11. Did either of you set any conditions for the marriage to take place? If so, what was the condition and who set it? Did the continuation of the union depend on this? Who knows about this?

V. The Wedding

1. Did either or both of you consent to marriage freely? If not, what are the reasons?
2. Describe anything unusual that might have happened at the wedding or the reception.
3. State your understanding of marriage at this time.
4. Did either of you have any serious doubts about going through with the wedding? If so, why? Did either tell anyone about your doubts?

VI. The Honeymoon and Attempts at Consummation

1. Did both of you go on a honeymoon? If so, describe where you went for the honeymoon and the length of time you stayed there.
2. Indicate any problems or any significant events that occurred on the honeymoon that prevented the consummation of the marriage.
3. Did anything unusual happen during the honeymoon?
4. Were artificial contraceptive measures used? If so, was it only at the early attempts of the consummation of the marriage or all the time? By whom? On whose insistence?
5. Did the male party use the withdrawal method or *coitus interruptus?* If so, was it only at the early attempts of the consummation of the marriage or all the time?

6. Was sexual intercourse between the parties attempted by some violent or forceful means, or by as putting the other party under hypnosis, drugs, medication, or by some other means wherein the conjugal act was not freely given or made by the affected party?

7. After the wedding, did both of you immediately establish common life? If so, where and for how long?

8. Are you related? If so, when did you discover this? Prior to or subsequent to the marriage ceremony?

9. Did you have sexual intercourse shortly after your marriage, in other words, was your marriage consummated? If not, why not?

10. In what religion were you and your ex-spouse raised? Does your religion or that of your former spouse teach some type of aversion to sexuality?

11. Did either of you contract a sexually transmitted disease? If so, was this before or after the marriage ceremony? When and how did you and your former spouse discover this?

12. Were you or your ex-spouse afraid of contracting a sexually transmitted disease?

13. What is the sexual orientation of you and of your former spouse? Did this become known to either or both parties during the courtship or after the wedding?

14. Did you or your ex-spouse suffer from any physical defect or infirmity? If so, please explain. Have any doctors been consulted in this regard? Do you have medical documents?

15. What do you think were the reasons or causes why you did not or could not have sexual intercourse?

16. Do you have physical or moral evidence that the marriage was not consummated?

17. Did you or your ex-spouse, either openly or confidentially discuss your marital problems with your parents, relatives, friends or other persons? If so,

please provide names and contact information.

18. Is there any other development of the sexual dimension of the relationship with reference to any problems or difficulties encountered?

VII. The Married Life

1. Describe the beginning of your married life. Were there signs of future problems?
2. Were there any changes of character or behavior? Please explain.
3. If you had children, when were they born? Did they affect the marriage?
4. If you had no children, what artificial contraceptive measures were used? By whom? On whose insistence?
5. If there were no children, what reasons was stated for the exclusion of children?

VIII. The Separation

1. Were there separations prior to the final separation? Why? When and for how long? What brought you back together?
2. Give the reason for the final separation; give the date; and how it came about.
3. What was the reaction of others at the news of the separation and divorce? Please explain.
4. If this is dissolved and you are permitted to marry in the Catholic Church, would it give rise to scandal, or criticism, or unfavorable publicity?
5. Have you anything else to add?
6. Do you affirm and attest that all the answers you provided above are true to the best of your knowledge.

IX.   The Present Situation

    1.   What is the present marital status of each party?
    2.   If you plan to marry, is the person free to marry in the Catholic Church?

_____ (*Signature*)   _____

Name   Date

4.12. *The Questionnaire for the Examination of the Witnesses*

WITNESS QUESTIONNAIRE FOR THE DISSOLUTION OF A NON-CONSUMMATED MARRIAGE

I.   General Questions

1.   Do you solemnly swear to tell the truth, the whole truth, and nothing but the truth, so help you God?
2.   What are your full names (including maiden name)?
3.   What is your address and telephone number?
4.   When and where were you born?
5.   By what means do you have to establish your identity (e.g., driver's license)?
6.   Please, describe your relationship to the parties? How long have you known each of them?

II.   Background and Personalities

1.   What was their home life like? Their relationship with parents? With others in their families? What influence did this have on their decision to marry?
2.   What had been their major experiences in childhood? In adolescence? In education? In the military? In work? In other relationships?
3.   Did either have any problem with discipline? With health? With drugs or alcohol?

4. Please note any problems or events that had a significant influence on their development.
5. How did you see each of them prior to and at the time of the marriage?
6. What is their respective religion? How well did each party practice his or her faith?

III. Dating Period and Engagement

1. Was the dating period harmonious? Was it sufficiently long? Given the benefit of hindsight, was the source of later problems evident during the dating period? Please explain.
2. What led them to decide to marry? Was there any pressure to marry exerted upon them? Did they have any real choice in deciding to marry?
3. Were they ready to make the commitment to marriage? What were their expectations? Please explain.
4. What was the attitude of their families toward the marriage? Did they receive any counseling or advice in preparing to marry?
5. Did they feel compelled to marry against their own will? Did either have any second thoughts about marrying? Did either want to call off the wedding? Please explain.
6. Did either, in order to obtain the consent of the other, hide anything from the other which after marriage became a source of tension and disruption?
7. What were their respective intentions and attitudes toward begetting children in the marriage?

IV. The Wedding

1. Was there anything usual during the wedding? The reception?
2. Did they go on a honeymoon?
3. Were there any problems on the honeymoon? In the initial adjustment to married life?

4. To the best of your knowledge, was the marriage ever consummated? How do you know this? When did you learn of this?
5. If the marriage was not consummated, were you informed of the cause? If so, who? And when?

V. The Marriage

1. Kindly describe the early stages of their married life?
2. Did their intentions and attitudes toward begetting children change during the marriage? If so, why?
3. When did serious difficulties emerge between the parties? What were they? How did they deal with them? Please note the roots of these difficulties and their seriousness. Was any counseling or medical treatment sought?

VI. The Separation

1. What caused their separation? Who departed from the marriage?
2. Before their separation, where they under one roof and sleeping in the same bed?
3. How did they deal with the separation? What was the reaction of others? What is the situation of each today?
4. Is there any possibility of reconciliation?
5. Kindly offer your personal reflections on the marriage.
6. Do you believe that either or both of them will be truthful in answering questions about this matter? Please give reasons for your answer.
7. Would there be scandal, criticism, or unfavorable publicity, if this marriage is dissolved?
8. Have you anything else to add?
9. Do you affirm and attest that all the answers you provided above are true to the best of your knowledge.

_____ (*Signature*)   _____
Name   Date

4.13. *The Medical Release Form*

Case

MEDICAL RELEASE FORM

I, _____, hereby consent and authorize
    Name (please print)
_____, a Medical Doctor,
    Name of Medical Doctor

Whose Office is situated at: _____
                    Mailing address of Medical Doctor

to provide to the Judicial Vicar of the Diocese of N. full and complete information pertaining to the medical examination of me by the above named medical doctor. I waiver the privileges and the confidentiality of such information in connection for the purpose of assisting the Tribunal in a pending ecclesiastical inquiry which is of an exclusively religious nature. This consent, authorization, and waiver extends only to revealing the information requested to the Tribunal of N. for the sole purpose of its use in connection with my petition for a dissolution of the bond of my marriage.

_____

Signature of Petitioner

_____

Date
============================

For the USA only

The Tribunal of the Diocese of N. understands that it is being given certain Protected Health Information from the provider identified by the petitioner. The Tribunal agrees:

- to use this information only for ecclesiastical purposes during this pending inquiry, and for no other reason; and

- to safeguard this information from misuse, inappropriate disclosure, and accidental or intentional destruction, or loss.

This provision complies with the requirements of the Health Insurance Portability and Accountability Act.

_____   _____
Tribunal Officer   Date

4.14. *The Appointment Decree of the Medical Examiner*[71]

Case

Decree
Appointment of the Medical Examiner

Re: Dispensation from the bond of the non-consummated marriage between:

N., Petitioner, and N., Respondent

Having heard the defender of the bond and having heard N., the Party who is to be examined, I, the undersigned Judge Instructor, hereby designate and appoint as medical expert Dr. N. for the purpose of the medical examination of the above-named Party in accordance with the requirements of the norms of canon law for the dispensation of a non-consummated marriage.

_____ (*Signature*)   _____
Name   Date
Defender of the Bond

_____ (*Signature*)   _____
Name   Date
Judge Instructor

_____

[71] If applicable to the case.

4.15. *The Oath of the Medical Examiner*

Case

I, the undersigned medical doctor, having been duly appointed in accordance with the norms of canon law for the purpose of conducting a medical examination on N., do hereby solemnly promise to perform the office committed to me faithfully and dutifully. I also promise to undertake the necessary tests and examination which medical science permits and which the teachings of the Church also permit regarding the medical determination of the consummation or the non-consummation of the marriage. I also promise to report truthfully a written report of the findings and to observe secrecy. So help me God.

_____ (*Signature*)   _____

Name   Date
Medical Examiner

4.16. *The Decree Appointment of the Matron, Nurse, or Medical Assistant*[72]

Case

Decree
Appointment of the Matron

Re: Dispensation from the bond of the non-consummated marriage between:

N., Petitioner, and N., Respondent

Having heard the defender of the bond and having heard N., the Party who is to be examined, I, the undersigned Judge Instructor, hereby designate and appoint as Matron (or Nurse, or Medical Assistant) N. to assist during the medical examination of

---

[72] If applicable to the case.

the above-named Party in accordance with the requirements of the norms of canon law for the dispensation of a non-consummated marriage.

_____ (*Signature*)   _____
Name   Date
Defender of the Bond

_____ (*Signature*)   _____
Name   Date
Judge Instructor

4.17. *The Oath of the Matron*

Case

I, the undersigned nurse (or medical assistant), having been duly appointed in accordance with the norms of canon law for the purpose of assisting during the medical examination on N., do hereby solemnly promise to perform the office committed to me faithfully and dutifully. I also promise to provide the assistance honestly and within the parameters of medical science and of the teachings of the Church and to observe secrecy. So help me God.

_____ (*Signature*)   _____
Name of Nurse   Date

4.18. *The Brief of the Defender of the Bond*

Case

The Observations of the Defender of the Bond

Re: Dispensation from the bond of the non-consummated marriage between:

N., Petitioner and N., Respondent

I, the undersigned Defender of the Bond, having been legitimately cited to present my observations regarding this case and having carefully examined the acts of the case, hereby presents this brief to the Court for consideration.

1. A petition for the dissolution of the marriage bond between N., Petitioner, and N., Respondent, on the grounds of non-consummation has been submitted to the Roman Pontiff by the Petitioner through the hand of the Bishop of N. (*name of the local diocese instructing the case*). By virtue of canon 1699 §1, Most Reverend N., Bishop of N. (*name of the local diocese instructing the case*) is competent to accept the case on behalf of the Roman Pontiff and to arrange for the instruction of the process.

2. The petition is well-founded. There is also a just cause for the petition. There is no hope of reconciliation between the parties. For example, one of the spouses, the Petitioner/Respondent has. (or, Both spouses have) entered into civil law marriage with another spouse. *State some other reasons for the just cause.*

3. I am satisfied that the process for the dissolution of ratified and non-consummated marriage have been observed in the instruction of the petition, in accordance with the Code of Canon Law and the supplementary norms issued by the Apostolic See.

4. There is a probable doubt that the marriage was ever consummated in accordance with the received jurisprudence of the Church with regards to what constitutes the canonical consummation of marriage. (*CIC,* cc. 1061 §1 and 1678 §4). Furthermore, "for a marriage to be consummated it is necessary that there be a human act on the part of both spouses; it is sufficient for it to be virtually voluntary, provided that it was not exhorted through violence. No juridic weight is given to other psychological elements which render the act easier or more loving." (Sacred Congregation for the Sacraments, December 20, 1986, Prot. No. 1400/86, *The Process for the Dispensation from a Ratified and Non-consummated marriage, in Communicationes* 20

(1988), pp. 78-84; in *Monitor Ecclesiasticus* 112 (1987) pp. 423-429).

5. *State the religious practice of the petitioner and of his/her current or intended spouse, as indicated in the letter of the pastor. For example*: The Petitioner is a Catholic/receiving religious instruction, who attends Mass regularly with his /her intended spouse. The Petitioner wishes to marry a baptized Catholic, N., who is Catholic and is free to marry.

6. There is no possibility of scandal or wonderment should the Roman Pontiff grant the dispensation. The community is aware of the Petitioner's prior marriage and that both parties have since moved on with their life.

7. The undersigned has no objection to placing this case before the Holy See for favorable consideration.

_____   _____

N.   Date
Defender of the Bond

4.19. *The Report of the Judge Instructor*

Case

Re: Dispensation from the bond of the non-consummated marriage between:

N., Petitioner, and N., Respondent

The Report of the Instructor

The Petitioner, N., a ___ (*religion*), has presented a petition for the dispensation from the bond of his/her marriage to the Respondent, N., a ___ (*religion*), on the grounds of the non-consummation of the marriage. The Petitioner wishes to marry N. a ___ (*religion*). The Petitioner is seeking the favor of the dispensation from the Roman Pontiff for his/her own spiritual good as well as for the spiritual good of his/her intended spouse. The Petitioner and his/her intended spouse attend Mass regularly in their parish.

State whether the petition was presented ab initio as a non-consummated marriage petition or it was initially submitted as a formal case, and it was later determined that the matter pertains to a non-consummated marriage. Give a brief procedural history of the case here.

The Petitioner married N. (*name of the respondent*), on ... (*date*). The Petitioner was __ years old and the Respondent was __ years old at the time of the marriage. They courted for about __ years and __ months before they got married.

State the facts and circumstances surrounding why the marriage was not ever consummated.

The marriage perdured for __ years and __ months. *State the reasons why the marriage ended in absolute divorce.* __ children were born to the union. They obtained a civil divorce in __.

It is my considered opinion that there is no hope of reconciliation between the parties. This determination is based on their attitude toward each other, which preclude reconciliation and a restoration of conjugal living between them. In addition, it has been ... years since they obtained a civil decree of absolute divorce and each of them has attempted civil marriage with another spouse.

The Petitioner attests to the non-consummation of the marriage. His/Her claim is corroborated by __ witnesses, among whom are his/her ___ (e.g., his mother, his father, his aunt, his brother, his sister, a family friend, etc.). They testified separate and apart from each other and under oath. In addition, there is no reason to doubt their credibility. They can be considered qualified witnesses to the fact of the non-consummation of the marriage.

The Respondent has cooperated/not cooperated with us. *If the respondent has cooperated, give a synopsis of his/her statement. If the respondent did not cooperate, give a brief report of the efforts made to cite or contact the respondent, and why all efforts to get him or her to participate in the process failed. Are there proofs of citation in the acts? If so, state it.*

The pastor of the intended spouse has testified to the credibility of the Petitioner and his intended spouse.

There is no possibility of scandal should the Petitioner be granted the dispensation in order to be married in the Catholic Church. The granting of this favor will be a great spiritual gift to the Petitioner and his/her intended spouse and it will also bring spiritual relief and peace of conscience to them.

_____   _____
Name   Date
Instructor

4.20. *The Votum of the Bishop*

Case

Re: Dispensation from the bond of the non-consummated marriage between:

N., Petitioner, and N., Respondent

The *Votum* of the Bishop

The Petitioner, N., a ___ (*religion*), has presented a petition for the dispensation from the bond of his/her marriage to the Respondent, N., a ___ (*religion*), on the grounds of the non-consummation of the marriage. The Petitioner wishes to marry N. a ___ (*religion*). The Petitioner is seeking the favor of the dispensation from the Roman Pontiff for his/her own spiritual good as well as for the spiritual good of his/her intended spouse.

I. COMPETENCE TO ACCEPT AND INSTRUCT THE PETITION

The undersigned Bishop is competent to accept the petition for the dispensation of the marriage by virtue of canon 1699 §1 of the Code of Canon Law. The Petitioner is domiciled within the jurisdiction of the Diocese of N. The basis for the petition is also well founded.

II. COURTSHIP AND CONJUGAL LIFE

The parties dated for __ years and __ months before they became engaged. The engagement lasted... years. The marriage was celebrated on ... (*date*), at ... (*place, city, state, and country*) before a Catholic Cleric/Justice of the peace/Rabbi/Non-Catholic Minister/etc.

III. THE NON–CONSUMMATION OF THE MARRIAGE

The acts and proofs gathered in the case strongly support the claim and argument of the Petitioner that the marriage, after its celebration, was never consummated. The Petitioner has submitted proofs and arguments to support this fact. His/Her witnesses also provided testimony under oath, which corroborate the petition of the Petitioner. The witnesses can be considered as above suspicion and as having obtained their information at a non-suspect time.

The Respondent also provided statements which support the fact of the non-consummation of the marriage. (or, The Respondent was cited according to the norm of law, but he/she neither responded to the citation nor appeared in person to provide testimony. Nonetheless, given the facts and circumstances surrounding the case, there can be no prudent and reasonable doubt regarding the non-consummation of the marriage).

IV. SEPARATION AND DIVORCE

The marriage lasted for __ years and __ months. State the principal causes of the break-up of the marriage.

V. THE IMPOSSIBILITY OF RECONCILIATION

There is no possibility of reconciliation. *State the reasons. For example:* The Petitioner has remarried and has children with his/her current spouse. The Respondent does not wish reconciliation. He/She has also remarried.

VI. JUST CAUSE FOR THE PETITION

The parties have a serious aversion towards each other without hope of reconciliation. They have obtained a civil decree of absolute divorce. They are in successive, successful marriages with other spouses. This is not an exhaustive list.

The Petitioner faithfully attends Mass with his/her intended spouse. *Are the petitioner and his/her intended spouse Catholics? Or is any of them currently taking instruction in the Catholic faith and has made a definite decision to be received into full communion with the Catholic Church?* His/Her intended spouse is a __ (*religion*), who is free to marry.

VII. DANGER OF SCANDAL

There is no danger of scandal. The community is aware that the Petitioner and the Respondent have since divorced and that they have since moved on with their life.

VIII. CREDIBILITY OF WITNESSES

The deponents are honest and trustworthy. There is no reason to doubt their veracity.

IX. THE BRIEFS OF THE INSTRUCTOR AND THE DEFENDER OF THE BOND

The Defender of the Bond is satisfied that the petition is well-founded and that there a just cause for the petition. There is no hope of reconciliation between the parties. He/She is also satisfied that the process for the dissolution of ratified and non-consummated marriage have been observed in the instruction of the petition, in accordance with the Code of Canon Law and the supplementary norms issued by the Apostolic See. He/She agrees that there is a probable doubt that the marriage was ever consummated.

Also, it is the opinion of the Instructor that the Petition is well founded and that a just cause exists for the granting of the favor.

X. CONCLUSION

We hereby request that the marriage of N., Petitioner and N., Respondent, be dissolved by the Roman Pontiff on the grounds of the non-consummation of the marriage and a rescript of dispensation be granted so that the Petitioner can be married in the Catholic Church. The granting of this favor will be a great spiritual gift to the Petitioner and his/her intended spouse and it will also bring spiritual relief and peace of conscience to them.

Given at ... (*Place*), on ... (*date*).

_____

Most Reverend N.
Bishop of N.

4.21. *The Authentication of the Acts*

Case

Re: Dispensation from the bond of the non-consummated marriage between:

N., Petitioner, and N., Respondent

I, the undersigned duly appointed notary in the above referenced case, do hereby certify that the attached documents, letters, and testimonies of the above-named and numbered case are true and genuine copies of the original acts placed in the Archives of the Tribunal of the Diocese of N.

_____   _____

Notary   Date

4.22. *The Index*

The index is the table of contents or list of all the documents, testimonies, and other acts of the case and the respective pages where they are to be found in the acts. For this reason, every page of the acts must be numbered clearly.

INDEX

Case Name & Prot. No.

DOCUMENT DESCRIPTION   PAGE

1. Index of the Acts
2. The Petition
3. Certificate of Marriage between N., Petitioner, and N., Respondent.
4. Decree of Civil Divorce.
5. Baptismal Certificate of (or Proof of Baptism of). N.
6. Decree of Commission of Officers
7. The Oath of the Instructor
8. The Oath of the Defender of the Bond
9. The Oath of the Notary
10. Deposition of the Petitioner
11. Deposition of the Respondent
12. Testimony of N., Witness
13. Testimony of N., Witness
14. Medical Release Form
15. Decree of the Appointment of the Medical Examiner
16. Oath of the Medical Examiner
17. Decree of the Appointment of the Matron
18. Oath of the Matron
19. Medical Report of the Medical Examiner
20. Observations of the Defender of the Bond
21. Report of the Instructor
22. *Votum* of the Diocesan Bishop
23. Certificate of Authentication of the Acts

4.23. *The Notification of the Apostolic Rescript to the Parties*

Case

Declaration of Freedom to Marry

On ..., His Holiness, Pope N., in accordance with the Code of Canon Law and other legal requirements of the Catholic Church, dissolved the marriage entered into by N. and N. at ___ Church in ___ on ___, at the request of N., Petitioner, on the grounds of its non-consummation. (The Apostolic Tribunal of the Roman Rota, Prot. N. ____/___).

The Parties are now free to contract another marriage, provided the requirements of canon law for entering into a valid and licit marriage have been duly fulfilled.

Given at ... (*Place*), on ... (*date*)

Signed by the judicial vicar and by the notary.
Tribunal seal

4.24. *The Notification Letters to the Churches of Baptism and Marriage*

Date

FOR ANNOTATION IN THE MARRIAGE REGISTER OF
YOUR PARISH IN ACCORDANCE WITH THE PRESCRIPTS
OF CANON 1706

CHURCH OF MARRIAGE:
CONTRACTING PARTIES:
DATE OF MARRIAGE:

The above named marriage has been dissolved by His Holiness, Pope N., on ..., in accordance with canon 1142 of the Code of Canon Law, that is, on the grounds of its non-consummation. (The Apostolic Tribunal of the Roman Rota, Prot. N. ____). The Pastor of the Church of Marriage of these parties is kindly requested, in accordance with canon 1706 to make the following notation in the marriage register and to send back to us the form provided below as proof of the annotation.

The marriage of N. and N. has been dissolved by His Holiness, Pope N., on ... as non-consummated. The Apostolic Tribunal of the Roman Rota, Prot. N. _____).

_____   _____
Very Reverend N.   Date
Judicial Vicar
===============================
The above notation has been duly made by the undersigned:

_____   _____
Name   Date
Title

NOTE: After you have completed this form, if you wish, you may fax it to: ___ ___ _____.
===

FOR ANNOTATION IN THE BAPTISMAL REGISTER OF YOUR PARISH IN ACCORDANCE WITH THE PRESCRIPTS CANON 1706

NAME OF PARTY:
DATE OF BAPTISM:
NAME OF SPOUSE:
CHURCH OF MARRIAGE:
DATE OF MARRIAGE:

The above named marriage has been dissolved by His Holiness, Pope N., on ..., in accordance with canon 1142 of the Code of Canon Law, that is, on the grounds of its non-consummation. (The Apostolic Tribunal of the Roman Rota, Prot. N. _____). The Pastor of the Church of Marriage of these parties is kindly requested, in accordance with canon 1706 to make the following notation in the marriage register and to send back to us the form provided below as proof of the annotation.

The marriage of N. and N. has been dissolved by His Holiness, Pope N., on ... as non-consummated. The Apostolic Tribunal of the Roman Rota, Prot. N. _____).

_____   _____

Very Reverend N.   Date
Judicial Vicar

================================

The above notation has been duly made by the undersigned:

_____   _____

Name   Date
Title

NOTE: After you have completed this form, if you wish, you may
fax it to: ____ ____ ____.

CHAPTER 7:   PAULINE PRIVILEGE

1. The Pauline Privilege is the dissolution of the marriage bond of two unbaptized parties by the very fact that a new marriage is contracted by the party who has received baptism, provided that the baptized party is not the prevalent cause of the break-up of the marriage, that the marriage was not consummated after the party received baptism, and that there is no hope of reconciliation.

2. It is called the Pauline Privilege because St. Paul granted this privilege or concession to converts to Christianity to aid and facilitate conversions. According to St. Paul: "If any brother has a wife who is an unbeliever, and she is willing to go on living with him, he should not divorce her; and if any woman has a husband who is an unbeliever, and he is willing to go on living with her, she should not divorce her husband. For the unbelieving husband is made holy through his wife, and the unbelieving wife is made holy through the brother. Otherwise your children would be unclean, whereas in fact they are holy. If the unbeliever separates, however, let him separate. The brother or sister is not bound in such cases; God has called you to peace."[73]

3. Thus, according to canon 1143 §§1-2: "A marriage entered into by two non-baptized persons is dissolved by means of the Pauline privilege in favor of the faith of the party who has received baptism by the very fact that a new marriage is contracted by the same party, provided that the non-baptized party departs. The non-baptized party is considered to depart if he or she does not wish to cohabit with the baptized party or to cohabit peacefully without affront to the Creator unless the baptized party, after baptism was received, has given the other a just cause for departing."[74]

---

[73] I Cor. 7: 12-15, NABRE.
[74] C. 1143 §§1-2.

1. **How to Determine a Pauline Privilege Case**

The following questions will help you determine whether you have a Pauline Privilege case:

1. ☐ YES ☐ NO Were both parties unbaptized and remained unbaptized throughout the marriage?
2. ☐ YES ☐ NO Is it true that there is no hope that the couple will be reconciled?
3. ☐ YES ☐ NO Is it true that the Petitioner is not the predominant cause of the break-up of the marriage?
4. ☐ YES ☐ NO Is it true that the Petitioner is not the one who refused to cohabit peacefully in the marriage?
5. ☐ YES ☐ NO Does the Petitioner wish to be validly baptized or has the Petitioner been validly baptized since the divorce?
6. ☐ YES ☐ NO Does the Petitioner have a fiancé or spouse whom he/she wishes to marry in the Catholic Church?
7. ☐ YES ☐ NO Is it true that the use of the Pauline Privilege by the Petitioner would not be a cause of scandal and criticism of the Catholic Church?

If the answer to each of the foregoing questions is YES, you may have a Pauline Privilege case. The final determination is made by the tribunal after it has gathered all the pertinent information and proofs in the case.

2. **The Requirements for the Invocation of the Pauline Privilege**

I. Both spouses were unbaptized prior to the marriage.

II. One of the spouses receives baptism subsequent to the marriage. The baptism can be in the Catholic Church or in a Christian Church whose baptism is considered valid by the Catholic Church. A baptism with water along with the recitation of the Trinitarian formula would be regarded as valid.

III. The unbaptized party departs the marriage. The departure can be physical or moral. Physical departure is verified when the spouses terminate their conjugal cohabitation or when the non-baptized party has taken another spouse and refuses to leave this person or is unable to do so. Moral departure is verified when the non-baptized spouse is not willing to cohabit peacefully without affront to the Creator or when the unbaptized party forbids the convert from practicing his or her faith, or when the unbaptized person is accustomed to making fun of the Catholic faith or ridiculing it, or when the unbaptized person commits adultery habitually or makes life unbearable for the baptized party. The departure of the non-baptized spouse must be the consequence of his or her personal free decision and not caused by the converting party. The departure can happen either before or after the baptism of one of the spouses.[75]

To ascertain the departure of the non-baptized party and whether or not the non-baptized party wishes to receive baptism, the law requires that interpellations should be made of the non-baptized party before the Pauline Privilege can be invoked. There are two required questions that must be asked of the non-baptized party, namely:

a). Whether he or she wishes to receive baptism.
b). Whether he or she wishes to live in peace with the baptized party without offense to the Creator.[76]

The non-baptized party may answer in any four possible ways:

---

[75] Augustine Mendonça, "Use of the 'Pauline Privilege,'" in *Studies in Church Law* 2 (2006) pp. 404-405.
[76] c. 1144 §1; *CCEO,* c. 855 §1.

1). If the non-baptized party responds negatively to both questions, the Pauline Privilege can be invoked. In the letter to the non-baptized party, it can be stated that failure to respond to the citation within the deadline given means that the Tribunal will presume his or her silence is negative to both questions.

2). If the non-baptized party replies affirmatively to both questions, the Pauline Privilege cannot be invoked. However, the Pauline Privilege can be invoked if it is *de facto* impossible to restore conjugal cohabitation because of distance, or because of the subsequent marriage of the baptized or converting party, or because of some other circumstances. Moreover, if the unbaptized party responds affirmatively to both questions but changes his or her mind and not only refuses to be baptized but also denies peaceful cohabitation, then a departure is verified. The ordinary or his delegate may concede the invocation of the Pauline Privilege to the convert.

3). If the non-baptized party responds that he or she does not wish to be baptized but declares that he or she is willing to live in peace with the baptized spouse, the Pauline Privilege cannot be invoked. However, if the non-baptized break his or her promise or if conjugal cohabitation be considered *de facto* impossible, the non-baptized is considered to have departed the marriage, and the baptized or converting party may enter a new marriage and invoke the Pauline Privilege.

4). If the non-baptized party replies that he or she wishes to be baptized but has no intention of cohabiting in peace with the baptized or converting party, the Pauline Privilege may be invoked provided the convert or converting party enters into a new marriage before the conversion and baptism of the other party. If the other party receives baptism before the convert marries, the Pauline Privilege cannot be invoked.

If the answers of the non-baptized party are evasive, vague, ambiguous, unclear, unreasonable, or insincere, the matter is to be resolved in favor of the baptized party.

IV. If a doubt exists regarding the application of the Pauline Privilege, whether the doubt pertains to the doubtful baptism of the baptized party (in such a case he or she can be baptized conditionally), or to the sincerity of the conversion of the converting party or convert, or to the cause of the departure, the judgment may be rendered in favor of the faith. "In a doubtful matter the privilege of faith possesses the favor of the law." (c. 1150).

V. The interpellation or interrogation of the non-baptized party is done after the baptism of the converting party. However for a grave reason, the local ordinary can permit the interrogation to be done before baptism, or even dispense from the interrogation entirely if it cannot be done or if it would be superfluous to do so. (c. 1144 §2).

VI. The pastor of the baptized party is to include, in addition to the petition form and other documents and the tribunal fees (if there is one) to the tribunal, a cover letter addressed to the local ordinary attesting to the extent of the instruction in Catholic faith and doctrine the petitioner has received, the indications of the practice of the faith by the petitioner, and the signs of sincerity of the petitioner.

3. The Procedures for the Invocation of the Pauline Privilege

The dissolution of a marriage bond by virtue of the Pauline Privilege (cc. 1143-1149) is an administrative process, which is placed under Book IV, Part 1, Title VII, Chapter IX, Article I, "Dissolution of the Bond" of the 1983 Code of Canon Law. The distinction between the declaration of the nullity of a marriage and the dissolution of a marriage must be kept in mind in regard to terminology. (DC, art. 7 §2). While the dissolution of the bond of marriage pertains to dissolving or dispensing from a valid marriage, the declaration of the nullity of marriage pertains to declaring a marriage null or invalid.

1. The Gathering of the Documents

For the proof of a Pauline Privilege marriage case, the following documents are required:

i. The Petitioner's Petition for the Pauline Privilege.
ii. A copy of the marriage certificate to be dissolved.
iii. A copy of the divorce decree.
iv. If applicable, the Petitioner's baptismal certificate, issued within the last 6 months.
v. Baptismal certificate of intended spouse, issued within the last 6 months.
vi. A letter of the pastor addressed to the bishop stating the length and extent of instruction in the Catholic faith and teachings the petitioner has received, the indications of the practice of the faith by the petitioner, the signs of sincerity of the petitioner, and whether or not the petitioner has attempted civil marriage.
vii. A freewill donation or the administrative processing fee.

2. The Completion and Submission of the Pauline Privilege Petition

When the documents have been gathered, the Pauline Privilege Petition is completed and submitted to the tribunal.

A sample form of the petition is provided under this chapter below.

3. The Decree of the Commission of the Officers

When the petition and the accompanying documents have been received and reviewed by the tribunal, the judicial vicar is to issue a decree by which the tribunal officers who will handle the case are commissioned. By means of this decree the judicial vicar also accepts the petition, establishes the competence of the tribunal over the case, and orders the citation of the defender of the bond and the parties.

A sample form of the decree of the commission of the officers is provided under this chapter below.

4. The Acknowledgment Letter to the Petitioner

Subsequent to the acceptance of the petition, an acknowledgment letter is written to the petitioner.

A sample form of the acknowledgment letter is provided under this chapter below.

5. The Citation of the Defender of the Bond

After the decree commissioning the officers has been issued, the defender of the bond is cited and the acts of the case are made available to him or her, if this has not already been done.

A sample form of the citation of the defender of the bond is provided under this chapter below.

6. The Citation and Interpellations of the Respondent

A letter is then written to the respondent notifying him or her of the petition. The respondent questionnaire or interpellations are enclosed in the letter.

The interpellation of the respondent is done after the baptism of the petitioner. However, for a grave cause, the local ordinary can permit the interpellation to be done before baptism. The local ordinary can dispense from the interpellation either before or after the baptism of the petitioner provided that it is evident at least by a summary and extrajudicial process that it cannot be done or that it would be superfluous to do so. (c. 1144 §2).

Thus, the diocesan bishop issue a decree granting the judicial vicar the general faculty to interpolate the respondent before the baptism of the petitioner for a grave reason. And if the need arises, the judicial vicar, on his part, can issue a decree *per casum* by which he orders the interrogation of a respondent before the baptism of the petitioner.

A sample form of the citation letter to the respondent is provided under this chapter below.

A sample form of the questionnaire or interpellations of the respondent is provided under this chapter below.

A sample form of the decree of the bishop granting the judicial vicar the faculty to interpolate the respondent prior to the petitioner's baptism is provided below.

A sample form of the decree of the judicial vicar directing that the respondent should be interpolated prior to the baptism of the petitioner is provided under this chapter below.

Sample forms of the decrees of the bishop and of the judicial vicar dispensing from the interpellation of the respondent are provided below under this chapter.

7. The Citation and Interpellations of the Witnesses

Subsequent to the citation and interpellations of the respondent, the witnesses are to be cited. The citation of the witnesses can be done on the same day as the citation of the respondent. In the citation of the witnesses, the witness questionnaire is to be enclosed.

For a sample form of the citation letter to the witnesses, see this chapter below.

For a sample form of the witness questionnaire, see this chapter below.

8. The Brief of the Defender of the Bond

When the instruction of the case has been completed, the defender of the bond is to submit a brief regarding the case.

For a sample form of the brief of the defender of the bond in Pauline Privilege cases, see this chapter below.

9. The Decree of the Invocation of the Pauline Privilege

When the instruction of the case has been completed, the Pauline Privilege decree is issued.

A sample form of the Pauline Privilege decree is provided below.

10. The Publication of the Decree to the Parties

Subsequent to the issuance of the decree permitting the petitioner to invoke the Pauline Privilege, a copy of the decree is mailed to both parties with a cover letter. The case sponsor or procurator or the cleric preparing the petitioner for marriage is also mailed a copy of the decree to be included in the pre-nuptial marriage file of the petitioner and his/her intended or civil law spouse.

4. The Sample Documents for the Invocation of the Pauline Privilege

4.1. *The Petition*

PAULINE PRIVILEGE PETITION

TYPE OR PRINT

Tribunal Use Only
Petitioner _____
Respondent _____
Protocol number _____

To his Excellency, the Bishop of N.

I, the undersigned Petitioner, respectfully present this petition to you to determine whether the conditions are present for me to invoke the Pauline Privilege in favor of the faith in accordance with canons 1143-1147 of the Code of Canon Law. I attest that the information presented herein is true to the best of my knowledge. I respectfully present the following information:

A. PETITIONER

Name _____
             First Maiden Name (if woman) Last Name

Place of Birth   _____
             City   *State*

Date of Birth   _____
             Month Date   Year

Address   _____
             Street/P.O. Box

             _____
             City   State   Zip Code

Telephone: Home: ___ Work:___ Cell: _____

Parish Church: _____

B. RESPONDENT

Name _____
             First Maiden Name (if woman) Last Name

Place of Birth   _____
             City   *State*

Date of Birth   _____
             Month   *Date*   *Year*

Address   _____
             Street/P.O. Box

             _____
             City   State   Zip Code

Telephone: Home:_____ Work: ____ Cell: _____

C. MARRIAGE

The marriage was contracted at:

Venue: _____

On: _____
              Date
In: _____
          City   *State*
By: _____
              Officiant

At the time of this marriage, neither the Respondent nor I was baptized by the pouring of water, immersion, or sprinkled as the words of the Trinitarian formula were said. I submit the following witnesses who can testify to this.

D. WITNESS FORMS

WITNESS FOR THE PETITIONER

First Witness
Name: _____

Address: _____

Relationship to the Parties: _____
Second Witness
Name: _____

Address: _____
Relationship to the Parties: _____

WITNESS FOR THE RESPONDENT

First Witness
Name: _____

Address: _____

Relationship to the Parties: _____

Second Witness
Name: _____

Address: _____

Relationship to the Parties: _____

E. SEPARATION AND DIVORCE

I separated from the Respondent,   on _____
                                            Date

Reasons for the break-up of the marriage:
_____
_____
_____
_____
_____

A divorce was obtained in:

_____, _____, _____ on _____
  City   *County*   *State*   *Date*

The divorce was petitioned by:

      ☐ the Petitioner
      ☐ the Respondent

I have resided in this Diocese since _____

F. CURRENT SITUATION OF PETITIONER

Select the appropriate one that applies to you. If none of the following questions applies, the petitioner does not meet the criteria for the Pauline Privilege.
I am presently:

☐ A Roman Catholic who has been baptized subsequent to my previous marriage, and I wish to marry someone who is free to marry in the Catholic Church.

I was baptized in _____
                          Name of Church
On_____ in _____.
      Month Day Year   *City   State*

☐ A baptized non-Catholic who received baptism subsequent to my previous marriage. I have taken instruction in the Catholic faith. I have made a definite decision to be received into full communion with the Catholic Church, and I wish to marry someone who is free to marry in the Catholic Church.

I was baptized in _____
                          Name of Church

On_____ in _____.
      Month Day Year   *City   State*

☐ Unbaptized. I am taking/have taken instructions in the Catholic faith. I wish to be baptized a Catholic and to marry someone who is free to marry in the Catholic Church.

I, the undersigned Petitioner, respectfully request Your Excellency to authorize the interpellation to be made in this case and to ask the Respondent:

- Whether he/she wishes to be converted and to be baptized in the Catholic faith;
- Whether he/she wishes to be reconciled with me and to cohabit without offense to the Creator, permitting me and our offspring the free exercise of my religion.

If the Respondent answers these questions in the negative, it is my desire to enter a marriage in the Catholic Church with the party whose name and information appears as follows:

Name _____

     First Maiden Name (if woman) Last Name

Place of Birth   _____

     City   *State*

Date of Birth   _____

     Month   *Date*   *Year*

Address   _____

     Street/P.O. Box

     _____

     City   *State*   *Zip Code*

Telephone: Home:_____ Work: ____ Cell: _____

Religion: _____

Parish Church:_____

Baptized: ☐ Yes ☐ No

Date of Baptism: _____

Church of Baptism: _____

     Name, City, State.

_____   _____

Signature of Petitioner   Date

G. ATTESTATION OF THE PROCURATOR

I, the undersigned Procurator, hereby attest that to the best of my knowledge and upon information and belief (*check applicable boxes*):

1. □ YES □ NO. Neither the Petitioner nor the Respondent was baptized prior to the marriage and remained unbaptized throughout the marriage.
2. □ YES □ NO. There is no hope of reconciliation between the parties.
3. □ YES □ NO. The Petitioner was not the predominant cause of the other party's departure from the marriage or of the breakdown of the marriage.
4. □ YES □ NO. The Petitioner was not the one who refused to live in peace with the other party.
5. □ YES □ NO. The Petitioner wishes to be validly baptized or has been validly baptized since the divorce.
6. □ YES □ NO. The Petitioner has a current or intended spouse whom he/she wishes to marry in the Catholic Church.
7. □ YES □ NO. The current or intended spouse of the Petitioner is free to marry in the Catholic Church.
8. □ YES □ NO. The Petitioner is in a civil marriage with the spouse he/she wishes to marry in the Catholic Church.
9. □ YES □ NO. The invocation of the Pauline Privilege by the Petitioner would not be a cause of scandal.
10. □ YES □ NO. The Petitioner has been receiving catechesis and religious instruction in the Catholic faith. If "YES," for how long now? Since _____ (*Please, specify duration*).
11. □ YES □ NO. The Petitioner has shown indications of sincerity in his/her conversion to the Catholic faith.
12. □ YES □ NO. The Petitioner has shown indications of sincerity in the practice of the Catholic faith.

I have also enclosed the following documents:

☐ The Petitioner's Petition for the Pauline Privilege.

- ☐ A copy of the marriage certificate to be dissolved.
- ☐ A copy of the divorce decree.
- ☐ If applicable, the Petitioner's baptismal certificate, issued within the last 6 months.
- ☐ Baptismal certificate of intended spouse, issued within the last 6 months.
- ☐ A letter of the pastor addressed to the bishop stating the length and extent of instruction in the Catholic faith and teachings the petitioner has received, the indications of the practice of the faith by the petitioner, and the signs of sincerity of the petitioner and whether or not the petitioner has attempted civil marriage.

Signature of Priest or Deacon   Date

Parish, Address, City, State, Zip Code

4.2. *The Decree of the Commission of the Officers*

When the petition and the accompanying documents have been received by the tribunal, and they have been presented in accordance with the norm of law, the judicial vicar is to issue a decree of competence, constitution, acceptance, and citation.

On tribunal letterhead

DECREE OF THE COMMISSION OF OFFICERS

CASE

On ... (*date*), N., (*name of the petitioner*), presented a petition for the dissolution of the marriage bond entered into with N. (*name of the respondent*) and for the invocation of the Pauline Privilege, in accordance with the norm of law. The petition was presented to the Tribunal of N., which is competent to accept the case by virtue of canon 1672, __°. Having been presented in the accordance with the norm of law, and the Tribunal having declared itself competent to adjudicate the case by virtue of the law, the petition is hereby decreed accepted for consideration and adjudication.

The following persons are hereby nominated and delegated:

Judge Instructor: N.
Defender of the Bond: N.
Notary: N.

So that they may instruct the process, in accordance with the norm of law, for the invocation of the Pauline Privilege. (cc. 1143-1150).

Furthermore, in accordance with canon 1688, I hereby cite the Parties and the Defender of the Bond to provide their response to the formula of the doubt. They are to respond within fifteen (15) days of the notification of this Decree. (c. 1676 §1).

This Decree is to be communicated to the Parties and the Defender of the Bond.

Given in ..., on this day ....

Signed by the Judicial Vicar and by the notary.

Official stamp

4.3. *The Citation of the Defender of the Bond*

On the tribunal letterhead

JUDICIAL MEMO:
CITATION OF THE DEFENDER OF THE BOND

To: The Defender of the Bond
From: The Judicial Vicar
Case:

Subject: Pauline Privilege Petition
Date:
==

A Pauline Privilege petition has been submitted to this Tribunal in accordance with the norm of law. According to canon 1143 §§1-2: "A marriage entered into by two non-baptized persons is dissolved by means of the Pauline privilege in favor of the faith of the party who has received baptism by the very fact that a new marriage is contracted by the same party, provided that the non-baptized party departs. The non-baptized party is considered to depart if he or she does not wish to cohabit with the baptized party or to cohabit peacefully without affront to the Creator unless the baptized party, after baptism was received, has given the other a just cause for departing."

Kindly submit a brief addressing the following elements of a Pauline Privilege case:

1. Whether the tribunal has the competence to accept the petition, whether the petitioner possesses legitimate standing in the trial, and whether the petition must be either admitted or rejected by decree. (c. 1505 §1; DC, art. 119 §§1-2).
2. Whether both spouses were unbaptized prior to the marriage and remained unbaptized throughout the duration of the marriage?
3. Whether one of the spouses has received baptism or wishes to receive baptism subsequent to the marriage.
4. Whether the unbaptized party has departed the marriage.
5. Whether there is no hope of reconciliation between the parties.
6. Whether the Petitioner was the predominant cause of the other party's departure from the marriage.
7. Whether the invocation of the Pauline Privilege by the Petitioner would not be a cause of scandal.

Copies of the acts of the case are attached for your review. Kindly submit your written brief regarding the case no later than … (*date*). Thank you.

4.4. *The Acknowledgment Letter to the Petitioner*

Case

Date

Name
Address

Dear N.:

This is to acknowledge the receipt of your petition for a decree of the ecclesiastical dissolution of the marriage bond you contracted with N., Respondent, which has been submitted to this Tribunal by N., your Procurator/Case Sponsor/Advocate. The law of the Catholic Church upholds the validity of a marriage until the contrary is proven. The burden of proof is on the party who alleges that the bond of his her previous marriage should be dissolved in favor of his or her Catholic faith. It is the duty of the Tribunal to gather the necessary proofs and determine, according to the laws of the Catholic Church, whether or not to issue a decree of the ecclesiastical dissolution of the marriage bond. Therefore, we ask that no definite plans for marriage are to be made before receiving the definitive decision of this Tribunal.

At this phase of the process, the Tribunal has notified the Respondent of your petition. Your case will be assigned to a Judge and a Defender of the Bond of Marriage for adjudication. As the process unfolds, the Tribunal will be in contact with you.

In obtaining proof of your claim, the Tribunal may contact you for more information. Please reply promptly, for your neglect in doing so for six months will end the process. Someone from the Tribunal or I may wish to meet with you to clarify the information you have submitted. We shall call you for an appointment at that time.

If you have any questions or concerns regarding this case, please contact us either by phone or in writing. If you have none, no further action is required on your part at this time.

Your petition has been assigned the above Case Name and Protocol Number. Please use this name and number to identify your petition when you contact the Tribunal so that we can easily locate your case file.

Yours Sincerely,

Signed by the judicial vicar.

4.5. The Citation Letter to the Respondent

CITATION LETTER TO THE RESPONDENT

Case

Date

Name
Address

Dear N.:

Your former spouse, N., has presented a petition to the Tribunal of the Diocese of N. requesting the dissolution of his marriage to you based on the Pauline Privilege. Pauline Privilege is when both parties were unbaptized before and throughout the marriage, or if they were baptized, they were not validly baptized. One of the parties (the Petitioner) subsequently receives a valid baptism or wants to be baptized in the Catholic Church and wishes to marry a Catholic who is free to marry.

According to the Bible: "If any brother has a wife who is an unbeliever, and she is willing to go on living with him, he should not divorce her; and if any woman has a husband who is an unbeliever, and he is willing to go on living with her, she should not divorce her husband. For the unbelieving husband is made holy through his wife, and the unbelieving wife is made holy through the brother. Otherwise your children would be unclean, whereas in fact they are holy. If the unbeliever separates, however, let him separate. The brother or sister is not bound in such cases; God has called you to peace." (I Cor. 7: 12-15, NABRE).

You will find enclosed a list of questions, which I ask you to answer and return to the Tribunal of the Diocese of N. no later than ... (*give 3 or 4 weeks*) in order that this petition may be processed in a timely manner.

I wish to assure you that this is strictly a Church matter. The Tribunal is concerned merely with determining whether N. (*name of the petitioner*) would be free to marry in the Catholic Church.

Thank you for your consideration of my request and for your assistance. If any of the foregoing needs clarification, please do not hesitate to call me at the phone number listed above.

Sincerely,

Name and signature of the tribunal official.

Encl.: Questionnaire for the Respondent

4.6. *The Interpellations of the Respondent*

On official letterhead

Case

QUESTIONNAIRE FOR THE RESPONDENT

1. Was your marriage to N. the first marriage for both of you?
   Answer:

2. Were you ever baptized, christened, sprinkled, dedicated, or initiated in any religious denomination or sect prior to the time of your marriage to N.?
   Answer:

3. Were you ever baptized, christened, sprinkled, dedicated, or initiated in any religious denomination or sect during

your marriage to N.?
Answer:

4. Were you ever baptized, christened, sprinkled, dedicated,
   or initiated in any religious denomination or sect
   subsequent to your marriage to N.?
   Answer:

5. Was N. ever baptized, christened, sprinkled, dedicated, or
   initiated in any religious denomination or sect prior to
   his/her marriage to you?
   Answer:

6. Was N. ever baptized, christened, sprinkled, dedicated, or
   initiated in any religious denomination or sect during
   his/her marriage to you?
   Answer:

7. Do you wish to be converted and to be baptized in the
   Catholic faith?
   Answer:

8. Is there any possibility that you and N. can reconcile and
   restore married life? If so, how probable is this?
   Answer:

9. When did you last live as husband and wife with your
   former spouse?
   Answer:

10. Have you anything to add?
    Answer:

11. Is this a complete and accurate report of your statements?
    Answer:

_____   _____
Name of the Respondent   Date

The Respondent is to complete, sign, date, and return this form to the Tribunal.

4.7. *The Decree of the Bishop Granting the Judicial Vicar the Faculty to Interpolate the Respondent Prior to the Baptism of the Petitioner*

PAULINE PRIVILEGE:
DECREE GRANTING THE JUDICIAL VICAR THE FACULTY
FOR THE INTERPELLATIONS OF RESPONDENTS PRIOR TO
THE BAPTISM OF PETITIONERS

I, the undersigned Bishop of the Diocese N., by virtue of canon 137, do hereby grant the Judicial Vicar of this Diocese, the general faculty so that the interpellations of the Respondents can be made on a case-by-case basis for a grave cause prior to the baptism of the Petitioner, in accordance with the norms of canon 1144 §2.

Given at ... (*Place*), on this day ... (*date*).

Signed by the ordinary and by the notary.

4.8. *The Decree of the Judicial Vicar Permitting the Interpellation of the Respondent Prior to Baptism*

Case

DECREE OF THE JUDICIAL VICAR PERMITTING THE INTERPELLATION OF THE RESPONDENT PRIOR TO THE BAPTISM OF THE PETITIONER

By virtue of the general faculty granted the Judicial Vicar by the Most Reverend N., Bishop of N., (*name of the ordinary who granted the faculty*) so that Respondents can be interpolated prior to the baptism of Petitioners for a grave cause,

I, the undersigned Judicial Vicar, hereby decree the interpellation of the Respondent prior to the baptism of the Petitioner, in the above referenced case. The grave cause that exists for the interpellation of the Respondent prior to the baptism of the Petitioner is that ... (*state the reason*).

Given at the Tribunal of N., (*City, State*) on ... (*Date*).

Signed by the judicial vicar and by the notary.

4.9. The Decrees Dispensing from the Interpellations of the Respondent

DECREE OF THE BISHOP GRANTING THE JUDICIAL VICAR THE GENERAL FACULTY TO DISPENSE FROM THE INTERPELLATION FOR A GRAVE CAUSE

I, the undersigned Bishop of the Diocese N., by virtue of canon 137, do hereby grant the Judicial Vicar of this Diocese the general faculty to dispense from the interpellation of the Respondent for a grave cause either prior to or subsequent to the baptism of the Petitioner provided that it is evident at least by a summary and extrajudicial process it cannot be done or it would be superfluous to do so, in accordance with the norms of canon 1144 §2.
Given at ... (*Place*), on this day ... (*date*).

Signed by the ordinary and by the notary.

DECREE OF THE JUDICIAL VICAR GRANTING DISPENSATION FROM THE INTERPELLATION OF THE RESPONDENT

CASE

By virtue of the general faculty given the Judicial Vicar by the Most Reverend N., (*name of the ordinary who granted the faculty*) to grant dispensation from the interpellations of the Respondent for a grave cause either prior to or subsequent to the baptism of the Petitioner provided that it is evident at least by a summary and extrajudicial process it cannot be done or it would be superfluous to do so, in accordance with the norms of canon 1144 §2,

I, the undersigned Judicial Vicar, hereby grant dispensation from the interpellation of the Respondent *in hoc casu*.

From the information and documents gathered in the case, it is evidently clear that … (*state the grave cause here* – for example):

- the whereabouts of the Respondent are unknown. The due and diligent investigations that have been made to ascertain his/her address have proved futile.
- the Respondent is hostile to the process.
- the Respondent has been legitimately cited but did not reply within the deadline stipulated for a reply to the citation of the Tribunal.
- *or state some other grave cause.*

Therefore, having considered the above facts and circumstances, it is hereby decreed that the interpellations of the Respondent is superfluous and cannot be done.

Given at the Tribunal of N., (*City, State*) on … (*Date*).

Signed by the judicial vicar and by the notary

4.10. *The Citation of Witnesses*

Case

Date

Name
Address

Dear N.:

You have been named as a witness by N. (*name of the party*) who has submitted a Petition for the Pauline Privilege of his/her marriage to N., (*name of the other party*).

Pauline Privilege is when both parties were unbaptized before and throughout the marriage, or if they were baptized, they were not validly baptized. One of the parties (the Petitioner) subsequently receives a valid baptism or wants to be baptized in the Catholic Church and wishes to marry a Catholic who is free to marry.

I have enclosed a questionnaire which I am confident you will take time to complete. Your observations and comments will assist the judge in making a decision about the case. The questionnaire is designed for your observations regarding the baptism or non-baptism of N. (*name of the petitioner*) and N. (*name of the respondent*). Kindly type or print your answers on the enclosed questionnaire. Please be candid and precise in your response.

Your testimony is needed so that the Tribunal can proceed with the decision of this petition. This process does not have any effect in civil law. The purpose of the Tribunal's process is to seek the facts regarding the baptism or non-baptism of N. (*name of the petitioner*) and N. (*name of the respondent*). Please return the completed questionnaire no later than ... (*give 3 or 4 weeks deadline*). Thank you.

Sincerely,

Name and signature of tribunal official.
Enclosure: The Witness Questionnaire

4.11. *The Interpellations of Witnesses*

On official letterhead

Pauline Privilege:
Questionnaire for Witnesses

Case:

Testimony of N. (name of witness):

Oath: Do you solemnly swear to tell the truth, the whole truth, and nothing but the truth, insofar as you know it, so help you God?

Questions Regarding Yourself

1. What are your full names (including maiden name)?
2. What is your address and telephone number?
3. What is your relationship to the petitioner?
4. How long have you known the petitioner?
5. How well do you know the petitioner?
6. What is your relationship to the respondent?
7. How long have you known the respondent?
8. How well do you know the respondent?

Questions Regarding Petitioner's Baptismal Status

1. Are the petitioner's parents living? If so, what are their names and addresses?
2. Was the petitioner raised by his/her natural parents? If not, please give names and addresses of the foster parents or guardians and the years of guardianship.
3. Did his/her parents or guardians attend church when he/she was in their charge? If so, in what denomination(s)?
4. Did his/her parents (or guardians) believe in the necessity of baptism, especially infant baptism?
5. Was the petitioner ever baptized, sprinkled, christened, or dedicated in any religious denomination or sect at any time prior to his/her former marriage? If so, when and where? If not, please give any reason that you know of why he/she was not baptized.
6. Was the former spouse ever baptized, sprinkled, christened, or dedicated in any religious denomination or sect at any time during his/her former marriage? If so, when and where? If not, please give any reason that you know of why he/she was not baptized.
7. Did he/she ever attend any church at any time before the final break-up of the marriage? If so, please give the denomination of any churches you know he/she attended.

8. Did he/she ever attend Sunday school or classes of religious instruction?
   If so, do you recall where or when or in what denomination(s)?
9. Were any of his/her brothers or sisters ever baptized (christened, sprinkled, etc.)?
   If so, please give their names and the time and place of baptism.
10. If any of them were baptized, can you give any reason why he/she would not have been baptized?
11. What is his/her religion now?
12. How does he/she practice it?
13. Would he/she be reliable and truthful in giving testimony in this case?

Questions Regarding Former Spouse's Baptismal Status

1. Are the former spouse's parents living? If so, what are their names and addresses?
2. Was the former spouse raised by his/her natural parents? If not, please give names and addresses of the foster parents or guardians and the years of guardianship.
3. Did his/her parents or guardians attend church when he/she was in their charge? If so, in what denomination(s)?
4. Did his/her parents (or guardians) believe in the necessity of baptism, especially infant baptism?
5. Was the petitioner ever baptized, sprinkled, christened, or dedicated in any religious denomination or sect at any time prior to the his/her former marriage? If so, when and where? If not, please give any reason that you know of why he/she was not baptized.
6. Was the former spouse ever baptized, sprinkled, christened, or dedicated in any religious denomination or sect at any time during his/her former marriage? If so, when and where? If not, please give any reason that you know of why he/she was not baptized. If so, when and where?

If not, please give any reason that you know of why he/she was not baptized.

7. Did he/she ever attend any church at any time before the final break-up of the marriage? If so, please give the denomination of any churches you know he/she attended.
8. Did he/she ever attend Sunday school or classes of religious instruction?
   If so, do you recall where or when or in what denomination(s)?
9. Were any of his/her brothers or sisters ever baptized (christened, sprinkled, etc.)?
   If so, please give their names and the time and place of baptism.
10. If any of them were baptized, can you give any reason why he/she would not have been baptized?
11. What is his/her religion now?
12. How does he/she practice it?
13. Would he/she be reliable and truthful in giving testimony in this case?

Questions Regarding Marriage in Question

1. When the petitioner and his former spouse married, was that the first marriage for both?
2. How long did they keep company with each other before marriage?
3. Did they both marry with the intention of a marriage having unity and indissolubility?
4. Did they both get married for the usual reasons?
5. How long did they live together in marriage?
6. When did the final separation occur?
7. What caused the marriage to fail?
8. Do you know who petitioned for divorce?
9. Is there any chance this marriage can be reconciled? Why or why not?
10. Were there any children born of this marriage? If so, what are their names and ages?

Oath: Do you solemnly swear that you have told the truth, the whole truth, and nothing but the truth, insofar as I know it, so help you God?

_____

Signature

Date: _____

Place: _____

4.12. *The Brief of the Defender of the Bond*

Case

PAULINE PRIVILEGE:
BRIEF OF THE DEFENDER OF THE BOND

I, the undersigned Defender of the Bond, after having examined the documents, hereby attest that I have no reasonable objection to propose against the dissolution of the marriage bond in the above referenced case.

1. The tribunal has the competence to accept the Petition, the Petitioner possesses legitimate standing in the trial, and the Petition has been accepted by the decree of the judicial vicar. (c. 1505 §1; *DC,* art. 119 §§1-2).
2. Neither the Petitioner nor the Respondent was baptized prior to the marriage and remained unbaptized throughout the marriage.
3. There is no hope of reconciliation between the parties.
4. The Petitioner was not the predominant cause of the other party's departure from the marriage or of the breakdown of the marriage
5. The Petitioner was not the one who refused to live in peace with the other party.
6. The Petitioner wishes to be validly baptized or has been validly baptized since the divorce.

7. The Petitioner has current or intended spouse whom he/she wishes to marry in the Catholic Church.
8. The invocation of the Pauline Privilege by the Petitioner would not be a cause of scandal.

_____ (*Signature*)   _____
Name   Date
Defender of the Bond

4.13. *The Pauline Privilege Decree*

DECREE
PAULINE PRIVILEGE

CASE

IN THE CASE OF
N.-N.
PROTOCOL NUMBER: _ _ _ _-_ _ _

IN THE NAME OF GOD. AMEN.

With His Holiness Pope N. as Supreme Pontiff, I, Most Reverend N., Bishop of N., hereby issue the following decree in accordance with the norms of canons 1143-1147 of the Code of Canon Law.

THE FACTS

1. The Petitioner, N., unbaptized, married the Respondent, N., unbaptized, in __ (*city*), __ (*state*), on __ (*date*) before a ___. (*civil official /minister* - e.g. a Civil Official/Methodist Minister). The length of their marital union lasted for __years and __months. They obtained a decree of civil divorce from the __ (civil court, city, state) on (date).
2. On … (*date*), N., (*name of the petitioner*) petitioned for the dissolution of his/her marriage to N., (*name of the respondent*) in favor of the faith so that he/she may invoke the Pauline Privilege.

3. After having carefully investigated the case and gathering the pertinent documents and after having carefully observed all the requirements of the law, the undersigned Bishop now renders this definitive decision regarding the case.

THE LAW

Canon 1143 §§1-2: A marriage entered into by two non-baptized persons is dissolved by means of the Pauline privilege in favor of the faith of the party who has received baptism by the very fact that a new marriage is contracted by the same party, provided that the non-baptized party departs. The non-baptized party is considered to depart if he or she does not wish to cohabit with the baptized party or to cohabit peacefully without affront to the Creator unless the baptized party, after baptism was received, has given the other a just cause for departing.

4. The foregoing apostolic privilege was granted by St. Paul – hence it is called the Pauline Privilege – to converts to Christianity. According to St. Paul: "If any brother has a wife who is an unbeliever, and she is willing to go on living with him, he should not divorce her; and if any woman has a husband who is an unbeliever, and he is willing to go on living with her, she should not divorce her husband. For the unbelieving husband is made holy through his wife, and the unbelieving wife is made holy through the brother. Otherwise your children would be unclean, whereas in fact they are holy. If the unbeliever separates, however, let him separate. The brother or sister is not bound in such cases; God has called you to peace." (I Cor. 7: 12-15, New American Bible Revised Edition).

5. Certain conditions must be verified before the Pauline Privilege can be invoked.

i. The parties to the marriage were both un-baptized before the marriage.

ii. One of them is baptized or desires to be baptized subsequent to the marriage. Subsequent to the marriage can mean either during the period of their marital co-habitation or after the civil divorce. The baptism can be a Catholic baptism or a baptism in an ecclesial community that is not in full communion with the Catholic Church provided the Catholic Church recognizes the validity of the baptism. The Decision of the Sacred Congregation for the Doctrine of the Faith, 30 August 1976, states that the person employing the Pauline privilege need not be baptized in the Catholic Faith provided the baptism is regarded as valid in the Catholic Church – Prot. No. 1681/79M. (See, *Canon Law Digest* 8, pp. 837-840).

iii. The un-baptized party departs the marriage. The departure can be before or after the baptism of the other spouse. However, the baptism of the spouse need not be the cause of the un-baptized party's departure. If the pre-baptismal behavior of the baptized or baptizing spouse led to the failure of the marriage, the Pauline privilege can be invoked inasmuch as baptism remits one's sins. Thus, "if the behavior that led to the failure of the marriage occurred before the spouse was baptized, this fault does not impede his or her use of the Pauline privilege 'since it has been blotted out by the bath of regeneration.'" (John Beal, "Dissolution of the Bond," in *New Commentary on the Code of Canon Law*. Eds. John P. Beal, James A. Coriden, and Thomas Green. New York/ Mahwah, NJ: Paulist Press, 2000. p. 1366).

However, if the baptized party, after the reception of baptism, gave the non-baptized spouse a just cause for departing the marriage, the Pauline privilege cannot be invoked. (c. 1143 §§1-2).

The un-baptized party is considered to have departed the marriage if he or she does not want to live at all with the baptized spouse. The un-baptized party is also considered to have departed the marriage if he or she is unwilling live peacefully with the baptized party without offense to the Creator.

iv. The spouse who has received baptism or who wishes to receive baptism is the one seeking to invoke the privilege for himself or herself on account of a new marriage. The privilege is for the one who is baptizing or converting or who has already received a valid baptism.

THE ARGUMENT

6. The sworn declarations of N., Petitioner, which are subject to no reasonable contradiction or exception, prove that neither N. (*name of the petitioner*) nor N. (*name of the respondent*) ever received baptism prior to or during their marriage.

7. *If the respondent was interpolated:* The interpellations of the Respondent likewise prove the fact of the non-baptism of both parties.

8. The sworn testimony of the Petitioner's __ witness(es) and the Respondent's __ witness(es) verify that that none of the parties ever received baptism prior to or during the marriage.

9. The credibility of the Petitioner, the Respondent, and Witnesses have been established beyond reasonable doubt.

(Use one of the applicable options below)

10. *If applicable:* N., (*name of the petitioner*) now wishes to convert and be baptized in the Catholic Faith and is in the Rite of Christian Initiation of Adults (R.C.I.A.) program at __, __, __, (*name of parish church, city, and state where the baptism is to take place*).

If applicable: N., has converted and received baptism in the Catholic Church at __ (*name of parish*), __ (*city and state of the parish*).

If applicable: N., has converted and received valid baptism in the ecclesial community of __ (*insert here the name of non-Catholic church the petitioner received baptism considered valid by the Catholic Church*) in __ (*city and state where that church is located*). He/She now wishes to be received into full communion with the Catholic Church at __, __, __, (*name of Roman Catholic parish church, city, & state where the reception into full communion is to take place*).

11. *If the respondent was interpolated:* The Respondent has been properly interrogated in accordance with canon 1144 §§1-2, and has shown that he/she neither wishes to receive baptism nor be reconciled with the Petitioner.

12. *If the ordinary has dispensed from the interpolations, state the*

reasons. For example: In accordance with canon 1144 §2, I have granted dispensation from the interpellations of the Respondent because it cannot be done or it would be superfluous to do so after having considered all the facts and circumstances of the case.

13. N., (*name of the petitioner*) in accordance with the norm of canon 1146, wishes to contract marriage in the Catholic Church with N., (*name of the present/ intended spouse of the petitioner*), a Catholic /a baptized non-Catholic/ unbaptized, who is free to marry.

WHEREFORE, having carefully considered the laws of the Catholic Church and the facts of the case I, the undersigned Bishop of N., by virtue of our ordinary power, do hereby permit and authorize N. (*name of the petitioner*) to invoke the Pauline Privilege so that he/she may contract a valid and licit marriage with N., (*name of the present/intended spouse of the petitioner*) provided the requirements of canon law for entering into a valid and licit marriage have been duly fulfilled and provided the civil law requirements of this jurisdiction have been fulfilled.

The bond of the previous marriage is dissolved at the moment the Petitioner contracts a new marriage in accord with the law of the Catholic Church. (c. 1143).

The newly converted spouse is reminded that this authorization to invoke the Pauline Privilege does not release this party from any natural, moral or civil obligations toward the other spouse and any children born of this union, in keeping with the norms of justice, Christian charity, and natural equity. (cc. 1148 §3; 1071 §1, 3°; and 1691 §1).

Given at ___ (*Place*), on ___ (*date*).

Signed by the bishop or the judicial vicar and by the notary.

CHAPTER 8:   PETRINE PRIVILEGE

1. Under Book IV, Part 1, Title VII, Chapter IX, Article I, "Dissolution of the Bond" of the 1983 Code of Canon Law is canon 1150, which states, to-wit: In a doubtful matter the privilege of faith possesses the favor of the law." This expression "the privilege of the faith" clearly includes the "dissolutions of non-sacramental marriages in favor of the faith by the Roman Pontiff."[77]

2. "If it is a question of a marriage between a non-baptized party and a *doubtfully* baptized party, recourse must be made to the Apostolic See in individual cases (cf. Supreme Sacred Congregation of the Holy See, Decree. 10 June 1937, in *AAS* 29 [1937] 305-306)."[78]

3. The terms, "privilege of the faith," and "favor of the faith" are not synonymous. The privilege of the faith is a concession which is granted on apostolic authority upon the fulfillment of certain conditions to facilitate conversion to the Catholic faith and to make that conversion possible by removing obstacles to the faith not only in matters of matrimony but also in other matters such as baptism, for example. The privilege of the faith is applicable not only to the Pauline Privilege, but also to all cases in which the marriage bond is dissolved in favor of the faith.

4. On the other hand, the expression, the "favor of the faith" is a concession which is granted on apostolic authority

---

[77] John P. Beal, "The Separation of Spouses," in the *New Commentary on the Code of Canon Law*, eds. John P. Beal, James A. Coriden, and Thomas J. Green (New York/Mahwah, NJ: Paulist Press, 2000) pp. 1373-1374. [Henceforth, "The Separation of Spouses"].

[78] The Supreme Tribunal of the Apostolic Signatura, January 23, 1996, "Defective Application of Canons 1608, §4 and 1150," Prot. 26689/96 VAR, in *Ministerium Iustitiae*, Jurisprudence of the Supreme Tribunal of the Apostolic Signatura, trans. and ed., William L. Daniel (Woodridge, IL: Midwest Theological Forum, 2011) p. 727. Also published in *Periodica* 85 (1996) pp. 357-360 and in *Roman Replies* (1996) pp. 40-42; 42-45.

upon the fulfillment of certain conditions to facilitate the acceptance and profession of the Catholic faith only in matters of the dissolution of non-sacramental marriages. Thus, while the privilege of the faith has application beyond cases of the dissolution of non-sacramental marriages, the favor of the faith, on the other hand, applies only to the dissolution of non-sacramental marriages.[79]

5. Thus, the favor of the faith applies to both the properly so-called Pauline Privilege and to the so-called Petrine Privilege inasmuch both forms of Privileges pertain to the dissolution of a non-sacramental marriage in favor of the faith. For in a Pauline Privilege, the dissolution is granted in favor of the faith of the converting party or converted party. "A marriage contracted before the baptism of either party is dissolved in favour of the faith (*in favorem fidei*) by the Pauline privilege. This is the first form or mode of dissolution of a marriage in favour of the faith."[80] And in a Petrine Privilege, so-called, the dissolution is granted in favor of the faith of the unbaptized spouse who now wishes to be baptized in the Catholic Church, or of the baptized non-Catholic party who now wishes to become Catholic, or of a Catholic party who is the intended or current civil law spouse of the petitioner who does not wish to convert at the present time. Therefore, both privilege cases pertain to the favor of the faith.

6. Therefore, to distinguish one favor of the faith case from the other, one is called the Pauline Privilege and the other Petrine Privilege. Nonetheless, it is not uncommon for the Petrine Privilege to be called also Favor of the Faith.

7. Moreover, unlike the Pauline Privilege which can be granted locally by the diocesan bishop, Petrine Privilege petitions can be granted only by the Supreme Pontiff.

---

[79] Beal, "The Separation of Spouses," p. 1374.

[80] Wojciech Kowal and William H. Woestman, *Special Marriage Cases and Procedures* (Ottawa, Canada: St. Paul University, 2008) p. 58.

1. How to Determine a Petrine Privilege Case

HOW TO DETERMINE A PETRINE PRIVILEGE CASE

"It is well known that under certain determined conditions the marriages between non-Catholics, at least one of whom is not baptized, can be dissolved in the favor of the faith and for the salvation of souls by the Roman Pontiff." (*Potestas Ecclesiae*, Congregation of the Doctrine of the Faith, 30 April 2001).

The following questions will help to determine whether you have a Petrine Privilege case.

1. ☐ YES ☐ NO: Was one party in the marriage unbaptized prior to the marriage and remained unbaptized throughout the duration of the marriage?
2. ☐ YES ☐ NO (*Check if applicable*): If the unbaptized party later became baptized, is it true both parties have not had conjugal relations since after his/her baptism?
3. ☐ YES ☐ NO: Is it true that the petitioner was not the exclusive or predominant culpable cause of the break-up of the marriage?
4. ☐ YES ☐ NO: Is it true that there is no hope of reconciliation between the petitioner and the respondent?
5. ☐ YES ☐ NO: If the Catholic party intends to contract or convalidate a new marriage with a person who is not baptized or with a baptized non-Catholic, is the Catholic party willing to sign the promise that he or she is prepared to remove dangers of defecting from the Catholic faith?
6. ☐ YES ☐ NO: If the petitioner or his/her intended or current spouse is not a Catholic, is the non-Catholic party willing to sign the promise to raise any children born of the new marriage as Catholics and not hinder the Catholic party's practice of the faith?
7. ☐ YES ☐ NO: Does the petitioner have a fiancé or spouse whom he/she wishes to marry in the Catholic Church?
8. ☐ YES ☐ NO: Is it true that the new fiancé or spouse was not the cause of the break-up of the marriage for which you are seeking a favor of the faith?

9. ☐ YES ☐ NO: Is the Catholic party actively practicing the faith?

10. ☐ YES ☐ NO: Is it true that the granting of the favor would not be a cause of scandal?

If all answers to the questions are YES, you may a Petrine Privilege case. Kindly send a copy of this completed form to the Tribunal. If the Tribunal determines that it is indeed a Petrine Privilege case, we shall then send you the Petrine Privilege petition and a list of the required documents. If a Petrine Privilege case cannot be proven, it may be necessary to complete the forms for a formal case.

If the answer to any of the questions is NO, then you have a case other than Petrine.

2. **The Requirements for the Granting of the Favor of the Faith Petition**

I. *At least one of the parties was unbaptized prior to the marriage and remained unbaptized throughout the duration of the Marriage*

"A marriage entered into by parties, of whom at least one is not baptised, can be dissolved in favour of the faith by the Roman Pontiff, provided that it has not been consummated after both parties have received baptism."[81]

II. *If one of the parties later became baptized, the parties did not afterwards exercise the conjugal act*

"A marriage entered into by parties, of whom at least one is not baptised, can be dissolved in favour of the faith by the Roman

---

[81] Congregation for the Doctrine of the Faith, 30 April 2001, *Norms on the Preparation of the Process for the Dissolution of the Marriage Bond in Favour of the Faith*, art. 1.

Pontiff, provided that it has not been consummated after both parties have received baptism."[82]

"If the unbaptised spouse is baptised at the time the favour of the dissolution is being sought, there must be an inquiry into the possibility of cohabitation after the baptism; witnesses are also to be questioned about this matter. The parties in the case are themselves to be asked whether they had any relationship after their separation and what kind, and especially whether they had engaged in a conjugal act."[83]

III. *There is no hope of reconciliation and restoration of conjugal life between the Parties*

"For the concession of the favour of the dissolution of the bond, at the moment it is given, it is required that:

1° there is no possibility of resuming the partnership of conjugal life."[84]

IV. *The petitioner is not the exclusive or predominate cause of the break-up of the marriage*

"For the concession of the favour of the dissolution of the bond, at the moment it is given, it is required that:

2° the petitioner was not exclusively or predominantly the culpable cause of the breakdown of the conjugal life, and that the

---

[82] Congregation for the Doctrine of the Faith, 30 April 2001, *Norms on the Preparation of the Process for the Dissolution of the Marriage Bond in Favour of the Faith,* art. 1.

[83] Congregation for the Doctrine of the Faith, 30 April 2001, *Norms on the Preparation of the Process for the Dissolution of the Marriage Bond in Favour of the Faith,* art. 17.

[84] Congregation for the Doctrine of the Faith, 30 April 2001, *Norms on the Preparation of the Process for the Dissolution of the Marriage Bond in Favour of the Faith,* art. 4, 1°.

party with whom the new marriage is to be contracted or convalidated was not at fault in provoking the separation of the spouses."[85]

V. *If the Catholic party intends to contract a new marriage with a person who is not baptized or with a baptized non-Catholic, the Catholic party must sign the promise that he or she is prepared to remove dangers of defecting from the faith*

"A Catholic party who intends to contract or to convalidate a new marriage with a person who is not baptised or with a baptised non-Catholic, is to declare that he or she is prepared to remove dangers of defecting from the faith and the non-Catholic party is to declare that he or she is prepared to allow the Catholic party the freedom to profess his or her own religion and to baptise and educate their children as Catholics. The favour of the dissolution is not conceded unless this declaration in writing has been signed by both parties."[86]

A sample form of the promises is provided below.

VI. *If the petitioner or his/her intended or current spouse is not a Catholic, the non-Catholic party must sign the promise to raise any children born of the new marriage as Catholics and not hinder the Catholic party's practice of the faith*

If the petitioner or his or her intended spouse or current civil law spouse is a non-Catholic, the non-Catholic party must declare in writing that he or she is prepared to allow the Catholic party the freedom to profess his or her own religion and to baptize and

---

[85] Congregation for the Doctrine of the Faith, 30 April 2001, *Norms on the Preparation of the Process for the Dissolution of the Marriage Bond in Favour of the Faith,* art. 4, 2°.

[86] Congregation for the Doctrine of the Faith, 30 April 2001, *Norms on the Preparation of the Process for the Dissolution of the Marriage Bond in Favour of the Faith,* art. 5, §§1-2.

educate their children as Catholics. The favor of the dissolution is not conceded unless this declaration in writing has been signed by both parties.[87]

A sample form of the promises is provided below.

VII. *The petitioner has not previously petitioned and obtained the dissolution of his or her previous marriage in favor of the faith from the Roman Pontiff*

"A process may not be instructed for the dissolution of the bond of a marriage contracted or convalidated after obtaining the dissolution in favour of the faith of a prior marriage, nor may it be presented to the Congregation for the Doctrine of the Faith for examination."[88]

If the petitioner had contracted a marriage after having obtained from the Roman Pontiff the dissolution of a prior marriage in favor of the faith, the process for the dissolution of another marriage by the same party should neither be undertaken by the ordinary nor should the ordinary propose such a case for examination by the Congregation for the Doctrine of the Faith. In other words, if the petitioner had previously petitioned the Roman Pontiff for the dissolution of a previous marriage in favor of the faith and if the previous marriage of the petitioner was dissolved by the Roman Pontiff, the petitioner is not to petition the Roman Pontiff again for the dissolution of any of the petitioner's subsequent marriages in favor of the faith.

Given the foregoing norm, the judicial vicar may remit the petition of a repeat customer of the favor of the faith case to a formal trial by decree, citing the applicable norm.

---

[87] Congregation for the Doctrine of the Faith, 30 April 2001, *Norms on the Preparation of the Process for the Dissolution of the Marriage Bond in Favour of the Faith,* art. 5 §§1-2.

[88] Congregation for the Doctrine of the Faith, 30 April 2001, *Norms on the Preparation of the Process for the Dissolution of the Marriage Bond in Favour of the Faith,* art. 6.

VIII. *It must be determined whether the marriage was contracted with dispensation from the impediment of the disparity of worship*

"A petition can be presented to the Supreme Pontiff for the dissolution of the bond of a non-sacramental marriage entered with a dispensation from the impediment of disparity of cult if the Catholic party intends to enter a new marriage with a baptised person."[89]

A petition for the dissolution of the non-sacramental bond of a marriage entered into between a Catholic party and an unbaptized party with dispensation from the impediment of the disparity of worship can be presented by the Catholic party to the Roman Pontiff if the Catholic party intends to contract a new marriage with a baptized person.

"In the same circumstances, a petition may be presented to the Supreme Pontiff if the unbaptised party intends to receive baptism and enter a new marriage with a baptised party."[90]

In other words, a petition for the dissolution of the non-sacramental bond of a marriage entered into between a Catholic party and an unbaptized party with dispensation from the impediment of the disparity of worship can be presented by the un-baptized party to the Roman Pontiff if the un-baptized party intends to receive baptism and enter a new marriage with a baptized person.

Thus, in a marriage which was entered into by a Catholic party and an unbaptized party with dispensation from the impediment of the disparity of worship, the Catholic party can petition for the dissolution of the marriage in favor of the faith from the Roman Pontiff if the Catholic party intends to contract a new marriage with a baptized person. If it is the unbaptized party in a marriage entered into with a Catholic party, with dispensation

---

[89] Congregation for the Doctrine of the Faith, 30 April 2001, *Norms on the Preparation of the Process for the Dissolution of the Marriage Bond in Favour of the Faith,* art. 7 §1.

[90] Congregation for the Doctrine of the Faith, 30 April 2001, *Norms on the Preparation of the Process for the Dissolution of the Marriage Bond in Favour of the Faith,* art. 7 §2.

from the impediment of the disparity of worship, who is petitioning for the dissolution of the marriage, the petition can be presented to the Roman Pontiff if the non-baptized party intends to receive baptism and enter into a new marriage with a baptized party. "The purpose of this restriction is to avoid the celebration of a second marriage with a dispensation from the impediment of disparity of worship. For such a marriage could, in principle, have the same outcome. [...]. The possibility of confusion concerning the Church's doctrine on indissolubility of marriage is also evident in such circumstances. Allowing the same person to marry in the Church several times, after successive dissolutions of previous non-sacramental marriages, could easily lead to the erroneous assertion that the Church permits divorce."[91]

In the case of the unbaptized party who wishes to receive baptism, the bishop must attain moral certainty regarding the sincerity of the conversion of the petitioner. "The Bishop is not to direct the petition to the Congregation for the Doctrine of the Faith if a prudent doubt should exist regarding the sincerity of conversion of the petitioner or the intended spouse even though the baptism has already been received by one or both of them."[92]

IX. *Is the petitioner a catechumen?*

"In the case of a catechumen entering marriage, the wedding is to be delayed until after the baptism; if for grave reasons this cannot be done, it is to be morally certain that the baptism will be received as soon as possible."[93]

---

[91] Kowal and Woestman, pp. 107-108.

[92] Congregation for the Doctrine of the Faith, 30 April 2001, *Norms on the Preparation of the Process for the Dissolution of the Marriage Bond in Favour of the Faith*, art. 7 §3.

[93] Congregation for the Doctrine of the Faith, 30 April 2001, *Norms on the Preparation of the Process for the Dissolution of the Marriage Bond in Favour of the Faith*, art. 8.

X. The terms of the divorce are being fulfilled or have been fulfilled

"The Bishop is to consult the Congregation whenever special difficulties exist in the way in which the petitioner intends to fulfill his or her obligations toward the former spouse and any children they may have had, or if there is a fear of scandal from the concession of the favour."[94]

There must be a determination that the petitioner is fulfilling his or her moral or legal requirements towards the prior spouse and towards the children who may have been born of that marriage. There is a provision in the questionnaire for the parties and the witnesses to ask this question. Furthermore, the divorce decree may stipulate the obligations one party has towards the other and to the children. Thus, the instructor must also gather information regarding the fulfillment of any moral or civil obligations towards the former spouse and any offspring which the parties may have had from the marriage. If the petitioner is experiencing special difficulties towards fulfilling his or her obligations towards the other spouse and, or, towards the children, the instructor is to note this in his or her report to the dicastery and the circumstances surrounding the difficulties.

Similarly, if the petitioner is having special difficulties towards fulfilling his or her obligations towards the other spouse and, or, towards the children, the bishop is to state this in his *votum* to the dicastery, the circumstances surrounding the difficulties, and seek the advice of the dicastery regarding the matter.

XI. The petitioner has provided, is providing, or will provide for the religious education of the children

"The instructor is to report whether the petitioner has had any children and in what way the petitioner has provided or intends to provide for their religious education in accordance with the

---

[94] Congregation for the Doctrine of the Faith, 30 April 2001, *Norms on the Preparation of the Process for the Dissolution of the Marriage Bond in Favour of the Faith*, art. 9.

law and the petitioner's capabilities. The instructor must also inquire about the existence of any obligations either moral or civil toward the former spouse and any offspring which they may have had."[95]

Thus, the instructor is also to indicate in his or her report information regarding whether the petitioner has children and if so, how many children? What are their respective ages? Is the petitioner providing, has provided, or will provide for their religious education?

XII. *There is no possibility of scandal should the favor of the faith be Granted*

"The Bishop is to consult the Congregation...if there is a fear of scandal from the concession of the favour."[96]

The bishop is to state in his *votum* whether scandal would arise if the favor were to be granted by the Roman Pontiff. If no possibility of scandal would arise, the bishop may also provide the reasons for his answer.

XIII. *There must be proof of the fact of non-baptism*

"The absence of the baptism of either spouse is to be demonstrated in such a way that every prudent doubt is removed."[97]

The proof of the non-baptism of the unbaptized spouse is to be demonstrated with moral certainty.

---

[95] Congregation for the Doctrine of the Faith, 30 April 2001, *Norms on the Preparation of the Process for the Dissolution of the Marriage Bond in Favour of the Faith*, art. 20 §§1-2.

[96] Congregation for the Doctrine of the Faith, 30 April 2001, *Norms on the Preparation of the Process for the Dissolution of the Marriage Bond in Favour of the Faith*, art. 9.

[97] Congregation for the Doctrine of the Faith, 30 April 2001, *Norms on the Preparation of the Process for the Dissolution of the Marriage Bond in Favour of the Faith*, art. 16 §1.

3. The Procedures for the Instruction of the Favor of the Faith Petition

I. *The Determination of the Competent Bishop*

"A marriage entered into by parties, of whom at least one is not baptised, can be dissolved in favour of the faith by the Roman Pontiff, provided that it has not been consummated after both parties have received baptism."[98]

"It is the competence of the Congregation for the Doctrine of the Faith to examine the individual cases and, if it is warranted, to submit the petition to the Supreme Pontiff requesting the favour."[99]

"A diocesan Bishop and those equivalent to him in law, or an eparchial Bishop, are competent to instruct the process."[100]

"For the concession of the favour of the dissolution of the bond, at the moment it is given, it is required that:

1° there is no possibility of resuming the partnership of conjugal life;

2° the petitioner was not exclusively or predominantly the culpable cause of the breakdown of the conjugal life, and that the party with whom the new marriage is to be contracted or convalidated was not at fault in provoking the separation of the spouses."[101]

---

[98] Congregation for the Doctrine of the Faith, 30 April 2001, *Norms on the Preparation of the Process for the Dissolution of the Marriage Bond in Favour of the Faith,* art. 1. Available in http://www.vatican.va/roman_curia/congregations/cfaith/documents/rc_con_cfaith_doc_20010430_favor-fidei_en.html.

[99] Congregation for the Doctrine of the Faith, 30April 2001, *Norms on the Preparation of the Process for the Dissolution of the Marriage Bond in Favour of the Faith,* art. 2.

[100] Congregation for the Doctrine of the Faith, 30 April 2001, *Norms on the Preparation of the Process for the Dissolution of the Marriage Bond in Favour of the Faith,* art. 3.

[101] Congregation for the Doctrine of the Faith, 30 April 2001, *Norms on the Preparation of the Process for the Dissolution of the Marriage Bond in Favour of the Faith,* art. 4.

The process for the instruction of a Petrine Privilege petition commences at the local church. The bishop of the diocese in which the petitioner is domiciled can instruct the petition personally or delegate it to one of the tribunal judges or other persons approved by him.

II. *The Gathering of the Documents*

Not infrequently, the process begins at the parish level when one of the spouses or his or her intended or current spouse approaches the pastor or another priest for assistance in presenting the dissolution of the previous marriage to the tribunal. After determining that it may be a case of Petrine Privilege, the documents required for the case are then gathered. Some of the important documents required are:

i. The certificate of the marriage between the petitioner and the respondent.
ii. The divorce decree. "A copy of the party's divorce decree or civil nullity sentence is to be presented."[102]
iii. Marriage certificate, divorce decree, and declaration of nullity of marriage/freedom to marry for the intended or current spouse, if previously married. "Copies are to be presented, where they exist, of any divorce decree or civil nullity sentence together with the dispositive part of the canonical nullity sentence for any marriages attempted by either of the intended spouses."[103] If the petitioner's present or intended spouse has a petition that is pending before the tribunal, the completion of the process for the dissolution of marriage in favor of the faith is to be suspended until the present or intended

---

[102] Congregation for the Doctrine of the Faith, 30 April 2001, *Norms on the Preparation of the Process for the Dissolution of the Marriage Bond in Favour of the Faith*, art. 19 §1.

[103] Congregation for the Doctrine of the Faith, 30 April 2001, *Norms on the Preparation of the Process for the Dissolution of the Marriage Bond in Favour of the Faith*, art. 19 §2.

spouse is determined by the tribunal to be free to marry in the Catholic Church.

iv. Baptismal certificate or proof of baptism of the baptized party.

v. Baptismal certificate of the intended or current spouse, if Catholic.

vi. Certificate of present marriage if the petitioner has remarried.

vii. Baptismal certificate for each child who is Catholic.

viii. A letter from the pastor of the petitioner and intended spouse attesting to the religious practices of the petitioner and the intended spouse.

ix. The promises or *cautiones in favorem fidei*, if the petitioner or his or her intended/present spouse is not Catholic. Both parties to a mixed marriage or disparity of worship marriage are required to make the declaration in the presence of a priest. "A Catholic party who intends to contract or to convalidate a new marriage with a person who is not baptised or with a baptised non-Catholic, is to declare that he or she is prepared to remove dangers of defecting from the faith and the non-Catholic party is to declare that he or she is prepared to allow the Catholic party the freedom to profess his or her own religion and to baptise and educate their children as Catholics. The favour of the dissolution is not conceded unless this declaration in writing has been signed by both parties."[104]

x. Any Freewill donation or the processing fee imposed by the diocese. In some dioceses, the cost of processing the petition is offset by the diocese, and in other dioceses, the petitioner bears some or all of the cost.

"Documents submitted in original form or in authentic copy are to be verified by the notary. The documentation transmitted

---

[104] Congregation for the Doctrine of the Faith, 30 April 2001, *Norms on the Preparation of the Process for the Dissolution of the Marriage Bond in Favour of the Faith*, art. 5 §§1-2.

to the Congregation for the Doctrine of the Faith is to be complete and the copies are to be authenticated by the Bishop's notary."[105]

Original documents or their copies, certified by the civil or ecclesiastical notaries as concordant with the originals are to be submitted. In any case, all the documents to be forwarded to the dicastery must be notarized by the ecclesiastical notary or a certificate of authenticity of the documents issued by the notary is to be included in the acts of the case transmitted to the dicastery.

The petition is completed by the petitioner with the assistance of a competent priest at the parochial level or of a tribunal official. In completing the petition forms, indicate, where appropriate, "Not Applicable," or "Don't know," or "Not sure." No lines and no boxes are to be left blank.

A competent deacon or lay person can assist with the completion of the petition forms. However, the Congregation for the Doctrine of the Faith requires that the petitioner's pastor attest in writing to the religious practices of the petitioner and the present or intended spouse.

When the documents have been gathered and the petition completed, they are submitted to the tribunal.

III. *The Commissioning of the Officers*

"With the assistance of a notary and the intervention of the defender of the bond, the Bishop is to conduct the instruction of the process himself or commit it to an instructor selected either from the judges of the tribunal or from persons (*ex personis*) whom he has approved for this work. This commission is to be made in writing and it must appear in the acts."[106]

The competent bishop can instruct the case himself or delegate one of the tribunal judges or someone else to instruct the

---

[105] Congregation for the Doctrine of the Faith, 30 April 2001, *Norms on the Preparation of the Process for the Dissolution of the Marriage Bond in Favour of the Faith*, art. 13 §§1-2.

[106] Congregation for the Doctrine of the Faith, 30 April 2001, *Norms on the Preparation of the Process for the Dissolution of the Marriage Bond in Favour of the Faith*, art. 11 §§ 1-2.

case. A defender of the bond and an ecclesiastical notary are also to be appointed to the case. Given that the text uses the word "*personis*," it seems clearly evident that a lay person can be appointed as the instructor in favor of the faith cases. In any case, the appointment of officers to the case must be done on or after the date the petition was submitted, but before the collection of testimony or the instruction of the case.

A sample decree of the commission of the officers to the case is to be found below.

IV.   *The Instruction of the Case*

There are several elements to the instruction of the case.

i.   If there is a positive doubt regarding the validity of the marriage

"If a positive doubt should arise on any ground about the validity of the marriage whose dissolution is being sought, either in the process under the Bishop's direction or in the examination of the case at the Congregation for the Doctrine of the Faith, the petition directed to the Roman Pontiff is to make mention of this doubt."[107]

On the one hand, the dissolution of a marriage in favor of the faith pertains to the dissolution of a valid marriage and, on the other hand, the declaration of the nullity of marriage pertains to declaration of an invalid marriage. The former pertains to a valid marriage and the latter to an invalid marriage. Furthermore, the process for the declaration of the nullity of marriage is different from the process for obtaining the dissolution of the marriage bond. Therefore the distinction between the declaration of the nullity of a marriage and the dissolution of a marriage must be kept clearly in mind also in regard to terminology.[108]

---

[107] Congregation for the Doctrine of the Faith, 30 April 2001, *Norms on the Preparation of the Process for the Dissolution of the Marriage Bond in Favour of the Faith,* art. 10.

[108] *DC,* art. 7 §2.

Consequently, if, during the instruction of a petition for the dissolution of the bond of marriage, there arises a positive doubt that the marriage-in-question might not be valid, but may have been invalidly contracted, the bishop is to make mention of this doubt in his *votum* to the dicastery. Similarly, independent of whether or not the bishop made mention of this positive doubt, if the dicastery has reasons to doubt the validity of the marriage, that is, there is a positive doubt in the dicastery that the marriage might have been invalidly contracted, the dicastery will make mention of this doubt to the Roman Pontiff.

A doubt is positive if there is a reason to decide a matter one way, and there is a reason also to decide the matter another way. Applied to the petition for the dissolution of a marriage bond in favor of the faith, it means either the bishop or the dicastery officials or both the bishop and dicastery officials have a reason to believe that the marriage may be valid and, therefore, they are dealing with a dissolution of the bond in favor of the faith case and, at the same time, there is a reason to believe that the marriage may be invalid and, therefore, they are dealing with a declaration of the nullity of the marriage, and not with a dissolution of the bond of a valid marriage.

If the positive doubt exists in the mind of the bishop, he is to process and complete the petition and forward the acts of the case to Rome with a notation in his *votum* regarding the existence of this positive doubt. At the level of the dicastery, if the dicastery officials, based on the acts of the case, perceive this doubt in their mind, they may either ask for a supplementary instruction of the case from the bishop or, if the proofs in the acts of the case are sufficient, they may make a recommendation about the matter to the Roman Pontiff for his definitive decision.

ii. The interview of the parties and the witnesses

"Assertions must be proven according to the norms of law, either with documents or the depositions of trustworthy witnesses. Both spouses are to be heard during the instruction. The force of full proof cannot be attributed to declarations by the parties unless there are other elements which wholly corroborate them and from which moral certitude can be acquired."[109]

"The examination of the parties and witnesses is conducted by the instructor who must be attended by the notary. The defender of the bond is to be cited for the examination. The instructor is to administer an oath to the parties and witnesses that they will tell the truth, or that what they have said is the truth; if, however, one refuses to take an oath, he or she is to be heard unsworn. The instructor is to question the parties and witnesses in accordance with a questionnaire prepared in advance either by the instructor or by the defender of the bond; if need be, the instructor may add other questions. The answers are to be signed by the party or the witness, the instructor and the notary."[110]

"If the other party or a witness refuses or is unable to appear before the instructor and give testimony, their declarations may be obtained either before a notary or in any other lawful manner, provided it is established that they are genuine and authentic. The absence of the other party from the process is to be declared in accordance with the law and is to be recorded in the acts."[111]

The parties, witnesses, and the intended or current spouse of the petitioner are to be interviewed by the instructor. The interview can take place at the tribunal or at a convenient location mutually agreed upon by the instructor and the deponent. The dicastery permits telephone interviews, inasmuch as the person on the other end is asked to identify himself or herself, telephone number, and address and these pieces of information correspond with the information in the acts of the case, the oral interview of

---

[109] Congregation for the Doctrine of the Faith, 30 April 2001, *Norms on the Preparation of the Process for the Dissolution of the Marriage Bond in Favour of the Faith*, art. 12 §§ 1-3.

[110] Congregation for the Doctrine of the Faith, 30 April 2001, *Norms on the Preparation of the Process for the Dissolution of the Marriage Bond in Favour of the Faith*, art. 14 §§ 1-3.

[111] Congregation for the Doctrine of the Faith, 30 April 2001, *Norms on the Preparation of the Process for the Dissolution of the Marriage Bond in Favour of the Faith*, art. 15 §§ 1-2.

the deponent by means of telephone is noted in the transcript itself, the pertinent information is asked, and the deponent, after reviewing the transcript afterwards, signs and dates it.

The instructor is also to administer the oath; however, if a person refuses to take the oath, he or she can be heard unsworn. The questions are prepared beforehand. Other questions can and should be added, if necessary, for clarification purposes or which will elucidate the matter.

Effort must be made to interview the other party in the marriage. If the other party was legitimately cited in accordance with the norm of law (c. 1509 §§1-2) and if he or she neither replied nor appeared in person at the tribunal, the proof of the citation of the other party must be included in the acts. Copies the proof of the citation of the other party must likewise be included as part of the acts which are transmitted to Rome. The instructor is to indicate in his or her report to the dicastery that the other party was legitimately cited, but neither responded to the citation nor appeared in person before the tribunal. If the other party was contacted also by telephone and the person did not answer or could not be reached, this is also to be noted in the acts that are sent to Rome, including the dates and number of times attempts were made to contact the other party. If the other party was declared absent from the process (cc. 1592-1593), this declaration is to be made clear in the acts.

iii. The proof of the non-baptism of the unbaptized party

The proof of the non-baptism of the unbaptized party must be proven beyond reasonable doubt. "The absence of the baptism of either spouse is to be demonstrated in such a way that every prudent doubt is removed. Witnesses are to be heard in view of their quality, such as the parents or relatives of the unbaptised party or those who knew the person as an infant and have knowledge about the entire course of the party's life. The witnesses are to be questioned not only about the absence of baptism but also about the circumstances and the other indications that would probably indicate that baptism had not been conferred. Care is to be taken that the baptismal registers are examined in those places where it is established that the party who claims to be unbaptised had lived as an infant, especially in those churches which the party may have frequented or in which the marriage was celebrated. If the marriage was celebrated with a dispensation from the impediment of disparity of cult, the instructor is to obtain copies of the dispensation and the prenuptial inquiry for the acts."[112]

Thus, the proof of the non-baptism of the unbaptized party is to be demonstrated with moral certainty. Witnesses are to be interviewed such as the parents or relatives of the unbaptized party or those who knew this person from childhood and who have knowledge of this party's life. It is the quality of the witnesses, rather than the quantity that matters. The witnesses are to be questioned not only regarding the absence of baptism but also regarding the reasons why they believe that the party is unbaptized.

Furthermore, inquiries should be made in those places where the unbaptized party lived as an infant, especially in those churches which the party may have frequented or in which the marriage was celebrated and their baptismal registers examined so as to establish that the party who claims to be unbaptized has not been baptized as an infant. If the marriage was celebrated with a dispensation from the impediment of disparity of cult, the instructor is to obtain copies of the dispensation and the prenuptial inquiry and include them in the acts to be later forwarded to the dicastery.

iv. Moral certainty regarding the non-cohabitation of the parties after the baptism of the baptized party

During the instruction of the case, the instructor is also to inquire regarding whether both parties have cohabited after baptism, if one of the spouses later received baptism and whether after the separation, they have engaged in a conjugal act with each

---

[112] Congregation for the Doctrine of the Faith, 30 April 2001, *Norms on the Preparation of the Process for the Dissolution of the Marriage Bond in Favour of the Faith*, art. 16 §§ 1-5.

other. "If the unbaptised spouse is baptised at the time the favour of the dissolution is being sought, there must be an inquiry into the possibility of cohabitation after the baptism; witnesses are also to be questioned about this matter. The parties in the case are themselves to be asked whether they had any relationship after their separation and what kind, and especially whether they had engaged in a conjugal act."[113]

Furthermore, the instructor is also to gather information regarding the current marital status of the other spouse. For example, has he or she married another spouse since after divorcing the petitioner? The instructor is also to question the parties and the witnesses regarding the cause of the separation or divorce in order to ascertain who was at fault for the break-up of the marriage or marriages, if the petitioner is petitioning at the same time for the dissolution of the bond of more than one marriage. "The instructor is to collect information on the state of life of the other party and to report whether that party has attempted a new marriage after the divorce. The instructor is to question the parties and witnesses about the cause of the separation or divorce, so that it is clear who was at fault for the breakdown of the marriage or marriages."[114]

The instructor is also to ask the parties and the witnesses regarding whether there are any possibility of the reconciliation and restoration of conjugal living. The instructor is to make a statement about this matter in his or her *votum*.

v.   Copies of civil or ecclesiastical public documents

The instructor is also required to obtain a copy of the civil divorce or civil nullity of the parties and of the dispositive part of any canonical sentence which may have been declared null by a

---

[113] Congregation for the Doctrine of the Faith, 30 April 2001, *Norms on the Preparation of the Process for the Dissolution of the Marriage Bond in Favour of the Faith,* art. 17 §§ 1-2.

[114] Congregation for the Doctrine of the Faith, 30 April 2001, *Norms on the Preparation of the Process for the Dissolution of the Marriage Bond in Favour of the Faith,* art. 18.

competent ecclesiastical tribunal. "A copy of the party's divorce decree or civil nullity sentence is to be presented. Copies are to be presented, where they exist, of any divorce decree or civil nullity sentence together with the dispositive part of the canonical nullity sentence for any marriages attempted by either of the intended spouses."[115]

vi. The moral and civil obligations of the petitioner towards the other party and the children

It is also the role of the instructor to inquire and report "whether the petitioner has had any children and in what way the petitioner has provided or intends to provide for their religious education in accordance with the law and the petitioner's capabilities. The instructor must also inquire about the existence of any obligations either moral or civil toward the former spouse and any offspring which they may have had."[116]

vii. The baptismal status of the petitioner and his or her intended spouse, their practice of the faith, and their freedom to marry

If the petitioner or the intended or current spouse of the petitioner has converted or has been baptized, the sincerity of the conversion must not only be ascertained from them, but also the reasons that lead to the conversion. These findings are to be included in the letter of the pastor to the bishop and in the report of the instructor to the dicastery. "If either the petitioner or the intended spouse has been converted and baptised, they are to be questioned regarding the time and intention of being baptised.

---

[115] Congregation for the Doctrine of the Faith, 30 April 2001, *Norms on the Preparation of the Process for the Dissolution of the Marriage Bond in Favour of the Faith*, art. 19 §§1-2.
[116] Congregation for the Doctrine of the Faith, 30 April 2001, *Norms on the Preparation of the Process for the Dissolution of the Marriage Bond in Favour of the Faith*, art. 20 §§1-2.

The parish priest is also to be questioned about the reasons for the baptism, and especially about the integrity of the parties."[117]

There is also to be a report in the acts about the religious practice of both the petitioner and of the intended or current spouse. "Explicit reference is to be made in the acts to the religious practice of both the petitioner and the intended spouse. Certificates of baptism or profession of faith or both are to be included in the acts."[118]

The acts of the case should also include indications that the intended or current spouse of the petitioner is free to marry. If the intended or current spouse has never been previously married, this should be stated; otherwise proof of this spouse's freedom to marry should be included. For example, decree of nullity of the previous marriage; or, if the person was in sacred orders or was a perpetually professed lay religious, proof of rescript of laicization or indult of departure or dismissal.

Samples of the questions for the petitioner, the respondent, the witnesses, and the intended or current spouse are provided under this chapter below.

V. *The Brief of the Defender of the Bond*

"When the instruction has been completed, the instructor is to give all the acts, without publishing them, together with a suitable report, to the defender of the bond whose responsibility to is to find reasons, if there are any, against the dissolution of the bond."[119]

---

[117] Congregation for the Doctrine of the Faith, 30 April 2001, *Norms on the Preparation of the Process for the Dissolution of the Marriage Bond in Favour of the Faith,* art. 21.

[118] Congregation for the Doctrine of the Faith, 30 April 2001, *Norms on the Preparation of the Process for the Dissolution of the Marriage Bond in Favour of the Faith,* art. 22.

[119] Congregation for the Doctrine of the Faith, 30 April 2001, *Norms on the Preparation of the Process for the Dissolution of the Marriage Bond in Favour of the Faith,* art. 23.

There is no publication of the acts in a Petrine Privilege case. Thus, subsequent to the completion of the instruction of the case, the acts are handed over to the defender of the bond so that he or she can submit a brief on the case.

A sample form of the brief of the defender of the bond is enclosed below.

VI. *The Report of the Instructor*

The instructor is also to prepare a report about the case, which will be part of the documents of the case that will be forwarded to Rome. The instructor's report should contain the following elements:

1. It should be addressed to the Cardinal Prefect of the Congregation for the Doctrine of the Faith.
2. The facts about the petitioner and the respondent regarding who is baptized and who is unbaptized.
3. The reason the petitioner is seeking the dissolution of the marriage, which is usually for his or her own spiritual good, the spiritual good of the intended spouse, and in favor of the faith of the Catholic party in the pending marriage between the petitioner and the intended spouse.
4. A statement about the practice of the faith of the Catholic party in the pending marriage.
5. The ages when the petitioner and the respondent married, the length of their courtship and engagement, the date and duration of the marriage, the prevailing reasons why the marriage ended, and the date of divorce.
6. The reason why there is no hope of reconciliation. For example, either or both parties have remarried or intend to marry, and one or both parties have begotten children in the subsequent marriage, if this is the case.
7. Did the respondent participate? If negative, provide proofs that he/she was legitimately cited, and he or she neither appeared nor responded to the citation.
8. Have witnesses corroborated the fact of the non-baptism of the unbaptized party? Who are these witnesses? State

their relationship to the party on whose behalf they provided testimony. Make a statement regarding their credibility, if you believe they are worthy of trust.

9. If the intended or current spouse is a practicing Catholic, state it. State why you believe he/she is not responsible for the break-up of the marriage for which you are seeking dissolution in favor of the faith. Are they currently married in the civil forum? Do the petitioner and the intended / current spouse have children together? If so, are they being raised in the practice of the Catholic faith?

10. Is there the possibility of scandal should the favor be granted? If no, state so.

11. Did the pastor of the Catholic party testify to the credibility of the Catholic party and the party's intended/ current spouse?

12. Does the petitioner wish to convert? Have both parties signed the Promises or *Cautiones?*

13. Append your name and signature at the end, with the date.

A sample form of the report of the instructor is provide under this chapter below.

VII. *The Votum of the Bishop*

"Having received all the acts, the Bishop is to write his opinion concerning the petition which indicates accurately whether the conditions for the concession of the favour have been fulfilled, and especially whether the promises, mentioned in art. 5, have been made. The reasons are to be given which recommend the concession of the favour, always including whether the petitioner has attempted a new marriage in any way or may be living in concubinage."[120]

---

[120] Congregation for the Doctrine of the Faith, 30 April 2001, *Norms on the Preparation of the Process for the Dissolution of the Marriage Bond in Favour of the Faith*, art. 24.

The brief of the defender of the bond and the report of the instructor have been written, the acts of the case are then sent to the bishop for his own *votum*. The *votum* of the bishop should indicate whether the conditions for the granting of the favor have been fulfilled in the case, the reasons why the favor should be granted, and whether the petitioner has entered into a new marriage. Thus, the elements to be included in the *votum* of the bishop are as follows:

i. The non-baptism of one of the parties in the marriage prior to the marriage and this party remained unbaptized throughout the duration of the marriage.

ii. Whether the unbaptized party later became baptized and whether both parties have had conjugal relations since after the baptism.

iii. Whether the petitioner was the exclusive or predominant culpable cause of the break-up of the marriage.

iv. Whether it is true that there is no hope of reconciliation between the petitioner and the respondent.

v. Whether if the petitioner or his/her intended or current spouse is not a Catholic, the non-Catholic party has signed the promise to raise any children born of the new marriage as Catholics and not hinder the Catholic party's practice of the Faith.

vi. Whether the petitioner has a fiancé or spouse whom he/she wishes to marry in the Catholic Church.

vii. Whether the petitioner's fiancé or spouse is free to marry in the Catholic Church.

viii. Whether it is true that the new fiancé or spouse was not the cause of the break-up of the marriage for which you are seeking a Favor of the Faith.

ix. Whether the Catholic party is actively practicing the Faith.

x. Whether it is true that the granting of the favor would not be a cause of scandal.

xi. The reasons why the favor should be conceded to the petitioner.

xii.   The current marital status of the petitioner.

If there is a request that the favor should be granted without the usual fee (*in forma pauperum*), the bishop is to indicate this in his votum.

The *votum*, which is addressed to the cardinal prefect of the congregation for the doctrine of the faith, is signed and dated by the bishop.

A sample from of the *votum* of the bishop which covers all the points raised above is to be found below.

VIII. *The Authentication of the Acts*

As already indicated above, the acts of the case are authenticated by the notary. A sample form of the certificate of the authentication of the acts is provided below.

IX.   *The Completion of the Summary and Index Forms*

The summary and index forms also are to be completed. The summary template form provided by the congregation for the doctrine of the faith is to be used. See below for more details. An index sample form is also provided under this chapter below.

X.   *The Transmission of the Acts to Rome via the Nunciature*

"The Bishop is to send three typewritten sets of the acts to the Congregation for the Doctrine of the Faith, together with his opinion and the observations of the defender of the bond, an index and the summary of the case."[121]

"Care is also to be taken that the acts of a case drawn up in the language and style of the place are translated into one of those recognized in the regulations of the Roman Curia and confirmed

---

[121] Congregation for the Doctrine of the Faith, 30 April 2001, *Norms on the Preparation of the Process for the Dissolution of the Marriage Bond in Favour of the Faith*, art. 25 §1.

with a sworn declaration that they have been faithfully translated and transcribed."[122]

Three copies each of the acts of the case, including the brief of the defender of the bond, the report of the instructor, and the votum of the bishop are sent via the Nunciature to the congregation for the doctrine of the faith.

The congregation for the doctrine of the faith recommends that the acts be arranged in the following order and each act numbered appropriately. Each act of the case and its corresponding page is, in turn, to be in the index. A statement that the documents are on "file in the chancery" is not sufficient. Every act and every case is to be given an individual attention. The acts of the case may be arranged in the following order:

1. The summary.
2. The petition.
3. The commission or constitution of the officers.
4. The testimony of the petitioner.
5. The testimony of the respondent/former spouse.
6. Baptismal certificate of the baptized party or of the profession of faith.
7. Records of baptismal searches.
8. Records of the pre-nuptial investigation in the case of a Catholic marriage.
9. Marriage certificate.
10. Divorce decree, or civil sentence of nullity of the marriage.
11. The dispositive part of the canonical sentence of nullity of marriage or the canonical decree of nullity of all the marriages attempted by either or both spouses, if applicable.
12. Baptismal certificate of the children born of the union, if applicable.
13. Testimony of witnesses.
14. Testimony of intended or current spouse.

---

[122] Congregation for the Doctrine of the Faith, 30 April 2001, *Norms on the Preparation of the Process for the Dissolution of the Marriage Bond in Favour of the Faith,* art. 25 §2.

15. Baptismal certificate of intended or current spouse, if catholic.
16. Proof of freedom to marry.
17. Civil marriage certificate of petitioner and current spouse, if they are already married civilly.
18. Baptismal certificates of the children of the petitioner and current spouse, if applicable.
19. Letter of pastor regarding the religious practice of the petitioner and the intended, or current, spouse of the petitioner.
20. The Promises (*Cautiones in Favorem Fidei*)
21. The Report of the Instructor.
22. The Observations of the Defender of the Bond.
23. The *Votum* of the Ordinary.
24. The Authentication of the Acts of the Case.
25. The Index.

The congregation usually acknowledges the receipt of the acts of the case when the acts have reached the dicastery.

4. The Sample Documents for the Instruction of a Petition of the Favor of the Faith Based on the Petitioner's Lack of Baptism

4.1. *The Petition*

Tribunal name, address, & logo

PETITION FOR FAVOR OF THE FAITH

BASED ON THE PETITIONER'S LACK OF BAPTISM
Please fill in all the blanks and answer all questions as completely as possible.

MOST HOLY FATHER:

I, _____, humbly present this petition for the dissolution of the natural bond of marriage in favor of the faith that I contracted with _____ on the _____ day of _____ in the year of our Lord _____ at _____. I was unbaptized prior to and throughout the duration of our marriage. My former spouse and I did not ever have conjugal relations after baptism, if later baptized. Neither my present/intended spouse nor I was the exclusive or prevailing culpable cause of the breakdown of my former marriage. There is no possibility of restoring the partnership of conjugal life. Neither my present/current spouse nor I have received dissolution in favor of the faith before. No public scandal would result should this dissolution be granted. I sincerely request that you as the Vicar of Christ dissolve my non-sacramental marriage in favor of the faith so that I may enter a new marriage validly and licitly according to the laws of God and of the Holy Catholic Church.

I am presently:

☐ A Roman Catholic. I intend to enter a new marriage with someone who is free to marry according to the laws of the Catholic Church.

☐ A baptized non-Catholic. I have never been married to a Roman Catholic. I am participating in catechesis. I wish to be received into the Catholic Church. I intend to enter a new marriage with someone who is free to marry according to the laws of the Catholic Church.

☐ A baptized non-Catholic. I have never been married to a Roman Catholic. I do not wish to become a Catholic at this time. I intend to enter a new marriage with a Catholic who is free to marry according to the laws of the Catholic Church.

☐ Unbaptized. I married a Roman Catholic and the Catholic party obtained dispensation from the impediment of disparity of worship to marry me. I wish to receive baptism in the Catholic Church. I intend to enter a new marriage with someone who is free to marry according to the laws of the Catholic Church.

☐ Unbaptized. I have never been married to a Roman Catholic. I do not wish to be baptized in the Catholic Church at this time. I intend to enter a new marriage with a Catholic who is free to marry according to the laws of the Catholic Church.

☐ Unbaptized. I have never been married to a Roman Catholic. I wish to be baptized in the Catholic Church. I intend to enter a new marriage with someone who is free to marry according to the laws of the Catholic Church.

I attest that the information presented herein is true to the best of my knowledge.

_____   _____

Signature of Petitioner   Date

4.2. The Parties and Witnesses Information Form

On separate sheets of paper
PARTIES AND WITNESSES INFORMATION

I. PETITIONER

FIRST NAME	MIDDLE NAME	CURRENT LAST NAME	MAIDEN NAME	
STREET ADDRESS			HOME PHONE	
CITY	STATE	ZIP CODE	CELL PHONE	WORK PHONE
AGE	BIRTHDAY (Mo. / Day / Year)	PLACE OF BIRTH	OCCUPATION	
BAPTIZED: ☐ YES ☐ NO		CHURCH OF BAPTISM	CITY	STATE
DATE OF BAPTISM	RELIGION (RAISED IN)		PRESENT RELIGION	

IF YOU AN-SWERED NO, HOW CERTAIN ARE YOU THAT YOU HAVE NEVER BEEN BAP-	ABSO-LUTELY CER-TAIN ☐	QUITE CER-TAIN ☐	NOT TOO CER-TAIN ☐	UNCERTAIN ☐
NAME AND ADDRESS OF THE PLACE YOU PRESENTLY WORSHIP:				
If Catholic, check and initial: ☐ ———	I am providing an annotated certificate of baptism which has been issued in the last six months by the Church in which I was baptized or received into the Catholic Church. I understand that it is the newly issued certificate bearing the parish seal that is required. A photocopy of it is not accepta-ble. If a baptized non-Catholic, I am providing a certificate or letter verifying baptism.			

II. PETITIONER'S PARENTS

   If deceased, please note.

FATHER

FIRST NAME	MIDDLE NAME	CURRENT LAST NAME	
STREET ADDRESS		HOME PHONE	
CITY STATE ZIP CODE		WORK PHONE	
RELIGIOUS AFFILIA-TION	WAS HE BAPTIZED: ☐ YES ☐ NO	NAME OF THE CHRISTIAN DENOMINATION IN WHICH HE WAS BAPTIZED	

MOTHER

FIRST NAME	MIDDLE NAME	CUR-RENT LAST NAME	MAIDEN NAME
STREET ADDRESS		HOME PHONE	
CITY STATE ZIP CODE		WORK PHONE	
RELIGIOUS AFFILIA-TION	WAS SHE BAPTIZED: ☐ YES ☐ NO	NAME OF THE CHRISTIAN DENOMINATION IN WHICH SHE WAS BAPTIZED	

III. FORMER SPOUSE

FIRST NAME	MIDDLE NAME		CUR-RENT LAST	MAIDEN NAME	
STREET ADDRESS				HOME PHONE	
CITY	STATE	ZIP CODE	CELL PHONE	WORK PHONE	
AGE	BIRTHDAY (Mo./Day/Year)		PLACE OF BIRTH	OCCUPATION	
BAPTIZED: ☐ YES ☐ NO		CHURCH OF BAP-TISM	CITY	STATE	
DATE OF BAPTISM (Mo./Day/Year)		RELIGION (RAISED IN)	PRESENT RELIGION		

IF YOU ANSWERED NO, HOW CERTAIN ARE YOU THAT HE/SHE HAS NEVER BEEN BAPTIZED? ABSOLUTELY CERTAIN ☐ QUITE CERTAIN ☐ NOT TOO CERTAIN ☐ UNCERTAIN ☐
NAME AND ADDRESS OF CHURCH PRESENTLY ATTENDING:

IV. FORMER SPOUSE'S PARENTS

If deceased, please note.

FATHER

FIRST MIDDLE LAST NAMES			RELIGION
STREET ADDRESS	CITY	STATE	ZIP CODE	HOME PHONE

MOTHER

FIRST MIDDLE LAST NAMES			RELIGION
STREET ADDRESS	CITY	STATE	ZIP CODE	HOME PHONE

V. WEDDING CEREMONY

LOCATION CITY CIVIL PARISH/COUNTY STATE		WEDDING DATE (Mo./Day/Year)
PETITIONER'S AGE AT WEDDING:	FORMER SPOUSE'S AGE AT WEDDING:	YOUR RELIGION AT TIME OF MARRIAGE:
WAS THIS MARRIAGE THE FIRST	YOUR FORMER SPOUSE'S RELIGION AT TIME OF MARRIAGE:	

FOR BOTH OF YOU? □ YES □NO	
□ ___ (check and initial) I have obtained and enclosed a certified copy of the marriage certificate.	
YEARS OF MARRIAGE	YEARS OF MARITAL COHABITATION

VI. CHILDREN BORN TO PETITONER AND FORMER
    SPOUSE

If any child has been baptized, please furnish a baptismal certificate.

BIRTH DATE Mo./ Day/ Year	N A M E	BAP TIZE D	IF YES, DATE OF BAP- TISM	RE- LI- GI ON OF BA PTI SM	RELI- GION CUR- RENTL Y BE- ING RAISE D IN	WHO HAS CUSTODY?
		□ YES □ NO				□ ME □ FOR-MER SPOUSE
		□ YES □ NO				□ ME □ FOR-MER SPOUSE
		□ YES □ NO				□ ME □ FOR-MER SPOUSE
		□ YES □ NO				□ ME □ FOR-MER SPOUSE

VII. DIVORCE/DISSOLUTION

APPROXI-MATE DATE OF LAST CO-HABITATION (Mo./Day/Year)	WHO FILED FOR DIVORCE? ☐ ME ☐ FORMER SPOUSE	DIVORCE DATE (Mo./Day/Year)	CIVIL PARISH/COUNTY	STATE
☐ ___ (check and initial) I have obtained and enclosed a certified copy of the divorce/dissolution decree from the Civil Parish or County Clerk's office.				

VIII. WITNESSES

WITNESS INFORMATION: Testimony of reliable witnesses in this case is required. We ask that you give us the names and complete addresses of two people whom you have contacted who are willing and can testify to whether or not your former spouse was baptized and the reasons thereof. The best witnesses are members of your former spouse's immediate family, e.g., father, mother, grandparents, older siblings, aunts, uncles, etc.

First Witness

1. _____
Title   First Name   Last Name
Address
City   State   Zip
Relationship

Second Witness

1. _____
Title   First Name   Last Name
Address _____
City   State   Zip _____
Relationship

LIST BELOW IN CHRONOLOGICAL ORDER ALL YOUR MARRIAGES

FULL (MAIDEN) NAME OF SPOUSE	WEDDING DATE (Mo. / Day / Year)	REASON FOR END OF THE MARRIAGE (CHECK ONE)	IFDIVORCED, HAS A DECLARATION OF NULLITY (ANNULMENT) BEEN GRANTED
		☐ DEATH ☐ DIVORCE	☐ YES ☐ NO
		☐ DEATH ☐ DIVORCE	☐ YES ☐ NO
		☐ DEATH ☐ DIVORCE	☐ YES ☐ NO
If you have obtained a declaration of nullity for a previous marriage, kindly provide the following information			(Arch)Diocese _____ Prot. No. _____

IX. PRESENT/INTENDED SPOUSE

FIRST	MIDDLE	CUR-RENT LAST	MAIDEN NAMES
STREET ADDRESS			HOME PHONE
CITY STATE ZIP CODE			WORK PHONE
AGE	BIRTHDAY (Mo. / Day / Year)	PLACE OF BIRTH	OCCU-PATION
BAPTIZED? ☐ YES ☐ NO	CHURCH OF BAPTISM	CITY	STATE
DATE OF BAPTISM (Mo. / Day / Year)	RELIGION (RAISED IN)		PRE-SENT RELI-
NAME AND ADDRESS OF CHURCH PRESENTLY AT-TENDING:			
Check and initial:☐ —	☐ My present/intended spouse is Catholic, I am providing an anno-tated certificate of baptism which has been issued within the last six months by the Church in which my present/intended spouse was bap-tized or received into the Catholic Church. ☐ My present/intended spouse is a baptized non-Catholic, I am providing a certificate or letter ver-ifying baptism. ☐ My present/intended spouse has received a declaration of nul-lity; I am providing the decree of the nullity of that marriage.		

X. CHILDREN BORN OF CURRENT MARRIAGE

If any child has been baptized, please furnish a baptismal certificate

BIRTH DATE Mo. / Day / Year	N A M E	BAP-TIZED	IF YES, DATE OF BAP-TISM	RELI-GION OF BAP-TISM	RELIGION CURRENTLY BEING RAISED IN
		☐ YES ☐ NO			
		☐ YES ☐ NO			
		☐ YES ☐ NO			
		☐ YES ☐ NO			
		☐ YES ☐ NO			
		☐ YES ☐ NO			

By my signature below, I affirm that all the answers recorded above are true to the best of my knowledge.

_____   _____
Signature of Petitioner   Date

_____   _____
Name of Church Parish   City, State

The above statement was signed in my presence.

_____
Signature of the Priest

_____
Printed Name of the Pastor

_____
Date

_____   _____
Name of Church Parish   City, State

4.3. *The Promises*

"A Catholic party who intends to contract or to convalidate a new marriage with a person who is not baptised or with a baptised non-Catholic, is to declare that he or she is prepared to remove dangers of defecting from the faith and the non-Catholic party is to declare that he or she is prepared to allow the Catholic party the freedom to profess his or her own religion and to baptise and educate their children as Catholics. The favour of the dissolution is not conceded unless this declaration in writing has been signed by both parties."[123]

_____

[123] Congregation for the Doctrine of the Faith, April 30, 2001, *Norms (Normae) on the Preparation of the Process for the Dissolution of the Marriage Bond in Favour of the Faith*, art. 5 §§1-2.

On a separate sheet of the tribunal letterhead

PROMISES
(cf. art. 5 *Normae*)

A. The Promises of the Catholic Party

In the presence of the undersigned priest, I hereby promise to practice my faith, and to fulfill to the best of my ability my obligation to have all children who may be born to our marriage baptized in the Catholic Church and carefully raised in the knowledge and practice of the Catholic faith.

Signature

B. The Promises of the Non-Catholic Party

In the presence of the undersigned priest, I hereby promise that I shall permit my spouse to practice the Catholic religion and to fulfill the solemn promise that all the children of our marriage will be baptized and raised only in the Catholic faith.

Signature

C. Certification

I, the undersigned priest, hereby certify that both parties have freely made the above promises in my presence.

Date

Signature

Parish Seal

4.4. *The Documents to be Submitted Along With the Petition*

On a separate page
DOCUMENTS REQUIRED

The following have been submitted with the Petition:

☐ The marriage certificate of the marriage between the Petitioner and the Respondent.
☐ Final divorce decree.
☐ Baptismal certificate or proof of Baptism of the baptized party.
☐ Baptismal certificate of the Intended Spouse, if Catholic.
☐ Certificate of present marriage if the Petitioner has remarried.
☐ Baptismal Certificate for each child who is Catholic.
☐ A letter from the Pastor of the Petitioner and the intended spouse attesting to the religious practices of the petitioner and the intended spouse.
☐ Marriage Certificate, Divorce Decree, and Declaration of Nullity/Freedom to Marry for the Intended Spouse, if previously married.
☐ Promises (*Cautiones In Favorem Fidei*), if you or your intended /present spouse is not Catholic.

4.5. *The Questions for the Petitioner Based on the Petitioner's Lack of Baptism*

On a separate sheet of paper
CASE

DEPOSITION OF THE PETITIONER - NAME

Oath: Do you solemnly swear to tell the truth, the whole truth, and nothing but the truth, so help you God?
Response:

A. Questions regarding Yourself

1. What are your full names, address, and telephone number?
2. What is the date and place of your birth?

B. Questions regarding your Baptismal Status

1. Were you unbaptized prior to the marriage?
2. How do you know this?
3. Did you remain unbaptized throughout the duration of the marriage?
4. Have you been baptized since the marriage ended in divorce?
5. Did you ever attend a Christian Church when you were growing up? If so, what is the name of the Church?
6. What is the name of your father?
7. What is his religion?
8. What is the name of the church?
9. What is the name of your mother?
10. What is her religion?
11. What is the name of the church?
12. Were you ever under the care or guardianship of others besides your parents? If so, whom?
13. Have you any brothers or sisters?
14. How many?
15. Were any of your brothers or sisters ever baptized?
16. Did your parents insist that their children attend church?
17. Did you ever attend any Christian church or Sunday school? If so, list out the churches or Sunday school you attended.
18. Do you intend at this time to become a Catholic?

C. Questions regarding your marriage to your former spouse

1. What are the names, address, and telephone number of your former spouse?
2. When and where was this person born?

3. Was your former spouse ever baptized christened, dedicated, or initiated in any religious denomination or sect?
4. How do you know this?
5. When and where did your marriage take place?
6. How long did you date your former spouse before marriage?
7. How long were both of you engaged?
8. How long did you live with your former spouse in marriage?
9. Were there temporary separations?
10. Please, state the principal causes for the break-up of the marriage
11. Were there any children born in the marriage? If so, how many?
12. Are the terms of the divorce decree, if any, toward your former spouse and/or children being met or have they been met? Please, explain.
13. Since the break-up of the marriage, have you had cause to resume, renew, or restore the partnership of conjugal life with your former spouse?
14. Do you wish to be reconciled with your former spouse and to live again as husband and wife? Give reasons for your answer.
15. Has your former spouse remarried?
16. Have you or your former spouse ever obtain the dissolution of a previous marriage in favor of the faith?

D. Questions regarding your present or intended spouse

1. Are you currently engaged or have you remarried civilly?
2. Please, give the full names of your present or intended spouse.
3. How long have you known her?
4. Briefly describe how both of you first met?
5. Does your present or intended spouse know your former spouse? If yes, explain how.

6. Was your present or intended spouse the predominant and culpable cause of the break-up of the marriage for which you are seeking dissolution in favor of the faith?
7. What is your present or intended spouse's religion?
8. Is this person baptized?
9. Does your intended spouse sincerely believe in and practice the Catholic faith?
10. Do you promise to allow the person you intend to marry freely to practice the Catholic religion?
11. Do you promise to raise the children that may be born of this marriage in the Catholic faith?
12. Has your present or intended spouse been previously married?
13. Have you had any children with this person?
14. Has your present or intended spouse been involved in this favor of the faith case?
15. If your former marriage is dissolved and you are permitted to marry in the Catholic Church, would it give rise to scandal, or criticism, or unfavorable publicity?
16. Have you anything else to add?

By my signature below, I affirm and attest that all the answers recorded above are true to the best of my knowledge.

_____   _____
Signature of Petitioner   Date

_____   _____
Instructor   Date

_____   _____
Ecclesiastical Notary   Date

4.6. *The Citation Letter to the Respondent*

LETTER TO THE RESPONDENT

CASE

Certified mail:

Date

Name
Address

Dear N.:

The Petitioner, N. (*name of the petitioner*), has presented to the Tribunal of N. a Petition for the dissolution of his/her marriage to you.

The dissolution of a former marriage is different from annulment. The dissolution of a former marriage does not question the validity of the marriage- or that the marriage never occurred. The dissolution of a former marriage acknowledges the existence of the validity of the marriage but the Petitioner wants the marriage bond dissolved by the Catholic Church either because the Petitioner wants to be a Catholic or because the Petitioner wants to marry a Catholic. Under certain conditions the marriages between non-Catholics, at least one of whom was not baptized prior to the marriage can be dissolved by the Pope in the favor of the faith. Also, a valid marriage between a baptized Catholic and an unbaptized non-Catholic can also be dissolved by the Pope in favor of the faith.

The Petitioner wants the bond of marriage between the two of you dissolved so that he/she can marry according to the laws of the Catholic Church. This is strictly a Church matter. The Tribunal is concerned merely with determining whether N. (*name of the petitioner*) is free to marry in the Catholic Church.

Thank you for your kind consideration of this matter. Either myself or someone from this Tribunal will be in contact with you in the next few days to make arrangement for a brief interview with you.

If you have any questions, please do not hesitate to contact us.

Sincerely,

Signed: Judicial Vicar (or Instructor)

4.7. The Questions for the Respondent Based on the Petitioner's Lack of Baptism

THE DECLARATIONS OF THE RESPONDENT

NAME OF THE RESPONDENT:

Oath: Do you solemnly swear to tell the truth, the whole truth, and nothing but the truth, insofar as you know it, so help you God?
Response:

A. Questions Regarding Yourself

1. What are your full names?
2. When and where were you born?
3. Where did you grow up?

B. Regarding Your Baptismal Status

1. Have you ever been baptized?
2. What is the name of the church?
3. Were you raised by your natural parents?
4. Are your parents living?
5. What was the religion of your father at the time of your birth and during your childhood and youth? Please, give specific denominations or religion.
6. Was he baptized or christened? How do you know this?
7. What was the religion of your mother at the time of your birth, during your childhood and youth? Please, give specific denomination or religion?
8. Was she baptized or christened? How do you know this?
9. Have you any brothers or sisters? How many?
10. Were any of your brothers or sisters ever baptized or christened?

11.   Are you currently attending any church, temple, or synagogue? If so, which one(s)?

C. Regarding Your Former Spouse

1.   What are the full names of your former spouse?
2.   Was your former spouse ever baptized prior to the marriage? How do you know this?

D. Regarding Your Former Marriage

1.   What was the date of the marriage?
2.   What is the city, civil parish/county, and state of the marriage?
3.   Was this marriage the first marriage for both of you?
4.   Who officiated at the wedding?
5.   How long did you keep company with each other before the marriage?
6.   How did both of you come to the decision to marry?
7.   What was your religion at the time of your marriage?
8.   What was your former spouse's religion at the time of your marriage?
9.   What were the principal causes of the break-up of your former marriage?
10.   Are the terms of the divorce decree being met?
11.   Were there children born of the marriage?
12.   Is there any possibility that you would be reconciled with your former spouse and live again as husband and wife? Please, give reasons for your answer.
13.   Have you remarried?
14.   Have you ever been involved with a favor of the faith case before that had to go to Rome?
15.   If your former marriage is dissolved in the Catholic Church, would it give rise to scandal, or criticism, or unfavorable publicity?
16.   Have you anything else to add?

By my signature below, I affirm and attest that all the answers recorded above are true to the best of my knowledge.

_____   _____
Signature of Respondent   Date

_____   _____
N.   Date
Instructor

_____   _____
Ecclesiastical Notary   Date

4.8. *The Interview Questions for the Witnesses Based on the Petitioner's Lack of Baptism*

On a separate sheet of paper

CASE

WITNESS DEPOSITION

NAME OF THE WITNESS:

Oath: Do you promise to tell the truth, the whole truth, and nothing but the truth, insofar as you know it, so help you God? Response:

A. Questions Regarding Yourself

1. What are your full names?
2. What is your full address and telephone number?
3. What is your date of birth?
4. What is your present religion?
5. What is your relationship to Name of the Petitioner?
6. How long have you known him/her?
7. What is your relationship to Name of the Respondent?
8. How long have you known him/her?

B. Questions Regarding the Petitioner's Baptismal Status

1. Has N. (*Name of the Petitioner*) ever been baptized, christened, sprinkled, dedicated, or initiated in any religious denomination or sect prior to the time of this marriage?
2. How certain of you of your answer?
3. How and when did you learn that N. (*Name of the Petitioner*) was never baptized?
4. Was N. (*Name of the Petitioner*) ever under the care or guardianship of anyone at any time when he/she was a youth? If yes, please give the name and address.
5. Has N. (*Name of the Petitioner*) ever been baptized, christened, sprinkled, dedicated, or initiated in any religious denomination or sect during the time of this marriage?
6. Did the parents of N. (*Name of the Petitioner*) profess any religion at the time of his/her birth and early childhood?
7. How certain of you of your answer?
8. Did they believe in infant baptism?
9. Did they believe that baptism is necessary for salvation?
10. Would he/she be reliable and truthful in giving testimony in this case?

C. Questions regarding the Respondent's Baptismal Status

1. Has N. (*Name of the Respondent*) ever been baptized, christened, sprinkled, dedicated, or initiated in any religious denomination or sect prior to or during the time of this marriage?
2. If yes, what is the year of baptism and what is name and address of the church?
3. How certain of you of your answer?
4. How and when did you learn that N. (*Name of the Respondent*) was baptized?
5. Was N. (*Name of the Respondent*) ever under the care or guardianship of anyone at any time when he/she was a youth? If yes, please give the name and address.

6. Did the parents of N. (*Name of the Respondent*) profess any religion at the time of his/her birth and early childhood?
7. Did they believe in infant baptism?
8. Did they believe that baptism is necessary for salvation?
9. Has N. (*Name of the Respondent*) received baptism after the marriage? If yes, did both parties exercise the conjugal act together after the baptism?
10. Would he/she be reliable and truthful in giving testimony in this case?

D. Questions Regarding the Marriage in Question

1. Was this marriage-in-question witnessed by: a) Catholic priest; b) minister of another denomination or faith; c) civil official; or d) other?
2. Was this the first marriage for each of the parties?
3. How long was the courtship before the marriage?
4. Briefly state the reasons why they got married to each other.
5. How long did they live together as husband and wife in the marriage?
6. When was the final separation?
7. Briefly state the reasons for the break-up of the marriage.
8. Was anyone in any way responsible for the break-up of the marriage? If yes, please give specific names and answers.
9. Did you believe they both entered the marriage with the intention of being faithful to each other?
10. Did you believe they both entered the marriage with the intention of indissolubility?
11. Do you know who petitioned for divorce?
12. Is there any chance this marriage can be reconciled? Why or why not?
13. Were there any children born of this marriage?
14. Are the terms of the divorce being met?

15. Would there be any scandal if the Holy Father were to grant this petition?
16. Do you have anything else to add?

By my signature below, I affirm and attest that all the answers recorded above are true to the best of my knowledge.

_____   _____
Signature of Witness   Date

_____   _____
N.   Date
Instructor

_____   _____
Ecclesiastical Notary   Date

4.9. *The Questions for the Intended or Current Spouse*

On a separate sheet of paper

CASE

DEPOSITION OF THE PRESENT/INTENDED SPOUSE

NAME:

Oath: Do you solemnly swear to tell the truth, the whole truth, and nothing but the truth, insofar as you know it, so help you God?
Answer:

A. Questions Regarding Yourself

1. What is your full name?
2. What is your full address and telephone number?
3. What is your date of birth?
4. What is your present religion?

5. Have you ever been baptized?
6. What is the Church of Baptism?
7. Can you provide us with a certificate of your baptism issued within the last 6 months?
8. How do you practice your religion?
9. What is your relationship to the Petitioner?

B. Questions Regarding Your Freedom to Marry

1. Have you been married before?
2. If yes, have you obtained a declaration of nullity of your previous marriage?

C. Questions Regarding Your Present or Intended Spouse

1. Has your intended spouse ever been baptized?
2. If no, why so?
3. What religion or faith does he/she practice?
4. Has your present or intended spouse ever been married before? If so, to whom?

D. Questions Regarding You and Your Present or Intended Spouse

1. When did you first begin a courtship with N. (*first and last names of Petitioner*)?
2. When you began courting N. (*first and last names of Petitioner*), was he/she still living at that time his/her former spouse, N. (*first and last names of Respondent*)?
3. Did you at any time influence N. (first and last names of Petitioner) or suggest to him/her that he/she separate from N. (*first and last names of Respondent*)?
4. Were you in any way responsible for the separation and divorce of N. (*first and last names of Petitioner*) and N. (*first and last names of Respondent*)? If yes, please, explain your answer.
5. What was the actual cause of their separation?
6. How do you know this?

7. Was N. (*first and last names of Petitioner*) in any way to be blamed for the separation and divorce from N. (*first and last names of Respondent*)? If yes, explain how.
8. Are you and N. (*first and last names of Petitioner*) civilly married?
9. Are you and N. (*first and last names of Petitioner*) living as husband and wife?

E. Questions Regarding Children

1. Do you and N. (first and last names of Petitioner) have children together?
2. Have the child/children been baptized? If so, in what religion is the child/are the children baptized?
3. If the child/children have not been baptized in the Catholic Faith, state the reason(s).
4. Do you solemnly promise that the child/children born, or to be born of your union with N. (first and last names of Petitioner) will be baptized and educated in the Catholic Faith? Please, give reasons for your answer:

F. Questions Regarding the Danger of Scandal

1. Would there be any reason for serious criticism or unfavorable publicity of the Catholic Church if the Favor of the Faith Petition is granted by the Pope and you are permitted to marry in the Catholic Church?
2. Have you anything else to add?

By my signature below, I affirm that all the answers recorded above are true to the best of my knowledge.

_____   _____
Signature of Present/   Date
Intended Spouse

N.	Date
Instructor	

Ecclesiastical Notary	Date

4.10. *The Guidelines for Writing the Pastor's Letter of Character Attestation for the Petitioner and the Intended or Current Spouse*

On a separate sheet of paper

GUIDELINES FOR PASTORS WHEN WRITING A LETTER TO THE ORDINARY OF THE DIOCESE FOR THE PETITIONER AND THE INTENDED SPOUSE IN FAVOR OF THE FAITH CASES

Part of the documents usually sent to the Congregation for the Doctrine of the Faith for a petition requesting the dissolution of a marriage in favor of the faith is the recommendation letter written by the pastor of the Catholic petitioner or of the petitioner's current or intended spouse who is Catholic attesting to their religious practices. Below is a guide to writing such a letter.

1. The letter should be on your parish letter head.
2. It should be a formal letter addressed to the diocesan bishop. However, include the letter itself as part of the other documents you are sending to the Tribunal regarding the case. This is to enable the Tribunal not only track all the documents pertaining to the case but also to have a complete checklist.
3. The content of the letter should answer the following questions:

   i. How well does the Catholic party practice his/her Catholic religion?

    ii.   Will the Catholic party do all in his/her power to live in accordance with his/her baptismal promises?

    iii.   What signs of sincerity in practicing the Faith has the Catholic party shown?

    iv.   If the other spouse or intended is a non-Catholic and does not wish to convert, what signs of sincerity or uprightness has he/she shown?

    v.   If the non-Catholic party is converting, how much religious instruction or catechesis has the person received in Catholic faith and doctrine?

    vi.   Would there be any scandal or wonderment if the marriage for which the favor is being sought is dissolved by the Pope?

    vii. Are there any other remarks or peculiar circumstances of the case, which you think might be of help to the petitioner and his/her current or intended spouse?

4. Sign your name and write below it your ecclesiastical office.

5. If you have a parish seal, please stamp it on the letter.

4.11. *The Decree of the Commission of the Officers*

On tribunal letterhead

DECREE OF THE COMMISSION OF OFFICERS

CASE

The undersigned Ordinary of the Diocese of N., in accordance with the prescriptions of the Code of Canon Law and the norms issued by the Congregation for the Doctrine of the Faith for the Dissolution of the Matrimonial Bond in Favor of the Faith, do hereby nominate and delegate the following persons

Instructor: N.

Defender of the Bond: N.
Notary: N.

So that they may instruct the process, in accordance with the norm of law, for the dissolution of the matrimonial bond in favor of the faith between

N., Petitioner

And

N., Respondent.

At the same time, I grant to the Reverend Judicial Vicar the faculty of nominating and sub-delegating other officials of the Tribunal as he may deem necessary for the instruction of the case.

Given in ..., on this day ....

Most Reverend N.
Ordinary of N.

Notary
Official stamp

4.12. The Observations of the Defender of the Bond Based on the Petitioner's Lack of Baptism

On tribunal letter head

OBSERVATIONS OF THE DEFENDER OF THE BOND:
PETITION IN FAVOR OF THE FAITH

CASE

The undersigned Defender of the Bond, having carefully examined the Acts of the above referenced marriage case, hereby submits the following animadversions:

1. I am satisfied that the case has been adequately instructed and that the proper canonical investigation has been carried out in accordance with the instructions of the Holy See.
2. It is certain that N., Petitioner, was not baptized prior to or during the marriage. This is corroborated by N. and N., Witnesses of the Petitioner.
3. The Petitioner is unbaptized. (*If applicable*) He/She attends Mass regularly with his/her intended spouse. The Petitioner wishes to marry N., who is Catholic, and is free to marry.
4. To the best of my knowledge, based on the acts of the case, N., (*name of the petitioner*), is not the one predominantly responsible for the failure of the marriage.
5. To the best of my knowledge, based on the acts of the case, N., the intended/current spouse, is not the cause of the break-up of the marriage.
6. There is no danger of scandal if the favor is granted since the community is aware of the Petitioner's prior marriage and there is no hope of reconciliation.
7. I find no reasons that stand in the way of the dissolution of the bond. (CDF *Potestas Ecclesiae*, art. 23).

The undersigned has no objection to presenting the Petition to the Holy See for a favorable consideration.

_____

N.
Defender of the Bond

4.13. *The Report of the Instructor*

Case

Date

His Eminence
N. Cardinal N.
Prefect of the Congregation for the Doctrine of the Faith
Address

Your Eminence:

THE REPORT OF THE INSTRUCTOR

The Petitioner, N., a non-baptized Person, wishes to marry N., a baptized Catholic. The Petitioner is seeking the privilege of the faith for his/her own spiritual good as well as for the spiritual good of his/her intended spouse. N. (*name of intended/current spouse*) attends Mass regularly in her/her parish. (*if applicable:* They both attend Mass regularly in their parish). *State any church ministries that the intended/current spouse is involved in his/her parish.*

The Petitioner married the Respondent, N., (*name of the respondent*), baptized Catholic/Non-Catholic, on ... (*date of marriage*). The Petitioner was ... years old at the time of the marriage, and the Respondent ... years old at the time of the marriage. They courted for about ... year(s) and ... month(s) before they became engaged. The engagement lasted for ... year(s) before they got married.

If either the petitioner or the respondent, or both of them have been previously married and if the previous marriage has been declared invalid, then state it. State the grounds on which that marriage was declared invalid and on whose part. Remember to state that a copy of the decree declaring the marriage invalid is enclosed in the acts to be sent to the Congregation. Ensure that a copy of the said decree is actually enclosed.

The marriage perdured for ... years and ... months until it ended as a result of ... (*state the cause of the break-up of the marriage*).

___ children were born to the union. The union ended in civil divorce on .... There is no hope of reconciliation. *Have the petitioner and the respondent married other spouses civilly? If so, state it.*

The Respondent has cooperated/refused to cooperate/ with the Tribunal. *If the respondent cooperated with the tribunal, give a summation of what he/she regarding the fact of his/her non-baptism. Did he/she provide witnesses? If so, who are they to him/her? Did they corroborate the fact of his/her non-baptism? If the respondent did not cooperate, what efforts were made to contact him/her? Are there proofs of the various attempts made to cite or contact him/her? If so, state that the proofs of the citation of the respondent are enclosed among the acts. And remember to actually include copies of the proofs as part of the acts to be sent to Rome.*

The Witnesses testified that the Petitioner, N., was not baptized prior to the marriage or subsequent to the marriage. They made the statement separately and individually and under oath. In addition, there is no reason to doubt their credibility. They can be considered qualified witnesses to the fact of the Petitioner's non-baptism.

N. (*name of the petitioner*) wishes to marry N. (*name of intended/current spouse*), a lifelong practicing Catholic, who is not responsible for the break-up of the marriage. *Did the petitioner and the intended/current spouse know each other during the marriage of the petitioner and the respondent? If so, state why you believe the intended/current spouse is not responsible for the break-up of the marriage between the petitioner and the respondent. You may also include, for example that the petitioner and the respondent testify to the fact that the intended/current spouse is not responsible for the demise of the marriage between the petitioner and the respondent. If the petitioner and the intended/current spouse only came to know each other after the divorce of the petitioner and the respondent, state this fact in your report.*

N. (*name of the petitioner*) and N. (*name of the intended/current spouse*) are currently/nor currently in a civil union. They have ... children. (*If there are children, state whether or not they have been baptized. If so, state the religious denomination in which they were baptized. For example:*)The children have not been baptized/have been in the Catholic Church. (*If the children have been baptized, include copies of their baptismal certificate as part of the acts to be sent to Rome*).

There is no possibility of scandal should the Petitioner be granted the privilege in order to be married in the Catholic Church.

The Pastor has testified to the credibility of the Petitioner and to the credibility of the Intended/Current Spouse of the Petitioner.

Does the petitioner wish to convert to the Catholic Church or not convert at this time? Or, is he/she already a convert to the Catholic Church? The Petitioner wishes to convert/does not wish to convert at this time. The Intended/Current Spouse wishes to use this opportunity humbly to request the Holy Father for a dispensation for mixed marriage (or disparity of worship) so that he/she can validly marry N. (*name of the petitioner*). They have signed the necessary *Cautiones.* The granting of this privilege would be a great spiritual gift to the Petitioner and to his/her Intended/Current Spouse.

Signed by the Instructor.

4.14. *The Votum of the Bishop Based on the Petitioner's Lack of Baptism*

On the bishop's letterhead

VOTUM OF THE BISHOP

CASE

Date

His Eminence
Name
Title
Address

Your Eminence:

This case pertains to the dissolution of the marriage bond between, N., Petitioner, who is unbaptized and N., Respondent, a baptized ... (*State the religious denomination in which the respondent was baptized, e.g., Catholic, Anglican (or Episcopalian), Methodist, Baptist, or a baptized member of the ...Church).*

1. THE FACT OF THE NON-BAPTISM

It is certain the Petitioner was not baptized prior to or subsequent to the marriage. Besides his/her own statement to the fact of his/her non-baptism, there are also credible witnesses who testify to the fact of his/her non-baptism.

If applicable: The unbaptized party later became baptized and both parties did not have conjugal relations since after the baptism.

If applicable: The unbaptized party remains unbaptized.

2. COURTSHIP AND CONJUGAL LIFE

N. (*name of the petitioner*) and N. (*name of the respondent*) dated for about ... years before they became engaged. They remained engaged for ... months/years. They were married before a ... (*civil official or religious denomination of the minister. For example: before a Catholic priest/non-Catholic Minister/Justice of the Peace*). The marriage lasted for ... five years and ... months.

3. SEPARATION AND DIVORCE

State the principal reason(s) for the separation and divorce.

Are the reason(s) for the divorce corroborated by the witnesses?

Are there any legal obligations arising from the marriage?

Was the petitioner the exclusive or predominant culpable cause of the break-up of the marriage?

Did the relationship between the petitioner and his/her intended or current spouse cause the failure of the marriage between the petitioner and the respondent?

4. NO HOPE OF RECONCILIATION

Is there hope of reconciliation? If negative, why is there no hope of reconciliation? For example: There is no hope of reconciliation. Both Parties have stated that there is no possibility of reconciliation. The Petitioner and the Respondent have each married other spouses civilly. *State other reasons pertinent to the case why there is no possibility of reconciliation between them.*

5. CHILDREN

Are there any children born of the union between the petitioner and the respondent? Is the petitioner fulfilling his/her obligations towards the children?

6.   PRESENT CONDITION OF THE PARTIES

Has the petitioner attempted a new marriage even if civilly or is he/she cohabiting with a third party? Has the respondent remarried?

7.   CONVERSION

Does the petitioner wish to convert to Catholicism?
Is the intended/current spouse a Catholic? And is he/she free to marry? Is the Catholic party actively practicing the Faith?
Have the petitioner and the intended/current spouse signed the Promises or *Cautiones?*
For example: The Petitioner wishes to convert/does not wish to convert at this time. However, he/she has signed the *Cautiones* with his/her intended spouse, who is free to marry.

8.   NO DANGER OF SCANDAL

There is no danger of scandal should this petition be granted.

9. CREDIBILITY OF WITNESSES

The deponents are honest and trustworthy. There is no reason to doubt their veracity.

10. THE DEFENDER OF THE BOND

Is the defender of the bond satisfied that the case has been properly instructed?

Is the defender of the bond also satisfied that the unbaptized party was not baptized before or during the marriage?

Did the defender of the bond also affirm that neither the petitioner nor the petitioner's current or intended spouse was the prevailing cause of the break-up of the marriage?

Is the defender of the bond also satisfied that the other requirements for a granting of the favor of the faith have been fulfilled? For example:

The Defender of the Bond is satisfied that the case has been properly instructed and that the required canonical investigation has been carried out. He/She is also satisfied that the Petitioner has not been baptized, the Petitioner was not the prevailing cause of the break-up of the marriage, and the Intended/Current Spouse was not also the prevailing cause of the break-up of the marriage. He/She is also satisfied that the other requirements for a granting of the favor of the faith have been fulfilled.

11. IN FORMA PAUPERUM

If there is a request that the favor be granted without the usual fee (*in forma pauperum*), the bishop is to indicate this in his votum; otherwise, this sub-title is deleted, or the bishop can state that the diocese will pay the tax for and on behalf of the petitioner.

12. CONCLUSION

It is my opinion that all the necessary information has been obtained in this case. I earnestly request that the marriage between N., (*name of the petitioner*) and N. (*name of the respondent*) be dissolved in favor of the faith and for the salvation of souls so that the Petitioner may enter into a valid marriage with N. (*name of intended/current spouse*).

With renewed sentiments of the highest esteem and sincere personal good wishes, I am

Signed and dated by the diocesan bishop.

4.15. The Authentication of the Acts

CERTIFICATE OF AUTHENTICATION
Case Name and Prot. No.

I, the undersigned Ecclesiastical Notary, attest that the Acts of the above referenced Petition contained herein are either original writings or exact duplicates of original writings and form the authentic Acts of this case, to be transmitted to the Congregation for the Doctrine of the Faith

The Acts are numbered sequentially from 1 - __.
This Certificate of the Authentication of the Acts is the final page of the Acts and it follows immediately after the last page of the Bishop's *votum*.

In attestation thereof I sign my name and affix the Seal of the Tribunal.

Date:

_____
N.
Ecclesiastical Notary

_____
N.
Instructor

N.B.: Triplicate copies of the acts are sent to the CDF via the Apostolic Nuncio in your country.

4.16. *The Index*

The index is the table of contents or list of all the documents, testimonies, and other acts of the case and the respective pages where they are to be found in the acts. For this reason, every page of the acts must be numbered clearly.

INDEX

Case Name & Prot. No.
DOCUMENT DESCRIPTION   PAGE

4.17. *The Summary Forms*

SUMMARY

The new *Summarium* (Summary) form released by the Congregation for the Doctrine of the Faith ("CDF") on June 23, 2015 (*Privilegium fidei*, Prot. 333/95M) pertaining to the instruction of *favor fidei* marriage cases permits the inclusion of more precise indications regarding the Parties' baptismal status, at the time of their marriage as well as at present.

The summary is an overview of the important information regarding the petitioner, the former spouse, and the future spouse. It facilitates the examination of the case at the congregation for the doctrine of the faith. The summary form is usually placed at the beginning of the acts immediately prior to the petition.

With regards to the taxes, besides indicating that a Petitioner is able to pay the full sum or that he/she asks for a complete remission of the taxes ("*in forma pauperum*"), the diocesan Curia may now also inform the CDF that a Petitioner is able to contribute *a part* of the costs, in accordance with the financial resources of the Petitioner and the Diocese. In such exceptional cases, please make sure that the reasons for this request are explained in the Acts.

In contrast with the previous version, the new Summary form does not contain the fields for the documentation of the Parties' further (former and/or subsequent) marriages. For this purpose the supplemental page is to be added to the Summary, whenever applicable.

You can download the forms from the Homepage of the Dicastery (*www.doctrinafidei.va*). There you will also find translations of the *Norms* of 2001 into various languages.

At *www.doctrinafidei.va*, under Documents: Complete List, you will see: Documents on Sacramental Questions. Click on the

Documents on Sacramental Questions. On the aforesaid webpage, scroll down until you come to Matrimony. You can also download the summary forms from: http://www.vatican.va/roman_curia/congregations/cfaith/doc_doc_index.htm

4.18. *The Rescript from the CDF*

The following rendition can serve as guidelines for translating most of the Rescripts from the Congregation for the Doctrine of the Faith pertaining to the dissolution of the bond of marriage in favor of the faith:

DISSOLUTION OF MARRIAGE IN FAVOR OF THE FAITH

If the Petition is based on the Petitioner's Lack of Baptism:
In the Curia of N. (*name of the diocese*) was completed the process for obtaining the dissolution, in favor of the faith, of the marriage contracted between N. (*name of the petitioner*), non-baptized and N. (*name of the respondent*), baptized Catholic/non-Catholic.
If the Petition is based on the Respondent's Lack of Baptism:
In the Curia of N. (*name of the diocese*) was completed the process for obtaining the dissolution, in favor of the faith, of the marriage contracted between N. (*name of the petitioner*), baptized Catholic/non-Catholic and N. (*name of the respondent*), non-baptized.
If the petitioner is a non-Catholic who wants to marry a Catholic in the Church:
The acts having been subjected to an examination and having matured, and everything in the case having been carefully considered, the question which is proposed to this Congregation, according to the doubt is: "Whether the petition presented to His Holiness for the dissolution, in favor of the faith, of the marriage of the above mentioned parties so that the petitioner may be permitted to enter into a mixed marriage before the Church, validly and licitly, after having observed the promises, with the Catholic party, N. (*name of the intended/current spouse*), according to the marriage rite." The petition, having been discussed and reviewed

according to the established statutes, is answered and decreed in the:

"AFFIRMATIVE."

If the petitioner is a Catholic who is marrying another Catholic in the Church:
The acts having been subjected to an examination and having matured, and everything in the case having been carefully considered, the question which is proposed to this Congregation, according to the doubt is: "Whether the petition presented to His Holiness for the dissolution, in favor of the faith, of the marriage of the above mentioned parties so that the petitioner, a Catholic, may be permitted to enter into a new marriage before the Church, validly and licitly, with the Catholic party, N. (*name of the intended/current spouse*), according to the marriage rite." The petition, having been discussed and reviewed according to the established statutes, is answered and decreed in the:

"AFFIRMATIVE."

Continue here: His Holiness, by divine Providence, Pope N., on ... (*date*), everything herein having been related to him, benignly conceded and granted the favor according to the Decree related above.

If the diocese has not paid the administrative fee to the dicastery. The expenses for the (Apostolic) Chancery: ___. .
If the diocese has paid the administrative fee to the dicastery. All expenses owed the Chancery have been paid.

In presenting the concession, it is also to be included, insofar as it is necessary, the dispensation from the impediment or the permission from the prohibition mentioned in canons 1086 and 1125 of the Code of Canon Law.

THE FOLLOWING ARE TO BE NOTED IN A DIVERSITY OF CASES:

1. A suitable penance is to be imposed on the Catholic party who is living in illicit cohabitation or who has attempted marriage with the party not yet converted to the faith; the same penance ought to be grave and salutary for each party whenever they may have attempted marriage after baptism or for the conversion of the non-Catholic party in the future.

2. The Pontifical favor must be communicated, if it can be done, to the former spouse, especially if this person has already attempted marriage with a Catholic party.

3. The converted party is to be admonished regarding the obligation of caring, inasmuch as it is possible, for the conversion of all the children born from the dissolved marriage. Any such children, if they are minors, are to be under the care and education of the converted party, who is assiduously and vigorously to prepare them towards accepting the faith after an appropriate instruction. If, indeed, the children have been entrusted to the non-Catholic party, the converted party should earnestly and vigorously, within all his or her powers, work for their conversion. This obligation is all the more grave for the one to whom the children who are minors have been entrusted.

4. The Catholic party is to be admonished regarding the obligation, by prayers and example, of converting the non-Catholic partner.

These things are to be observed by law, anything to the contrary notwithstanding.

Given in Rome, on ... (*date*).

Name
Title of the dicastery official

4.19. *The Letter Notifying the Cleric of the CDF Rescript*

Case

Date

Reverend N.

Parish Name
Address
City, State, ZP

Dear Father N.:

This is to advise you that His Holiness, Pope N., has granted the dissolution of the bond of marriage between N. (*name of the petitioner*) and N. (*name of the respondent*) in favor of the faith. Enclosed is a copy of the Decree of the Dissolution of the Marriage.

Kindly ensure that the copy of the decree of dissolution of the dissolved marriage is placed in the marriage file of N. (*name of the petitioner*) and N. (*name of the intended/current spouse*) proof of their freedom to marry in the Church. The Pre-nuptial investigation should be completed as usual prior to the marriage. The notification of the marriage should also be made in their baptismal records.

The following norms are to be observed, if applicable to this case:

A suitable penance is to be imposed on the Catholic party who is co-habiting with the party not yet converted to the faith or who has attempted civil marriage with the party not yet converted to the faith. The same penance ought to be grave and salutary for each party whenever they may have attempted marriage after baptism or for the conversion of the non-Catholic party in the future.

The converted party must be admonished regarding the obligation of ensuring, inasmuch as it is possible, the conversion of all the children born from the dissolved marriage. Any such children, if they are minors, are to be under the care and education of the converted party, who is assiduously and vigorously to prepare them towards accepting the faith after an appropriate instruction. If, indeed, the children have been entrusted to the non-Catholic party, the converted party should earnestly and vigorously, within all his or her powers, work for their conversion. This obligation is all the more grave for the one to whom the children who are minors have been entrusted.

The Catholic party is to be admonished regarding the obligation, by prayers and example, of converting the non-Catholic partner.

These things are to be observed by law, notwithstanding anything to the contrary.

This dissolution has no civil effects, and it does not dispense both parties from any natural or legal obligations they may have towards the other spouse and any children born of the union.

If I can be of further assistance to you, please do not hesitate to contact me.

Sincerely Yours in Christ,

Very Reverend N., J.C.L./J.C.D.
Judicial Vicar
Enclosure

4.20. *The Letter Notifying the Petitioner of the CDF Rescript*

Case
Date

Name
Address
City, State, ZP

Dear Mr./Ms./Mrs. N.:

This is to advise you that His Holiness, Pope N., has granted the dissolution of your marriage N. (*name of the other party*) in favor of the faith.

A copy of the decree has been sent to Reverend N., your Procurator, with appropriate instructions on how to proceed. Kindly be in contact with him at your earliest convenience regarding the celebration of your marriage.

This dissolution has no civil effects, and it does not dispense both parties from any natural or legal obligations they may have towards the other spouse and any children born of the union.

If I can be of further assistance to you, please do not hesitate to contact me.

Wishing you every grace and blessing, I am

Sincerely Yours,

Very Reverend N., J.C.L./J.C.D.
Judicial Vicar

4.21. *The Letter to the Respondent of the CDF Rescript*

Case

Date

Name
Address
City, State, ZP

Dear Mr./Ms./Mrs. N.:

This is to advise you that His Holiness, Pope N., has granted the dissolution of your marriage N. (*name of the other party*) in favor of the faith.

This dissolution has no civil effects, and it does not dispense both parties from any natural or legal obligations they may have towards the other spouse and any children born of the union.

If I can be of further assistance to you, please do not hesitate to contact me.

Wishing you every grace and blessing, I am

Sincerely Yours,

Very Reverend N., J.C.L./J.C.D.
Judicial Vicar

5. The Sample Documents for the Instruction of a Petition of the Favor of the Faith Based on the Respondent's Lack of Baptism

5.1. *The Petition*

PETITION FOR FAVOR OF THE FAITH BASED ON THE RESPONDENT'S LACK OF BAPTISM

(*Please fill in all the blanks and answer all questions as completely as possible*).

MOST HOLY FATHER:

I, _____, humbly present this petition for the dissolution of the natural bond of marriage in favor of the faith that I contracted with _____ on the _____ day of _____ in the year of our Lord _____ at _____. I was unbaptized prior to and throughout the duration of our marriage. My former spouse and I did not ever have conjugal relations after baptism, if later baptized. Neither my present/intended spouse nor I was the exclusive or prevailing culpable cause of the breakdown of my former marriage. There is no possibility of restoring the partnership of conjugal life. Neither my present/current spouse nor I have received dissolution in favor of the faith before. No public scandal would result should this dissolution be granted. I sincerely request that you as the Vicar of Christ dissolve my non-sacramental marriage in favor of the faith so that I may enter a new marriage validly and licitly according to the laws of God and of the Holy Catholic Church.

I am presently:

☐ A Roman Catholic. I intend to enter a new marriage with someone who is free to marry according to the laws of the Catholic Church.

☐ A baptized non-Catholic. I have never been married to a Roman Catholic. I am participating in catechesis. I wish to be received into the Catholic Church. I intend to enter a new marriage with someone who is free to marry according to the laws of the Catholic Church.

☐ A baptized non-Catholic. I have never been married to a Roman Catholic. I do not wish to become a Catholic at this time. I intend to enter a new marriage with a Catholic who is free to marry according to the laws of the Catholic Church.

☐ Unbaptized. I married a Roman Catholic and the Catholic party obtained dispensation from the impediment of disparity of worship to marry me. I wish to receive baptism in the Catholic Church. I intend to enter a new marriage with someone who is free to marry according to the laws of the Catholic Church.

☐ Unbaptized. I have never been married to a Roman Catholic. I do not wish to be baptized in the Catholic Church at this time. I intend to enter a new marriage with a Catholic who is free to marry according to the laws of the Catholic Church.

☐ Unbaptized. I have never been married to a Roman Catholic. I wish to be baptized in the Catholic Church. I intend to enter a new marriage with someone who is free to marry according to the laws of the Catholic Church.

I attest that the information presented herein is true to the best of my knowledge.

_____   _____
Signature of Petitioner   Date

5.2. *The Parties and Witness Information*

See the "Parties and Witness Information" under the "Petition for Favor of the Faith Based on the Petitioner' Lack of Baptism" above.

5.3. The Promises

See "Promises" under the "Petition for Favor of the Faith Based on the Petitioner' Lack of Baptism" above.

5.4. The Documents to be Submitted Along with the Petition

See the "Documents Required" under the "Petition for Favor of the Faith Based on the Petitioner' Lack of Baptism" above.

5.5. The Questions for the Petitioner Based on the Respondent's Lack of Baptism

PETITION FOR FAVOR OF THE FAITH
BASED ON THE RESPONDENT'S LACK OF BAPTISM

DEPOSITIONS OF THE PETITIONER: *NAME OF THE PETITIONER*

Oath: Do you solemnly swear to tell the truth, the whole truth, and nothing but the truth, so help you God?
Response:

A. Questions regarding Yourself

1. What are your full names, address, and telephone number?
2. What is the date and place of your birth?

B. Questions regarding your Baptismal Status

1. Have you ever been baptized?
2. Please, state the date of your baptism.
3. Please, state the name, city, and state of the church in which you were baptized?
4. Were you baptized in this church in the name of the Father, the Son, and the Holy Spirit?
5. What is the name of your father?

6. What is his religion?
7. What is the name of the church?
8. What is the name of your mother? What is her religion?
9. What is the name of the church?
10. Are your parents still living?
11. Were you ever under the care or guardianship of others besides your parents?
12. Have you any brothers or sisters? How many?
13. Were any of your brothers or sisters ever baptized or christened?
14. What is the name and address of the church in which they were baptized or christened?
15. Do you have the baptismal record of your baptism? Please give the names, addresses, and telephone numbers of witnesses who can testify that you were baptized at the time of your marriage.

C. Questions regarding your marriage to your former spouse

1. What are the names, address, and telephone number of your former spouse?
2. When and where was this person born?
3. Was this person ever baptized christened, dedicated, or initiated in any religious denomination or sect?
4. Was your former spouse unbaptized prior to the marriage? How do you know this?
5. Prior to your marriage, do you know whether your former spouse ever attended church services with some degree of regularity?
6. If known, please give us the name(s) and address(es) of the church(es) and approximate dates of attendance.
7. If known, did your former spouse ever live for an extended period of time with anyone other than his/her parents when he/she was a child? If so, please furnish information below.
8. Did your former spouse receive baptism during the entire time you lived together in marriage?

9. Has your former spouse received baptism since the marriage ended in divorce?
10. When and where did your marriage take place?
11. How long did you date your former spouse before marriage?
12. How long were both of you engaged?
13. How long did you live with your former spouse in marriage?
14. Were there temporary separations?
15. What were the principal causes of the break-up of the marriage?
16. Were there any children born in the marriage? If so, how many?
17. Are the terms of the divorce decree, if any, toward your former spouse and/or children being met or have they been met? Please, explain.
18. Since the break-up of the marriage, have you had cause to resume, renew, or restore the partnership of conjugal life with her?
19. Do you wish to be reconciled with your former spouse and to live again as husband and wife? State the reasons for your answer.
20. Has your former spouse remarried?
21. Have you or your former spouse ever obtained the dissolution of a previous marriage in favor of the faith?

D. Questions regarding your present or intended spouse

1. Are you currently engaged or have you remarried civilly?
2. What are the full names of your present or intended spouse?
3. How long have you known this person?
4. Briefly describe how both of you first met?
5. Does your present or intended spouse know your former spouse? Please, explain your answer.

6. Is your present or intended spouse the predominant and culpable cause of the break-up of the marriage for which you are seeking dissolution in favor of the faith?
7. What is your present or intended spouse's religion?
8. Is your present or intended spouse baptized?
9. Can this person provide a proof of baptism?
10. Does your present or intended spouse sincerely believe in and practice the Catholic faith?
11. Do you promise to allow the person you intend to marry freely to practice the Catholic religion?
12. Do you promise to raise the children that may be born of this marriage in the Catholic faith?
13. Has your present or intended spouse been previously married?
14. Have you had any children with this person?
15. Has your present or intended spouse been involved in this favor of the faith case?
16. If your former marriage is dissolved and you are permitted to marry in the Catholic Church, would it give rise to scandal, or criticism, or unfavorable publicity?
    Have you anything else to add?

By my signature below, I affirm and attest that all the answers recorded above are true to the best of my knowledge.

_____   _____
Signature of Petitioner   Date

_____   _____
Name   Date
Instructor

_____   _____
Ecclesiastical Notary   Date

5.6. *The Citation Letter to the Respondent*

The citation letter to the respondent is same as the "Letter to the Respondent" under the "Petition for Favor of the Faith Based on the Petitioner' Lack of Baptism" above.

5.7. *The Questions for the Respondent Based on the Respondent's Lack of Baptism*

PETITION FOR FAVOR OF THE FAITH
BASED ON THE RESPONDENT'S LACK OF BAPTISM

THE DECLARATIONS OF THE RESPONDENT: *NAME*
Oath: Do you solemnly swear to tell the truth, the whole truth, and nothing but the truth, insofar as you know it, so help you God?
Response:

A. Questions Regarding Yourself

1. What are your full names?
2. When and where were you born?

B. Regarding Your Baptismal Status

3. Have you ever been baptized?
4. How do you know this?
5. Were you ever baptized at any time prior to the marriage?
6. Did you receive baptism during the marriage?
7. Were you raised by your natural parents?
8. Are your parents living?
9. What was the religion of your father at the time of your birth and during your childhood and youth? Please, give specific denominations or religion.
10. Was he baptized or christened? How do you know this?

11. What was the religion of your mother at the time of your birth, during your childhood and youth? Please, give specific denomination or religion.
12. Was she baptized or christened? How do you know this?
13. Have you any brothers or sisters? How many?
14. Were any of your brothers or sisters ever baptized or christened?
15. Are you currently attending any church, temple, or synagogue? If so, which one(s)?

C. Regarding Your Former Spouse

16. What are the full names of your former spouse?
17. Was your former spouse ever baptized christened, dedicated, or initiated in any religious denomination or sect?
18. What is the name of the church, denomination, or sect?

D. Regarding Your Former Marriage

19. What was the date of the marriage?
20. What is the city, civil parish/county, and state of the marriage?
21. Was this marriage the first marriage for both of you?
22. Who officiated at the wedding?
23. How long did you keep company with each other before the marriage?
24. How did both of you come to the decision to marry?
25. What was your religion at the time of your marriage?
26. What was your former spouse's religion at the time of your marriage?
27. What were the principal causes of the break-up of your former marriage?
28. Are the terms of the divorce decree being met?
29. Were there children born of the marriage?
30. Is there any possibility that you would be reconciled with your former spouse and live again as husband and wife? Please, give reasons for your answer.

31. Have you remarried?
32. Have you ever been involved with a favor of the faith case before that had to go to Rome?
33. If your former marriage is dissolved in the Catholic Church, would it give rise to scandal, or criticism, or unfavorable publicity?
34. Have you anything else to add?

By my signature below, I affirm and attest that all the answers recorded above are true to the best of my knowledge.

_____   _____
Signature of Respondent   Date

_____   _____
Name   Date
Instructor

_____   _____
Ecclesiastical Notary   Date

5.8. The Questions for the Witnesses Based on the Respondent's Lack of Baptism

See the "Questions for the Witnesses Based on the Petitioner's Lack of Baptism" under "Petition for Favor of the Faith Based on the Petitioner's Lack of Baptism" above.

5.9. The Interview Questions for the Intended or Current Spouse of the Petitioner Based on the Respondent's Lack of Baptism

See the "Questions for the Intended/Current Spouse" under the "Petition for Favor of the Faith Based on the Petitioner's Lack of Baptism" above.

5.10. *The Guidelines for Writing the Pastor's Letter of Character Attestation for the Petitioner and the Intended or Current Spouse*

See the "Guidelines For Pastors When Writing A Letter To The Ordinary Of The Diocese For The Petitioner And The Intended Spouse In Favor Of The Faith Cases" under the "Petition for Favor of the Faith Based on the Petitioner's Lack of Baptism" above.

5.11. *The Decree of Commission of Officers*

See the "Decree of Commission of Officers" under the "Petition for Favor of the Faith Based on the Petitioner's Lack of Baptism" above.

5.12. *The Observations of the Defender of the Bond Based on the Respondent' Lack of Baptism*

On tribunal letterhead

OBSERVATIONS OF THE DEFENDER OF THE BOND

PETITION IN FAVOR OF THE FAITH

CASE

The undersigned Defender of the Bond, having carefully examined the Acts of the above referenced marriage case, hereby submits the following animadversions:

1. I am satisfied that the case has been adequately instructed and that the proper canonical investigation has been carried out in accordance with the instructions of the Holy See.
2. It is certain that N., Respondent, was not baptized prior to or during the marriage. This is corroborated by the Witnesses, N. and N.

3. The Petitioner, N., is a Catholic/Christian (*or name of the Christian denomination*). (*If the next sentence is applicable*) He/She attends Mass regularly with his/her intended spouse. The Petitioner wishes to marry N., who is Catholic, and is free to marry.
4. To the best of my knowledge, based on the acts of the case, N., (*name of the petitioner*), is not the one predominantly responsible for the failure of the marriage.
5. To the best of my knowledge, based on the acts of the case, N., the intended/current spouse, is not the cause of the break-up of the marriage.
6. There is no danger of scandal should the favor be granted since the community is aware of the Petitioner's prior marriage and there is no hope of reconciliation.

The undersigned has no objection to petitioning this case before the Holy See for a favorable consideration.

_____

N.
Defender of the Bond

5.13. *The Instructor's Report Based on the Respondent's Lack of Baptism*

Case

Date

His Eminence
N. Cardinal N.
Prefect of the Congregation for the Doctrine of the Faith
Address

Your Eminence:

REPORT OF THE INSTRUCTOR

The Petitioner, N., a validly baptized non-Catholic, wishes to marry N., (*name of the intended/current spouse*) a baptized Catholic. The Petitioner is seeking the privilege of the faith for his/her own spiritual good as well as for the spiritual good of his/her intended spouse. N., (*name of the intended/current spouse*) attends Mass regularly in his/her parish. (*if applicable:* They both attend Mass regularly in their parish).

The Petitioner married N. (*name of the respondent*), the non-Baptized party, in ... (*year of marriage*). The Petitioner was ... years old at the time of the marriage while the Respondent was .... They courted for about ... year(s) and ... month(s) before they became engaged. The engagement lasted for ... year(s) before they got married.

The marriage perdured for ... years and ... months until it ended as a result of ... (*state the cause of the break-up of the marriage*). There is no hope of reconciliation. ___ children were born to the union. The union ended in civil divorce on ....

The Respondent has cooperated/refused to cooperate/ with the Tribunal. *If the respondent cooperated with the tribunal, give a summation of what he/she regarding the fact of his/her non-baptism. Did he/she provide witnesses? If so, who are they to him/her? Did they corroborate the fact of his/her non-baptism? If the respondent did not cooperate, what efforts were made to contact him/her? Are there proofs of the various attempts made to contact him/her? If so, include copies of the proofs as part of the acts to be sent to Rome.*

The Witnesses testify that the Respondent, N., was not baptized either prior to the marriage or subsequent to the marriage. They made the statement separately and individually and under oath. In addition, there is no reason to doubt their credibility. They can be considered qualified witnesses to the fact of the Respondent's non-baptism.

N. (*name of the petitioner*) wishes to marry N. (*name of the intended/current spouse*), a lifelong practicing Catholic, who is not responsible for the break-up of the marriage. Did the petitioner and the intended/current spouse know each other during the marriage of the petitioner and the respondent? If so, state why you believe the intended/current spouse is not responsible for the break-up of the marriage between the petitioner and the respondent. You may also include, for example that the petitioner and the respondent testify to the fact that the intended/current spouse is not responsible for the demise of the marriage between the petitioner and the respondent. If the petitioner and the intended/current spouse only came to know each other after the divorce of the petitioner and the respondent, state this fact in your report.

N. (*name of the petitioner*) and N. (*name of intended/current spouse*) are currently/nor currently in a civil union. They have ... children. (*If there are children, state whether or not they have been baptized. If so, state the religious denomination in which they were baptized. For example:*) The children have not been baptized/have been in the Catholic Church. (*If the children have been baptized, include copies of their baptismal certificate as part of the acts to be sent to Rome*).

The Pastor has testified to the credibility of the Petitioner and to the credibility of the Intended/Current Spouse of the Petitioner.

Does the petitioner wish to convert to the Catholic Church or not convert at this time? Or, is he/she already a convert to the Catholic Church? The Petitioner has already converted/wishes to convert /does not wish to convert at this time. The Intended/Current Spouse wishes to use this opportunity humbly to request the Holy Father for a dispensation for mixed marriage (or disparity of worship) so that he/she can validly marry N. (*name of the petitioner*). They have signed the necessary *Cautiones*. The granting of this privilege would be a great spiritual gift to the Petitioner and to his/her Intended/Current Spouse.

Signed by the Instructor

5.14. The Votum of the Bishop Based on the Respondent's Lack of Baptism

On the bishop's letterhead

VOTUM OF THE BISHOP

CASE

Date

His Eminence
Name
Title
Address

Your Eminence:

This case pertains to the dissolution of the marriage bond between, N., Petitioner, who is a baptized ... (*State the religious denomination in which the respondent was baptized, e.g., Catholic, Anglican (or Episcopalian), Methodist, Baptist, or a baptized member of the ...Church*) and N., Respondent, who is unbaptized ....

1. THE FACT OF THE NON-BAPTISM

It is certain the Respondent was not baptized prior to or subsequent to the marriage. Besides his/her own statement to the fact of his/her non-baptism, there are also credible witnesses who testify to the fact of his/her non-baptism.

2. COURTSHIP AND CONJUGAL LIFE

N. (*name of the petitioner*) and N. (*name of the respondent*) dated for about ... years before they became engaged. They remained engaged for ... months/years. They were married before a ... (*civil official or religious denomination of the minister. For example: before a Catholic priest/non-Catholic Minister/Justice of the Peace*). The marriage lasted for ... five years and ... months.

3. SEPARATION AND DIVORCE

State the principal reason(s) for the separation and divorce.
Are the reason(s) for the divorce corroborated by the witnesses?

Are there any legal obligations arising from the marriage?

Was the petitioner the exclusive or predominant culpable cause of the break-up of the marriage?

Did the relationship between the petitioner and his/her intended or current spouse cause the failure of the marriage between the petitioner and the respondent?

4. NO HOPE OF RECONCILIATION

Is there hope of reconciliation? If negative, why is there no hope of reconciliation? For example: There is no hope of reconciliation. Both Parties have stated that there is no possibility of reconciliation. The Petitioner and the Respondent have each married other spouses civilly. *State other reasons pertinent to the case why there is no possibility of reconciliation between them.*

5. CHILDREN

Are there any children born of the union between the petitioner and the respondent? Is the petitioner fulfilling his/her obligations towards the children?

6. PRESENT CONDITION OF THE PARTIES

Has the petitioner attempted a new marriage even if civilly or is he/she cohabiting with a third party? Has the respondent remarried?

7. CONVERSION

Does the petitioner wish to convert to Catholicism?

Is the intended/current spouse a Catholic? And is he/she free to marry? Is the Catholic party actively practicing the Faith?

Have the petitioner and the intended/current spouse signed the Promises or *Cautiones?*

For example: The Petitioner wishes to convert/does not wish to convert at this time. However, he/she has signed the *Cautiones* with his/her intended spouse, who is free to marry.

8. NO DANGER OF SCANDAL

There is no danger of scandal should this petition be granted.

9. CREDIBILITY OF WITNESSES

The deponents are honest and trustworthy. There is no reason to doubt their veracity.

10. THE DEFENDER OF THE BOND

Is the defender of the bond satisfied that the case has been properly instructed?

Is the defender of the bond also satisfied that the unbaptized party was not baptized before or during the marriage?

Did the defender of the bond also affirm that neither the petitioner nor the petitioner's current or intended spouse was the prevailing cause of the break-up of the marriage?

Is the defender of the bond also satisfied that the other requirements for a granting of the favor of the faith have been fulfilled? For example:

The Defender of the Bond is satisfied that the case has been properly instructed and that the required canonical investigation has been carried out. He/She is also satisfied that the Respondent has not been baptized, the Petitioner was not the prevailing cause of the break-up of the marriage, and the Intended/Current Spouse was not also the prevailing cause of the break-up of the marriage. He/She is also satisfied that the other requirements for a granting of the favor of the faith have been fulfilled.

11. IN FORMA PAUPERUM

If there is a request that the favor be granted without the usual fee (*in forma pauperum*), the bishop is to indicate this in his votum;

otherwise, this sub-title is deleted, or the bishop can state that the diocese will pay the tax for and on behalf of the petitioner.

12. CONCLUSION

It is my opinion that all the necessary information has been obtained in this case. I earnestly request that the marriage between N., (*name of the petitioner*) and N. (*name of the respondent*) be dissolved in favor of the faith so that the Petitioner may enter into a valid marriage with N. (*name of intended/current spouse*).

With renewed sentiments of the highest esteem and sincere personal good wishes, I am

Signed and dated by the diocesan bishop.

5.15. *The Authentication of the Acts*

See the "Authentication of the Acts" under the "Petition for Favor of the Faith Based on the Petitioner's Lack of Baptism" above.

5.16. *The Index*

See the "Index" under the "Petition for Favor of the Faith Based on the Petitioner's Lack of Baptism" above.

5.17. *The Summary Forms*

See the "Summary Forms" under the "Petition for Favor of the Faith Based on the Petitioner's Lack of Baptism" above.

5.18. *The Apostolic Rescript*

See "The Apostolic Rescript" under the "Petition for Favor of the Faith Based on the Petitioner's Lack of Baptism" above.

5.19. *The Notification of the Rescript to the Procurator and to the Parties*

See "The Notification of the Rescript to the Procurator and to the Parties" under the "Petition for Favor of the Faith Based on the Petitioner's Lack of Baptism" above.

SECTION 3:   HOW TO DETERMINE THE CORRECT TYPE OF MARRIAGE NULLITY CASE

CHAPTER 9: HOW TO DETERMINE THE CORRECT TYPE OF MARRIAGE NULLITY CASE

1. How to Determine Lack of Canonical Form Case

1. ☐ YES ☐ NO Was one of the contracting parties a Catholic at the time of the wedding?
2. ☐ YES ☐ NO Did the marriage take place before a Catholic bishop, priest, or deacon and two witnesses?
3. ☐ YES ☐ NO Did the Catholic party obtain a dispensation to be married in a ceremony other than a Catholic one?
4. ☐ YES ☐ NO Was the marriage ever subsequently witnessed or validated by a Catholic bishop, priest, or deacon?
5. ☐ YES ☐ NO Was the marriage ever subsequently sanated by a Catholic bishop or his delegate.

If the answer to question 1 is YES and the answers to questions 2, 3, 4, and 5 are NO, it may be a lack of form case. The tribunal, however, will provide a definitive answer, based on the totality of the facts and circumstances of the case. For more information.

2. How to Determine Defect of Form Case

2.1. *How to Determine Defect of Canonical Form Based on Lack of Proper Delegation*

1. ☐ YES ☐ NO Was one of the contracting parties a Catholic at the time of the wedding?
2. ☐ YES ☐ NO Did the marriage take place before a Catholic bishop, priest, or deacon?
3. ☐ YES ☐ NO Did the marriage also take place before two witnesses?
4. ☐ YES ☐ NO Did the Catholic bishop, priest, or deacon who officiated at the wedding have the faculty or proper delegation from the pastor or the local ordinary to officiate at the wedding?

5. ☐ YES ☐ NO Was the marriage ever subsequently convalidated by a Catholic bishop, priest, or deacon who had the faculty or proper delegation and before two witnesses?
6. ☐ YES ☐ NO Was the marriage ever subsequently sanated by a Catholic bishop or his delegate?

If each of the answers to questions 1, 2, and 3 is YES and if each of the answers to questions 4, 5, and 6 is NO, it may be a case of defect of canonical form due to lack of proper delegation. The tribunal will make the final determination based on the totality of the facts and circumstances of the case.

2.2. How to Determine Defect of Canonical Form Based on Lack of Two Witnesses

1. ☐ YES ☐ NO Was one of the contracting parties a Catholic at the time of the wedding?
2. ☐ YES ☐ NO Did the marriage take place before a Catholic bishop, priest, or deacon?
3. ☐ YES ☐ NO Did the Catholic bishop, priest, or deacon who officiated at the wedding have the faculty or proper delegation to officiate at the wedding?
4. ☐ YES ☐ NO Did the marriage also take place before two witnesses?
5. ☐ YES ☐ NO Was the marriage ever subsequently convalidated by a Catholic bishop, priest, or deacon before two witnesses?
6. ☐ YES ☐ NO Was the marriage ever subsequently sanated by a Catholic bishop or his delegate?

If each of the answers to questions 1, 2, and 3 is YES and if each of the answers to questions 4, 5, and 6 is NO, you may have a case of defect of canonical form due to lack of two witnesses. The tribunal will provide a definitive answer, based on the totality of the facts and circumstances of the case.

3. A Comparison of Lack of Form Case and Defect of Form Case

No.	Lack of Form	Defect of Form Due to Lack of Proper Delegation	Defect of Form Due to Lack of Two Witnesses
1.	One of the contracting parties was a Catholic at the time of the wedding. ☐ Yes ☐ No	One of the contracting parties was a Catholic at the time of the wedding. ☐ Yes ☐ No	One of the contracting parties was a Catholic at the time of the wedding. ☐ Yes ☐ No
2.	The marriage did not take place before a Catholic bishop, priest, or deacon and two witnesses. ☐ Yes ☐ No	The marriage took place before a Catholic bishop, priest, or deacon and two witnesses, but the Catholic cleric lacked the faculty or proper delegation to officiate at the wedding. ☐ Yes ☐ No	The marriage took place before a Catholic bishop, priest, or deacon who possessed the faculty or proper delegation to officiate at the wedding. ☐ Yes ☐ No
3.	The Catholic party did not obtain a dispensation to be married in a ceremony other than a Catholic one. ☐ Yes ☐ No	The marriage was not subsequently convalidated by a Catholic bishop, priest, or deacon who had the faculty or proper delegation to officiate at the wedding. ☐ Yes ☐ No	There were no two witnesses present at the wedding. ☐ Yes ☐ No

4.	The marriage was not subsequently witnessed or validated by a Catholic bishop, priest, or deacon. ☐ Yes ☐ No	The marriage was not subsequently sanated by a Catholic bishop or his delegate. ☐ Yes ☐ No	The marriage was not subsequently convalidated by a Catholic bishop, priest, or deacon. ☐ Yes ☐ No
5.	The marriage was not subsequently sanated by a Catholic bishop or his delegate. ☐ Yes ☐ No		The marriage was not subsequently sanated by a Catholic bishop or his delegate. ☐ Yes ☐ No

If the answer to each of the questions on the Lack of Form Column is YES, you may have a Lack of Form case.

If the answer to each of the questions on the Defect of Form Due to Lack of Proper Delegation Column is YES, you may have a Defect of Form Due to Lack of Proper Delegation case.

If the answer to each of the questions on the Defect of Form Due to Lack of Two Witnesses Column is YES, you may have a Defect of Form Due to Lack of Two Witnesses case.

4. How to Determine Non-Consummated Marriage Case

1. ☐ YES ☐ NO. Is there a probable doubt that the marriage was not ever consummated?
2. ☐ YES ☐ NO. Is there a just cause to dissolve the marriage bond?
3. ☐ YES ☐ NO. Is it true there is no hope of reconciliation between the parties and that conjugal living cannot be restored?
4. ☐ YES ☐ NO. Is it true there would be no scandal if the pope were to grant the dissolution?

If each of the answers to all 4 questions is "YES," you may have a ratified and non-consummated marriage case.

5. How to Determine Pauline Privilege Case

1. ☐ YES ☐ NO Were both parties unbaptized and remained unbaptized throughout the marriage?
2. ☐ YES ☐ NO Is it true that there is no hope that the couple will be reconciled?
3. ☐ YES ☐ NO Is it true that the Petitioner is not the predominant cause of the break-up of the marriage?
4. ☐ YES ☐ NO Is it true that the Petitioner is not the one who refused to cohabit peacefully in the marriage?
5. ☐ YES ☐ NO Does the Petitioner wish to be validly baptized or has the Petitioner been validly baptized since the divorce?
6. ☐ YES ☐ NO Does the Petitioner have a fiancé or spouse whom he/she wishes to marry in the Catholic Church?
7. ☐ YES ☐ NO Is it true that the use of the Pauline Privilege by the Petitioner would not be a cause of scandal and criticism of the Catholic Church?

If the answer to each of the foregoing questions is YES, you may have a Pauline Privilege case. The final determination is made by the tribunal after it has gathered all the pertinent information and proofs in the case.

6. How to Determine Petrine Privilege Case

1. ☐ YES ☐ NO: Was one party in the marriage unbaptized prior to the marriage and remained unbaptized throughout the duration of the marriage?
2. ☐ YES ☐ NO (*Check if applicable*): If the unbaptized party later became baptized, is it true both parties have not had conjugal relations since after his/her baptism?
3. ☐ YES ☐ NO: Is it true that the petitioner was not the exclusive or predominant culpable cause of the break-up of the marriage?

4. ☐ YES ☐ NO: Is it true that there is no hope of reconciliation between the petitioner and the respondent?
5. ☐ YES ☐ NO: If the Catholic party intends to contract or convalidate a new marriage with a person who is not baptized or with a baptized non-Catholic, is the Catholic Party willing to sign the promise that he or she is prepared to remove dangers of defecting from the Catholic faith?
6. ☐ YES ☐ NO: If the petitioner or his/her intended or current spouse is not a Catholic, is the non-Catholic party willing to sign the promise to raise any children born of the new marriage as Catholics and not hinder the Catholic party's practice of the faith?
7. ☐ YES ☐ NO: Does the petitioner have a fiancé or spouse whom he/she wishes to marry in the Catholic Church?
8. ☐ YES ☐ NO: Is it true that the new fiancé or spouse was not the cause of the break-up of the marriage for which you are seeking a favor of the faith?
9. ☐ YES ☐ NO: Is the Catholic party actively practicing the faith?
10. ☐ YES ☐ NO: Is it true that the granting of the favor would not be a cause of scandal?

If the answers to all questions are YES, you may have a Petrine Privilege case. However, the tribunal, after considering the law and facts of the case, will advise the petitioner. If the answer to any of the questions is NO, then you have a case other than Petrine.

7. A Comparison of Pauline Privilege Case and Petrine Privilege Case

No.	Pauline Privilege	Petrine Privilege
1.	Both parties were unbaptized and remained unbaptized throughout the marriage. ☐ Yes ☐ No	At least one of the parties was unbaptized prior to the marriage and remained unbaptized throughout the marriage. ☐ Yes ☐ No

2.		If the unbaptized party later became baptized during or after the marriage, both parties have not had conjugal relations since after his/her baptism. ☐ Yes ☐ No ☐ N/A
3.	One of the parties later became baptized during or after the marriage. ☐ Yes ☐ No	The unbaptized party remains unbaptized. ☐ Yes ☐ No
4.	The baptized party wishes to convert, or is converting, or has converted to the Catholic Church. ☐ Yes ☐ No	The unbaptized party does not wish to convert to the Catholic Church. ☐ Yes ☐ No
6.	There is no hope of reconciliation between the parties. ☐ Yes ☐ No	There is no hope of reconciliation between the parties. ☐ Yes ☐ No
7.	The petitioner is not the predominant cause of the break-up of the marriage. ☐ Yes ☐ No	The petitioner is not the predominant cause of the break-up of the marriage. ☐ Yes ☐ No
8.		The petitioner's fiancé or civil law spouse is not the cause of the break-up of the marriage for which the petitioner is seeking the favor of the faith. ☐ Yes ☐ No
9.	The unbaptized party refuses to cohabit peacefully with the baptized party. ☐ Yes ☐ No	The non-Catholic party is willing to sign the promise to allow the Catholic-party to practice the faith and to raise the children born of their marriage as Catholics.

		☐ Yes ☐ No
10.	The petitioner has a fiancé or spouse whom he or she wishes to marry in the Catholic Church. ☐ Yes ☐ No	The petitioner has a fiancé or spouse whom he or she wishes to marry in the Catholic Church. ☐ Yes ☐ No
11.	The invocation of the Pauline Privilege by the petitioner will not be a cause of scandal. ☐ Yes ☐ No	The granting of the Petrine Privilege will not be a cause of scandal. ☐ Yes ☐ No

If the answer to each of the questions on the Pauline Privilege Column is YES, you may have a Pauline Privilege case.

If the answer to each of the questions on the Petrine Privilege Column is YES, you may have a Petrine Privilege case. Or, if the answer to question 1 and question 2-11 on the Petrine Privilege Column is YES, and the answer to the question 2 is N/A, you may have a Petrine Privilege case.

8. How to Determine Prior Bond Case

1. ☐ YES ☐ NO Was the respondent's marriage to the petitioner the respondent's first marriage?
2. ☐ YES ☐ NO If the respondent had been previously married, was the respondent's previous marriage ever declared invalid by a tribunal of the Catholic Church or dissolved by the death of the respondent's former spouse, or by the diocesan bishop, or by the Apostolic See before the petitioner and the respondent married?
3. ☐ YES ☐ NO Was the respondent's former spouse in the respondent's previous marriage deceased at the time of the respondent's marriage to the petitioner?

If each of the answers to all the above questions is "NO," then you may have a prior bond case. Your local tribunal will give a definitive answer based on the totality of the documents and facts gathered in the case.

9. How to Determine Disparity of Worship Case

9.1. *How to Determine Disparity of Worship if the Marriage Took Place in a Catholic Church*

1. ☐ YES ☐ NO Was one of the contracting parties a Catholic at the time of the wedding?
2. ☐ YES ☐ NO Was one of the contracting parties unbaptized prior to and throughout the duration of the marriage?
3. ☐ YES ☐ NO Did the parties exchange marital consent before a Catholic bishop, priest, or deacon and two witnesses?
4. ☐ YES ☐ NO Is there a document of the Catholic Diocese where the marriage took place which proves that the Catholic party was granted dispensation to marry an unbaptized person?
5. ☐ YES ☐ NO Was the marriage ever subsequently convalidated by a Catholic bishop, priest, or deacon and before two witnesses?
6. ☐ YES ☐ NO Was the marriage ever subsequently sanated by a Catholic bishop or his delegate?

If the answers to questions 1, 2, and 3 are YES and the answers to questions 4, 5, and 6 are NO, you may have a case of lack of dispensation from the disparity of worship.

The tribunal will provide a definitive answer, based on the totality of the facts and circumstances of the case.

9.2. *How to Determine Disparity of Worship if the Marriage Took Place in a Non-Catholic Religious Ceremony*

1. ☐ YES ☐ NO Was one of the contracting parties a Catholic at the time of the wedding?
2. ☐ YES ☐ NO Was one of the contracting parties unbaptized prior to and throughout the duration of the marriage?

3. ☐ YES ☐ NO Did the parties exchange marital consent before a non-Catholic religious minister or in a non-Catholic religious ceremony?
4. ☐ YES ☐ NO Is there a document of the Catholic Diocese where the marriage took place which proves that the Catholic party was granted dispensation from canonical form?
5. ☐ YES ☐ NO Is there a document of the Catholic Diocese where the marriage took place which proves that the Catholic party was granted dispensation to marry an unbaptized person?
6. ☐ YES ☐ NO Was the marriage ever subsequently convalidated by a Catholic bishop, priest, or deacon and before two witnesses?
7. ☐ YES ☐ NO Was the marriage ever subsequently sanated by a Catholic bishop or his delegate?

If the answers to questions 1, 2, 3, and 4 are YES and the answers to questions 5, 6, and 7 are NO, you may have a case of lack of dispensation from disparity of worship.

If the answers to questions 1, 2, and 3 are YES and the answers to questions 4, 5, 6 and 7 are NO, you may have a case of lack of canonical form, and not lack of dispensation from disparity of worship. This is so because there is no dispensation from canonical form regarding the marriage.

In any case, the tribunal will provide a definitive answer, based on the totality of the facts and circumstances of the case.

10. How to Determine Ordinary Process Case

1. ☐ YES ☐ NO Was the marriage contracted by two Catholics in the presence of a Catholic bishop, priest, or deacon and two witnesses?
2. YES ☐ NO Was the marriage contracted by a Catholic and a baptized non-Catholic with dispensation from canonical form?
3. YES ☐ NO Was the marriage contracted by a Catholic and an unbaptized person with dispensation from canonical

form and, or, with dispensation from disparity of worship?
4. □ YES □ NO Was the marriage contracted by two validly baptized non-Catholics?
5. Did the case fail to meet the requirements of the law for lack of form, radical sanation, *non-consummatum*, Pauline Privilege, Petrine Privilege, prior bond, and defect of form?

If the answer to any one of the foregoing question is "YES," it may be a formal case. However, the tribunal will make the final determination regarding the case.

11. How to Determine Abbreviated Process Case

1. □ YES □ NO Was the petition proposed by both parties or by one of them with the written consent of the other?
2. □ YES □ NO Are there facts and circumstances in the case which make a more detailed investigation of the marriage redundant and which make the nullity of the marriage manifest?
3. □ YES □ NO Was the petition submitted with supportive testimonies and with medical, psychiatric, psychological, or police reports which render a tribunal expert report superfluous and which make the nullity of the marriage manifest? (c. 1683, 1°- 2°).
4. □ YES □ NO Will the oral deposition of the parties and the witnesses be held within 30 days after the judicial vicar has issued the decree of the formula of the doubt? (c. 1686).

If the answer to each of the four questions above is "YES," then it is possible that it is an abbreviated process case. However, if the nullity of the marriage cannot be proven by means of the abbreviated process, it may be necessary to remit the case to the ordinary or formal process case. The tribunal will make the final determination regarding the case.

SECTION 4:   MARRIAGE ANNULMENT FREQUENTLY
ASKED QUESTIONS

CHAPTER 10: GLOSSARIES

Question 1: What is Marriage?

Marriage is a contractual agreement or a covenant by which a man and a woman establish between themselves a partnership of the whole of life and by which of its nature is ordered to the good of the spouses and to the procreation and education of offspring. Christ the Lord has raised marriage to the dignity of a sacrament between the baptized. For this reason, a valid matrimonial contract cannot exist between the baptized without it being by that fact a sacrament.[1]

Question 2: What is Matrimonial Consent?

Matrimonial consent is an act of the will by which a man and a woman mutually give and accept each other through an irrevocable covenant in order to establish marriage.[2]

Question 3: What is Marriage Annulment?

Annulment, properly called "declaration of marriage nullity," is an official declaration by the Catholic Church that a marriage which was celebrated in good faith by at least one of the spouses is in fact invalid from the moment of the exchange of the marital consent and, therefore, is not sacramental or binding for life. The consent must be an act of the will of each of the contracting parties, free of coercion or grave external fear. If this freedom is lacking the marriage is invalid.[3] To be free to contract marriage and to express marital consent freely means that one is not under constraint and one is not impeded by any natural or ecclesiastical law.[4] Thus, the Catholic Church, after an examination of the mar-

---

[1] c. 1055 §§1-2.
[2] c. 1057 §§1-2.
[3] Catechism of the Catholic Church, n. 1628.
[4] Catechism of the Catholic Church, n. 1625.

riage by the competent ecclesiastical tribunal, can declare the nullity of a marriage because one or both parties were canonically impeded from contracting a valid marriage at the time of the exchange of vows or because the consent of one or both parties was defective at the time of the exchange of consent.

The annulment of a marriage does not mean that there was no wedding; there was a wedding and the couple lived through the marriage. However, marriage annulment, as the Catholic Church understands it, means that the marriage from the moment of the exchange of vows did not meet the laws and teachings of Jesus Christ and the Catholic Church for the marriage to be binding for life. The declaration of the nullity of the marriage, therefore, frees the parties from the bond of that marriage. Oftentimes, the reasons why some people petition for the annulment of their marriage are to bring peace to their conscience, to reconcile with the Church and return to the sacraments or to start receiving the sacraments, to learn more about themselves and from their past mistakes, to heal wounds and hurts that resulted from the previous marital relationship, and to put some closure to that particular marriage.

Question 4:   Why do People Petition for Annulment?

Oftentimes, the reasons why some people petition for the annulment of their marriage are to bring peace to their conscience, to reconcile with the Church and return to the sacraments or to start receiving the sacraments, to learn more about themselves and from their past mistakes, to heal the wounds and hurts of theirs that resulted from the previous marital relationship, to be sacramentally and spiritually freed from the bond of that marriage, and to put spiritual closure to that particular marriage.

Question 5: What are the Differences Between Divorce and Ecclesiastical Annulment?

There are fundamental differences between divorce and an ecclesiastical annulment. A divorce is a legal declaration by the civil authority that a civilly valid marriage has ended; it is the legal termination of a valid marriage. On the other hand, an annulment or an ecclesiastical annulment is a declaration by the competent Church authority that a marriage, from its very beginning, is invalid; it is the ecclesiastical termination of an invalid marriage. Moreover, in the ecclesiastical annulment of marriages, the Tribunal focuses primarily on the laws of the Church and on the intentions, behaviors, attitudes, expectations, facts, circumstances, and family, social, and religious backgrounds of the parties prior to the marriage. The events and behaviors that occurred during the marriage are seen as evident manifestation of what was already present, absent, missing, lacking, or defective in either or both parties and ignored prior to the marriage. Also, while divorce terminates a marital relationship from a specific, later date, annulment terminates what was once thought to be a valid marriage and declares it to be invalid from the moment of consent.

Question 6: What is the Difference Between Annulment and Dissolution?

An annulment declares a marriage invalid, while dissolution dissolves a valid marriage. The difference is that in an annulment the marriage is declared invalid, but in a dissolution the marriage is not declared invalid; it retains its validity except that a dispensation is granted to one of the parties to contract marriage in the Church in favor of the faith.

Thus, the favor of the faith means that either one of the parties is converting or has converted to the Catholic Church or that one of the parties does not wish to convert to the Catholic Church, but he or she intends to marry a Catholic who is free to marry in the Catholic Church. If the party does not wish to convert to the Catholic Church, then the marriage is dissolved in favor of the faith of the Catholic he or she intends to marry in the Catholic Church or has already married in the civil forum.

Examples of marriage annulment are lack of canonical form and formal cases, while examples of marriage dissolution are the Pauline Privilege and the Petrine Privilege.

In conclusion, an annulment annuls an invalid marriage, while a dissolution dissolves a valid marriage.

Question 7:   What is a Diriment Impediment?

A diriment impediment is a personal quality in a person or an external factor which disqualifies or prohibits a person from contracting marriage validly in the Catholic Church. Examples of diriment impediments are:

- age, that is, a man under the age of sixteen cannot marry validly, and a woman under the age of fourteen cannot marry validly.
- impotence that both predates the marriage and continues throughout marriage.
- prior bond, that is, a person, whether Catholic or non-Catholic, who has been previously married cannot validly marry another person in the Catholic Church unless the previous marriage is declared null or dissolved by the Catholic Church.
- disparity of worship, that is, a Catholic cannot marry an unbaptized person without dispensation or authorization from the diocesan bishop or his delegate.
- spiritual relationship, that is, for Eastern Catholics, a Godparent and a Godchild cannot marry validly.

Each one of the foregoing impediments is a canonical ground for which a marriage can be declared invalid.

Question 8:   What is Defect of Consent?

Defect of consent is the lack or absence of some quality in the intellect or will of a person which renders the person incapable of contracting marriage validly. For example, the lack of sufficient use of reason, or discretion of judgment, or psychological capacity, or freewill in choosing one's marriage partner. Defect of consent also means the deliberate intention, prior to the marriage, to marry a person for the wrong reasons, to exclude fidelity, procreation of children, or permanence from the marriage, to say or do things that would be harmful and detrimental to one's future spouse, or to deceive one's future spouse in order to marry the person. When there is a defect of consent on the part of one or both parties, the marriage is considered to have been contracted invalidly. "The Church holds the exchange of consent between the spouses to be the indispensable element that makes the marriage."[5] If consent is lacking or is deficient, there is no marriage.

The grounds of defect of consent are

i. Insufficient use of reason at the time of the exchange of marital consent on the part of one or both parties.[6]

ii. Grave defect of discretion of judgment concerning the essential matrimonial rights and duties to be mutually given and accepted by the spouses.[7]

iii. Incapacity to assume the essential obligations of marriage due to psychological causes on the part of one or both parties.[8]

iv. Fraud or deceit.[9]

v. Total simulation or marriage for extraneous reasons or for improper motives.[10]

vi. The exclusion of fidelity.[11]

vii. The exclusion of the good of children.[12]

viii. The exclusion of the good of the spouse.[13]

ix. The exclusion of the good of the sacrament or indissolubility.[14]

---

[5] Catechism of the Catholic Church, no. 1626.
[6] c. 1095, 1°.
[7] c. 1095, 2°.
[8] c. 1095, 3°.
[9] c. 1098.
[10] c. 1101 §§1-2.
[11] c. 1101 §§1-2.
[12] c. 1101 §§1-2.
[13] c. 1101 §§1-2.
[14] c. 1101 §§1-2.

x.   Condition.[15]

xi.   Force and fear.

Question 9:   What is Insufficient Use of Reason?

Insufficient use of reason is a canonical ground of marriage nullity in which, at the time of the exchange of marital consent, at least one of the parties was not in possession of his or her mental faculties.[16] For example, at the time of saying "I do" one or both spouses were under the influence of alcohol or drugs, or under heavy sedation, or under hypnosis.

Question 10:   What is Grave Defect of Discretion of Judgment?

Grave defect of discretion of judgment is a canonical ground of marriage nullity in which, at the time of the exchange of vows and throughout the duration of the marriage, one or both parties lacked due knowledge concerning the essential matrimonial rights and duties to be mutually given and accepted by the spouses.[17] It is also a case of grave defect of discretion of judgment if one of both parties lacked due knowledge of oneself and due deliberation and due internal freedom to choose the marriage and the marriage partner. For example, one or both spouses, prior to and during the marriage, suffered from psychological immaturity or affective immaturity. Other examples of grave defect of discretion of judgment are when the parties entered into the marriage because of a pre-marital pregnancy or when one or both parties, prior to and during the marriage, suffered from a grave misunderstanding or lack of understanding of the rights and duties of marriage.

Grave defect of discretion of judgment also occurs when, for a serious reason, there is a change of mind on the part of one of the parties about going on with the proposed marriage; however,

---

[15] c. 1102 §§1-3.

[16] c. 1095, 1°.

[17] c. 1095, 2°.

the party feels obligated to proceed with the marriage for various reasons. For example, shortly before the marriage, one of the parties comes to the definite conclusion that he or she should not marry this person; however, the wedding invitation cards have been sent out, the hall has been booked, guests have started arriving, or a large amount of money has been spent in preparation for the wedding. Other reasons are that he or she has invested so much in the relationship that it is too late for him or her to pull out or call off the wedding, or he or she does not want to hurt the feelings of other person or embarrass family and friends. However, some of these cases, depending on the facts and circumstances of the case, can also be a case of total simulation.

Grave defect of discretion of judgment or lack of discretion also pertains to a situation in which the petitioner or the respondent, at the time of the marriage, was affected by some serious psychological anomaly that rendered one or both of them unable properly to evaluate the decision to marry or rendered one or both of them unable to create a true marital relationship. These factors could include but are not limited to: immaturity of judgment, affective immaturity, lack of proper preparation, peer pressure, going against the sound opinion of parents, family, or friends regarding the marriage, infatuation, or impulsivity in choosing to marry. These factors can prove that a person was unable to make a mature, stable, well informed decision regarding the marriage. Thus, while psychological, or affective, immaturity is one of the factors of grave lack of due discretion, grave defect of discretion of judgment, however, is broader than immaturity.

Question 11:   What is Incapacity to Assume the Essential
              Obligations of Marriage?

The incapacity to assume the essential obligations of marriage is a canonical ground of marriage nullity in which a marriage was not contracted validly due to causes of a psychological nature on the part of one or both parties.[18] For example, one or both parties, prior to and subsequent to the exchange of vows, suffered from

---

[18] c. 1095, 3°.

some grave psychological dysfunctionality or grave personality disorder which rendered the party unable to assume and fulfill the essential obligations of marriage. For example, narcissistic, or histrionic, personality disorder, drug abuse, alcoholism, etc.

Question 12:   What is Fraud?

Fraud is a canonical ground of marriage nullity in which a party was maliciously deceived by the other party or by a third party in order for both parties to contract the marriage. The fraud or deceit must concern some quality about one of the parties which, upon discovery during the marriage by the party who was deceived, caused grave problems in the marriage and gravely caused the break-up of the marriage.[19] Fraud is also the deliberate and malicious deception of one party by the other party or by a third party for the deceived party to contract the marriage. The deception is called positive when something was done or said which deceived the party or which led the deceived party into error. It is called negative when something was not said or done or when there is a keeping quiet about something so that the parties can contract the marriage.

Question 13:   What is Total Simulation?

Total simulation is a canonical ground of marriage nullity in which there is a deliberate and willful intention of marrying someone for reasons extraneous to marriage. For example, marriage in order to obtain permanent residency or citizenship, or marriage solely to reduce one's income tax, or marriage solely to increase one's pay check, or marriage solely to enhance one's class, prestige, and status in the society, or marriage as a means to get out of an abusive home environment. When someone marries with an improper or ulterior motive in mind or for selfish reasons, the marriage becomes a means to achieve an end that is extraneous, foreign, alien, or contrary to the true and proper purposes of marriage as taught by Christ and His Church.

---

[19] c. 1098.

Total simulation is also the willful and deliberate intention of exchanging marital vows without actually intending to keep the commitments and obligations of marriage and actually not keeping the commitments and obligations during the marriage.[20]

Total simulation or exclusion of marriage exists when the only reason for which one gets married is extraneous to marriage. It also entails the positive and willful exclusion of marriage itself. In total simulation, a person does not want the marriage at all, but goes through the marriage ceremony and the marriage itself either as a sham or solely as a means to achieve some end totally extrinsic to marriage.

Question 14:   What is the Exclusion of the Good of Fidelity?

The exclusion of the good of fidelity is a canonical ground of marriage nullity in which one or both parties, prior to the marriage, married with the intention of committing adultery during the marriage and actually committing adultery during the marriage.[21] It is also a ground of marriage nullity in which a party was unfaithful prior to the marriage and continued to be unfaithful with the same or multiple people during the marriage. It is also called the intention against the good of fidelity.

Question 15:   What is the Exclusion of the Good of Children?

The exclusion of the good of children is a canonical ground of marriage nullity in which one or both parties, prior to the marriage, with the intention that he or she or both of them would exclude the begetting of children from the marriage and actually excluded or prevented the begetting of children in the marriage.[22] It is also called the intention against the good of children.

---

[20] c. 1101 §§1-2.
[21] c. 1101 §§1-2.
[22] c. 1101 §§1-2.

Question 16:   What is the Exclusion of the Good of the
Spouse?

The exclusion of the good of the spouse is a canonical ground
of marriage nullity in which one of the parties married the other
party with the intention of saying and doing things that would be
against the good and well-being of the other party and really saying and doing things which actually became harmful and detrimental to the good of the other spouse and which gravely caused
the break-up of the marriage.[23] It is also called the intention
against the good of the spouse.

Question 17:   What is the Exclusion of the Good of Indissolubility?

The exclusion of the good of indissolubility is a canonical
ground of marriage nullity in which, prior to the marriage, one or
both parties contracted the marriage with the intention of divorcing one's spouse and actually divorcing one's spouse or causing
one's spouse to divorce him or her.[24] It is also called the intention
against the good of indissolubility, or the intention against the
permanence of marriage, or the intention against the good of the
sacrament. It is also called the exclusion of the permanence of
marriage or the exclusion of the good of the sacrament.

Question 18:   What is Condition?

Condition or conditioned consent is a canonical ground of
marriage nullity in which one or both parties entered into the
marriage based on a condition concerning the future.[25] For example, one of the parties says to the other: "I will marry on the condition that you inherit a fortune from your parents," or "I will
marry you on the condition that you will earn or continue to earn
a 6-figure salary per annum," etc. Thus, the marriage is based on

---

[23] c. 1101 §§1-2.
[24] c. 1101 §§1-2.
[25] c. 1102 §§1-3.

some condition concerning the future such that if the condition is not fulfilled or is broken during the marriage by the other spouse or by a third party, then the person who placed the condition terminates the marriage. The condition is so important to the person who placed the condition that when the condition was not fulfilled or was not kept during the marriage, the person ended the marriage and divorced his or her spouse. Thus, the condition is more important to the person who placed the condition than the marriage itself.

Question 19:   What is Force and Fear?

Force and fear is a canonical ground of marriage nullity in which one or both parties contracted the marriage against his or her will in order to avoid a greater evil.

For example, a minor or adult male person impregnates a girl who is a minor. The male person is told by the parents of the girl to either marry the girl, a minor, with parental consent, or face the possibility of spending up to 20 years in jail for statutory rape. The person chooses to marry the girl in order to avoid rape charges, embarrassment to family and friends, and imprisonment. Or, for example, a person marries another person due to the reverential fear of one's parents; that is, the person was forced into the marriage by parents or other family members against his or her will. "The consent must be an act of the will of each of the contracting parties, free of coercion or grave external fear. No human power can substitute for this consent. If this freedom is lacking the marriage is invalid."[26]

Force is the act, threat, pressure, or duress which is exerted on a person and which compelled the person to marry against his or her free will.[27] Fear is the result of the force. The fear made the person to marry against his or her will in order to avoid a greater evil. There cannot be a valid marriage based on force and fear because the matrimonial covenant requires a great degree of internal freedom and will. The force can be physical or moral. It is

---

[26] Catechism of the Catholic Church, no. 1628.
[27] c. 1103.

physical force when the movement of the person is restrained by an external agent or when a violent act was exerted on the person. It is moral force when the person was threatened such that the person chose the marriage in order to avoid the threatened evil. Therefore, a gun need not be pointed at a person in order for the person to contract the marriage due to force and fear. The evil threatened was of such nature that the person had no other viable choice than to marry the other person. The marriage, as it were, is the lesser of two evils.

In some cases, however, force and fear, based on the facts and circumstances of the case, can be a case of grave defect of discretion of judgment. (c. 1095, 2°).

Question 20: What is a Petitioner?

A petitioner is the person who has petitioned a Catholic tribunal for the declaration of the nullity of his or her marriage to his or her former spouse. Catholics and non-Catholics, baptized or unbaptized, can petition the Tribunal for a declaration of the nullity of their former marriage.

Question 21:   What is a Respondent?

A respondent is the person whose former spouse has petitioned a Catholic tribunal to have their marriage declared invalid by the tribunal.

Question 22:   What is a Witness?

A witness is a person who is distinct from the petitioner, from the respondent, and from the judge and who has been named by either the petitioner or the respondent as someone who knows the parties prior to and subsequent to the marriage and who can provide information to the tribunal about the parties and the marriage. Parents, siblings, relatives, and friends, whether or not they are Catholics, can serve as witnesses.

Children of the parties are not permitted to be witnesses because, in most cases, they would not have been born prior to the marriage and, therefore, have no first-hand information to provide to the tribunal about their parents and their parents' marriage and because children should not be made to take sides against their parents. Although children from a previous marriage may act as witness, however, it is up to the judge to determine whether a child from a previous marriage can be admitted to be a witness in the case.

Question 23:   What is a Procurator?

A procurator is a person who has been approved by the diocesan bishop to act on behalf of parties before the tribunal in marriage annulment cases. The role of the procurator is to assist the party he or she is representing to gather together the required documents for the annulment process, to guide the party in answering the annulment questionnaire, to explain the process to the party, and to defend the person's rights and interests before the tribunal. Just as a petitioner can have a procurator, so also a respondent can also have a procurator. In some dioceses, the procurator is called the case sponsor. In most dioceses, the procurator or case sponsor are priests and deacons. Lay people who have been trained in the annulment process are also designated and appointed as procurators.

Question 24:   What is a Case Sponsor?

A case sponsor is a priest, deacon, religious, or lay person who has been trained in the annulment process and who assists a petitioner in gathering the documents required for the annulment process, who submits the documents to the tribunal on behalf of the petitioner, and who guides the petitioner through the process. In some dioceses, the case sponsor is called the procurator.

Question 25:   What is an Advocate?

An advocate is a person who is knowledgeable in canon law and in matrimonial jurisprudence and who writes defense brief for a party and submits to the tribunal. An advocate is different from a procurator. For example, a procurator is not required to have a degree in canon law and is not required to submit a legal brief. Canon law, however, requires an advocate to have a canon law degree. However, one person can function both as a procurator and an advocate, especially if the person has a decree in canon law.

Question 26:   What is a Judicial Vicar?

The judicial vicar is the priest who has been appointed by the diocesan bishop to head the tribunal and to be the principal canonical adviser to the bishop. In marriage nullity process, the judicial vicar, among other things, determines, in accordance with canon law, whether a petition is to be accepted for trial or rejected and whether the case should be remitted to the ordinary process or to the abbreviated process. The judicial vicar also establishes the grounds on which the case is to be tried. He also assigns judges, the defender of the bond, the promoter of justice, the assessors, the auditor, and the ecclesiastical notary to cases.

Question 27:   What is a Judge?

A judge is a person who has been trained in canon law and who has been appointed to process marriage nullity cases and to decide, in accordance with the laws of the Church and the facts of the case, whether the alleged nullity of the marriage has been proven in the case.

Question 28:   What is a Defender of the Bond?

A defender of the bond is an official of the tribunal who has been appointed by the diocesan bishop to defend the validity of marriages. The principal function of the defender of the bond is to propose any proofs, responses, and objections, without prejudice to the truth of the matter, which can contribute to the upholding of the validity of the marriage bond (cf. can. 1432).

The defender of the bond can never argue in favor of the nullity of the marriage. The defender of the bond has the right by law to appeal a decision which declares a marriage invalid.

Question 29:   What is a Promoter of Justice?

A promoter of justice is an official of the tribunal who has been appointed by the bishop to ensure that canonical procedures are observed in the tribunal, to protect the rights of the parties and the common good of the Church, and to challenge the validity of some apparently invalid marriages before the tribunal.

Question 30:   What is an Assessor?

An assessor is an official of the tribunal who has been appointed by either the bishop or the judicial vicar to assist and advise the judge in those areas of a case in which the assessor is eminently qualified, knowledgeable, and experienced.

Question 31:   What is an Ecclesiastical Notary?

An ecclesiastical notary is an official of the tribunal who has been appointed by the diocesan bishop to docket, file, maintain, and update records at the tribunal, to assign a case name and number to each newly submitted petition, to send notices to the parties and the procurators regarding the status of their case, and to take a variety of actions on behalf of the judge or tribunal. The ecclesiastical notary also advises the parties and procurators about tribunal procedures, arranges appointments and meetings for the judges, provides answers to questions asked about cases by the parties and their procurators, and prepares and notarizes ecclesiastical documents.

Question 32:   What is a Court Expert?

A court expert is a clinical psychologist, or a licensed therapist or counselor, or a social worker who has been appointed by the judge to advise the judge on any psychological issues that may have been latent, dormant, present, or manifest in the parties prior to and subsequent to the marriage.

Question 33:   What is the Code of Canon Law?

The Code of Canon Law is the book published by the Apostolic See which contains the principal legislative, executive, and judicial norms and other fundamental laws of the Catholic Church. Thus, besides those ecclesiastical laws contained in the Code of Canon Law, other ecclesiastical laws are also to be found in other legislative documents of the Church. For example, Church marriage laws are not only contained in the Code of Canon Law, but also in other books and documents published by the Apostolic See.

Question 34:   What is Canon Law?

Canon law is the ordinance which is enacted by the supreme legislator of the Church, the pope. The principal legislative document of the Church is the Code of Canon Law. However, the laws of the Church are found in other legislative documents of the Church. Canon law is church law or ecclesiastical law. Church law which applies everywhere throughout the Catholic world is universal law, that which applies only to a diocese is particular law, and that which applies only to a religious institute or society is proper law.

Question 35:   What is a Canonist?

A canonist, also called a canon lawyer, is a person who has at least a licentiate in canon law from a university which has been approved by the Apostolic See to award degrees in canon law.

Question 36:   What is the Roman Rota?

The Apostolic Tribunal of the Roman Rota, for short, the Roman Rota, is the tribunal in Rome established by the Pope to hear marriage nullity cases from across the world that have been appealed to it, to safeguard rights within the Church, to foster unity of jurisprudence, and, by virtue of its own decisions, to provide assistance to lower tribunals. In rare and exceptional cases, it can hear marriage nullity cases in first instance. In most cases, the Roman Rota adjudicates marriage cases which have been decided by ecclesiastical tribunals across the Catholic world and which have been appealed to it.[28]

Question 37:   What is the Apostolic See?

The Apostolic See, also called the Holy See, refers to the Pope, the Vatican Secretariat of State, and the other dicasteries or departments of the Roman Curia, through which the Pope governs the universal Church.[29]

Question 38:   What is Lack of Canonical Form?

Lack of canonical form, for short, lack of form, is the canonical ground for declaring a marriage invalid in those cases in which a Catholic contracted marriage before a justice of the peace or before a civil magistrate or before a non-Catholic religious minister without dispensation or authorization from the bishop of the Catholic party.

See section 3 of this book on "How to Determine a Lack of Form" case.

Question 39:   What is Prior Bond?

Prior bond or *Ligamen* is the impediment which prohibits marriage by a person who has been previously married and whose previous marriage, except it ended in death, was not de-

---

[28] *Pastor Bonus,* art. 126 and 128.
[29] c. 361.

clared invalid or dissolved legitimately and certainly by the competent ecclesiastical authority or tribunal before the person entered another marriage.[30]

A person who has been previously married cannot enter into a valid marriage in the Catholic Church, unless the prior marriage has been declared null by the Catholic Church. This law applies to both Catholics and non-Catholics, baptized and unbaptized. Even if the prior marriage is believed invalid or dissolved for any reason, it is not on that account permitted to contract another before the nullity or dissolution of the prior marriages has been established legitimately and certainly by the Tribunal.[31]

See section 3 of this book on "How to Determine a Prior Bond" case.

Question 40:   What is Favor of the Faith?

The favor of the faith is the favor or concession which is granted by the pope or by the diocesan bishop to a petitioner who was unbaptized prior to the marriage and who remained unbaptized subsequent to the marriage so that the previous marriage bond is ecclesiastically dissolved in favor of the Catholic faith of the petitioner who is now converting or has converted to the Catholic Church or in favor of the Catholic faith of the fiancé or current civil law spouse of the petitioner, if the petitioner does not wish as yet to convert to the Catholic faith. In a favor of the faith case, the petitioner is converting or has converted to the Catholic Church and wants to marry in the Church or the petitioner does not wish to convert but wants to marry a Catholic in the Church. Thus, the petitioner's previous marriage, which the Church considers valid, is dissolved for the sake of his or her Catholic faith or for the sake of the Catholic faith of the Catholic person whom he or she wishes to marry. Thus, there are two kinds of favor of the faith cases, namely: Pauline Privilege and Petrine Privilege.

---

[30] *CIC*, c. 1085 §§1-2; *CCEO*, c. 802 §§1-2.
[31] c. 1085, §§1-2.

Question 41:   What is Pauline Privilege?

Pauline Privilege is the dissolution of the marriage bond of an unbaptized man and an unbaptized woman in favor of the Catholic faith of one of the parties who has received baptism or is converting to the Catholic faith by the very fact that a new marriage is contracted by the baptized or converting party, provided that the unbaptized party departs from the marriage.[32] The Pauline Privilege is based on the words of St. Paul in First Corinthians, chapter 7, verses 12-15: "If a man has a wife who is an unbeliever, and she is willing to go on living with him, he should not divorce her; and if any woman has a husband who is an unbeliever, and he is willing to go on living with her, she should not divorce her husband. For the unbelieving husband is made holy through his wife, and the unbelieving wife is made holy through the brother. Otherwise your children would be unclean, whereas in fact they are holy. If the unbeliever separates, however, let him separate. The brother or sister is not bound in such cases; God has called you to peace."

Therefore, based on the privilege granted by St. Paul that a spouse can leave a marriage on account of the Christian faith, the law of the Church states that a marriage entered into by two non-baptized persons is dissolved by virtue of the Pauline Privilege in favor of the faith of the party who has received baptism by the very fact that a new marriage is contracted by the same party, provided that the non-baptized party departs the marriage and the baptized party was not the principal cause of the non-baptized party departing the marriage. The non-baptized party is considered to have departed the marriage if he or she does not wish to remain married to the baptized party or to remain in the marriage peacefully without affront to the Creator unless the baptized party, after baptism was received, has given the other a just cause for departing."[33]

See section 3 of this book on "How to Determine a Pauline Privilege" case.

---

[32] *CIC*, c. 1143 §§1-2.
[33] c. 1143 §§1-2.

Question 42:   What is Petrine Privilege?

Petrine Privilege is the concession which is granted by the Roman Pontiff by which the marriage bond of two parties, of whom at least one was unbaptized prior to the marriage and remained unbaptized throughout the duration of the marriage, is dissolved in favor of the Catholic faith and for the salvation of souls.

It is called the Petrine Privilege because it is granted by the Pope who occupies the Chair of Peter. "It is well known that under certain determined conditions the marriages between non-Catholics, at least one of whom is not baptized, can be dissolved in the favor of the faith and for the salvation of souls by the Roman Pontiff."[34]

See section 3 of this book on "How to Determine a Petrine Privilege" case.

Question 43:   What are the Differences Between Pauline
                Privilege and Petrine Privilege?

First, a Pauline Privilege pertains to two unbaptized persons prior to the marriage, and a Petrine Privilege pertains in most cases to one baptized party and one unbaptized party. Secondly, in Pauline Privilege, there is required a conversion or baptism of the petitioning party and as such the Privilege is invoked in favor of the faith of the convert. In Petrine Privilege, however, a conversion to the Catholic faith is not required. If the petitioning party is not converting, then the Privilege is invoked in favor of the Catholic party he or she intends to marry in the Church. However, if the petitioning party is converting or has converted, the Privilege is invoked in favor of his or her Catholic faith.

---

[34] Congregation of the Doctrine of the Faith, April 30, 2001, *Potestas Ecclesiae*.

Question 44:   What is a Formal Case?

A formal case is a marriage nullity case in which two Catholics married in the Catholic Church, or in which two validly baptized non-Catholics married in their ecclesial community or church or before a justice of the peace, or in which a Catholic and a non-Catholic, baptized or unbaptized, married in a Catholic or non-Catholic religious ceremony with dispensation or authorization from the bishop of the Catholic party. Formal case is also applied if the marriage does not meet the requirements of the law for the application of other kinds of marriage annulment cases.

Question 45:   What is a *Vetitum*?

A *vetitum* or prohibition is an injunction imposed by a tribunal on a party which prohibits a party from marrying in the Catholic Church until certain conditions are fulfilled. The purposes of imposing the prohibition on a person are to protect the sanctity of marriage and to preclude the party from contracting another invalid marriage.

The prohibition is imposed in those cases in which the cause that led to the nullity of the marriage is still present in the party and in which little or nothing has been done to address the cause and that the cause might probably render a future marriage invalid. For example, if a marriage was declared invalid principally because of a party's pre and post marital gambling, alcoholic, or pornographic problem which deprived him or her of the ability to assume the essential obligations of marriage and nothing has been done to address the problem, the judge can impose a *vetitum* on the party by which the party is barred from a future marriage in the Church until the issue of the gambling, pornography, or alcoholism has been adequately addressed.

However, there are conditions for lifting a *vetitum*. Most local tribunals have the conditions or requirements for lifting a *vetitum*.

CHAPTER 11: THE PROCESS AND FEES

Question 46:   Is the Annulment of my Marriage Guaranteed?

No. The alleged nullity of the marriage must be proven by the petitioner. The burden of proof of the alleged nullity of the marriage lies on the petitioner.[35] Divorce is not a proof of the invalidity of a marriage. All marriages are presumed valid until the contrary is proven by the petitioner before the tribunal court.

However, some of the ways to increase the chances of getting an annulment are to be forthright with the truth, to do some soul-searching, and to provide as much information as possible on the family backgrounds of both parties and on the attitudes, behaviors, and events that occurred prior to the marriage. One of the mistakes that is frequently made by some people is to focus less on family backgrounds or on the events that occurred prior to the marriage and pay more attention to the events that occurred during the marriage, on the cause of the break-up of the marriage, and on the divorce. Catholic Church annulments focus primarily on family dynamics, defect of due discretion, psychological disorders, intentions, attitudes, red flags, and warning signs which were already present before the marriage took place but which were missed or ignored. The events that occurred during the marriage usually point to the dysfunctionality, red flags, and warning signs that were already present in either or both parties prior to the marriage.

Question 47:   How Long Does the Marriage Annulment Process Take?

First of all, there is no definitive guarantee on how long a marriage annulment case will take from start to finish. For example, some cases such as lack of canonical form, depending on the availability of all the documents and information require, can take up from one day to up two to four weeks. Other kinds of

---

[35] c. 1526.

cases such as prior bond and Pauline Privilege cases can, depending on the tribunal and other facts, take between three-six months. Petrine Privilege cases, which are sent to Rome, and formal cases can, depending on several factors in some tribunals, take between twelve to eighteen months. Each time frame is achievable if the petitioner submits all the documents and information requested by the tribunal in a timely manner, the witnesses respond to the citation in a timely manner, appointments with the tribunal on the part of the parties and witnesses are done in a timely fashion, and none of the parties employs delay tactics to prolong the resolution of the case. In any case, there is no guarantee that at the end of the process an affirmative decision will be issued by the tribunal.

Question 48:   What Tribunal Has Jurisdiction Over my Annulment Petition?

A tribunal has jurisdiction over the following marriage nullity cases only:

1. If the marriage was contracted within the territories of the diocese. (c. 1672, 1°).
2. If either the petitioner or the respondent is domiciled within the boundaries of the diocese. (c. 1672, 2°).
3. If the diocese is the jurisdiction in which most of the proofs will be collected or in which most of the witnesses reside. (c. 1672, 3°).

Question 49:   What are the Steps Involved in the Annulment Process?

A summary of the marriage annulment process in a formal case is as follows:

1. The petitioner meets with his or her procurator, case sponsor, parish priest, or pastor and talks about the annulment of his or her previous marriage. They then begin the process of gathering documents, of answering the annulment

questionnaire of the tribunal, and of completing the applicable documents.

2. The petition and related documents are submitted to the tribunal.
3. The tribunal checks the petition and documents to ensure that the required documents have been completed and submitted.
4. If all is in order with the petition and related documents, the judicial vicar accept the case for trial; otherwise, more information is requested. If the case lacks merit or the tribunal lacks jurisdiction over the case, then the petition may be rejected.
5. If the case has been accepted for trial, the petitioner is notified by mail and the respondent is notified of the petition and acceptance of the petition. A copy of the petition is usually sent to the respondent. The respondent is usually given 3-4 weeks to respond to the citation.
6. Having heard from the respondent or the deadline given to the respondent to respond to the citation having elapsed, the judicial vicar then appoints judges and other officials of the tribunal to the case.
7. The grounds are also established for the case.
8. The parties are notified of the grounds and of the names of the tribunal officials assigned to the case.
9. Witnesses are cited.
10. Witness testimony is collected.
11. The parties are notified that witness testimonies have been collected. The parties are also given the opportunity to go to the tribunal and read the information and testimonies submitted by the other party and by the witnesses. Each party is given the opportunity to submit a written response following the inspection of the evidence, if he or she chooses to do so, within a given time.
12. The defender of the bond submits his or her defense briefs. If advocates have been appointed for any of the parties, they are requested to submit a canonical brief on behalf and in defense of their party.

13. The judge renders a decision in the case, which either upholds the validity of the marriage or declares the nullity of the marriage proven.
14. The parties are notified of the decision of the judge and of the right to appeal the decision.
15. If there is no appeal within 3-4 weeks after the decision has been communicated to the parties and if the marriage has been annulled by the tribunal, a decree of nullity of the marriage is then issued by the tribunal. The decree is then mailed to the parties, and the party who wishes to marry in the Church is then free to do so.
16. The decree of nullity of the marriage, if the marriage has been declared null, is mailed to the parties.

Question 50:   Who Can Petition for Marriage Annulment?

Catholics and non-Catholics alike can petition for the annulment of their marriage to the tribunal in their diocese if any one of the following conditions is fulfilled in the case, namely:

1. The marriage ceremony took place within the territory of the diocese.
2. At least one of the parties is domiciled in the diocese.
3. The diocese is the place where most of the proofs will be collected or where most of the witnesses reside.

Question 51:   Do I Have to Appear at the Tribunal for an Oral Interview?

Some tribunals require that at least the petitioner must be interviewed either face-to-face or by telephone; some tribunals make an attempt also to interview the respondent, and some tribunals use questionnaire. The decision as to whether a party or a witness will be interviewed or sent questionnaire is decided by each tribunal.

Question 52:   How do I Know Whether I have a Case?

Some people have been told that they have a case, but the tribunal did not see any merit in their case. At other times, other people have been told that they do not have a case; however, the tribunal saw probable cause for the nullity of their marriage and annulled the marriage. Therefore, it is the tribunal that decides whether or not a person's petition has merit. If a person's petition lacks merit, the tribunal will usually provide the reason and, if applicable, the possible ways the situation can be remedied.

Question 53:   Will I Meet Face-to-Face with my Former Spouse?

No. The parties, that is, the petitioner and respondent, do not meet face-to-face. Court hearings, the inspection of the evidence gathered in the case, and the other events related to the case are arranged in such a way that the parties come to the tribunal on different days and at different times.

Question 54:   What If My Former Spouse Refuses to Participate in the Annulment Process?

The refusal of the respondent to participate in the process may delay the process, but it will not stop the process. The annulment process will continue if the respondent has been cited and has been given sufficient time to respond, but he or she refuses to do so.

Question 55:   What If My Former Spouse Objects to My Petition for Annulment?

Canon law presumes that every marriage is valid, until the contrary is proven in an ecclesiastical tribunal. It is the obligation of the petitioner to prove that the marriage is invalid. As required by canon law, the tribunal is obliged to notify the respondent of the petition. In some cases, the respondent is cited, and he or she objects to the petition or to the reasons for the petition. The reasons given by the respondent for objecting to the petition may or may not be founded. On the other hand, the reasons given by the petitioner for the annulment may or may not be supported the facts of the case, by witnesses, or by the other evidences in the case. Therefore, whether or not the respondent objects to the annulment, there is no guarantee that a petition for annulment will be granted or denied.

Question 56:   What If I Do Not Know the Address of My Former Spouse?

Your former spouse has a right to be contacted by the tribunal and be informed that you have petitioned the tribunal for the declaration of the nullity of your marriage. There should be diligent efforts on your part to locate the whereabouts of your former spouse. For example, through children, if any, born of the marriage, parents, siblings, or relatives, friends, internet searches, place of employment, etc. The efforts made to know the address of your former spouse must be documented and turned over to the tribunal as evidence of the diligent efforts that you have made to locate his or her whereabouts. The tribunal may conduct its own investigation into the whereabouts of your former spouse. If the tribunal is certain that the whereabouts of your former spouse cannot be located, then the tribunal will continue with the case.

Question 57:   Why Do I Need Witnesses?

Marriage annulment proceedings in the Catholic Church are not decided on the words of the parties alone. The statements of the petitioner and of the respondent, if the respondent participated in the process, require corroboration by witnesses and other forms of proofs. Witnesses help to support the statements of one party or to rebuff the statement of the other party. The nullity of a marriage is not proven on the words of the parties alone;

it must be supported by proofs which thoroughly corroborate the claim of the parties for or against the validity of the marriage.[36]

Question 58:   Who Reviews My Annulment Case?

Documents submitted to the tribunal are treated with confidentiality. Both the petitioner and the respondent have a right to review the statements of the other spouse, if there is one and the statements of the witnesses. The procurators or the advocates of the parties also have a right to review the statements in order to mount a defense on behalf of the party they are representing before the tribunal. The statements of the parties and witnesses are also reviewed by the court-appointed psychological expert for and on behalf of the tribunal. Lastly, the members of the Tribunal staff who have been assigned to the case also have a right to review the materials. In all cases, everyone who has a right to review the case and the psychological expert are sworn to confidentiality.

Question 59:   Is Annulment Not Another Term for Catholic Divorce?

A Catholic Church annulment is not Catholic divorce. The Catholic Church does not believe in divorce. The Church has a duty to protect, defend, and teach the sacred dignity of marriage, which is a source of divine grace and a means of sanctification for the spouses and for the Church. While the parties have a right to challenge the validity of their marriage through a petition for an annulment, the Church has a duty to protect the sanctity of marriage and accordingly has enacted a series of substantive and procedural norms to serve this purpose.

Moreover, in marriage annulment, the Church focuses primarily on the intentions, behaviors, expectations, warning signs, and familial, religious, and environment background of the parties prior to the marriage. What occurred during the marriage are of secondary concern to the tribunal. The tribunal views the post-

---

[36] c. 1536 §2.

nuptial difficulties, problems, and challenges of the marriage as indications and manifestations of the problems, issues, warning signs or red flags that were already present in either or both parties prior to the marriage. The events that occurred during the marriage are seen as pointers to what was already present before the marriage but which one or both parties ignored, overlooked, or dismissed. In addition, while divorce ends a valid marriage and ends it on the date of the divorce, annulment declares that the marriage *ab initio,* that is, from its beginning was not validly contracted and, therefore, does not bind on the parties for life.

Question 60: What Are the Financial Costs for My Annulment?

Some dioceses charge administrative fee, and some do not. However, the administrative fee is not payment for the annulment; rather it a fraction of what it costs the diocese to process a case from its commencement to its completion.

Question 61: I Didn't Get My Annulment the First Time. Can My Case be Heard Again?

The same or another tribunal of first instance can hear a marriage nullity case again if the annulment was not granted the first time and if there is new information or new insight into the case. However, the same or another tribunal cannot hear the same case again based on the same ground. Thus, a matrimonial cause which has been judged by one tribunal can never be judged again by the same or another tribunal of the same grade based on the same ground of nullity unless the sentence happens to have been declared null.[37]

Furthermore, a tribunal cannot retract its decision regarding the validity or nullity of a marriage. "A valid definitive sentence cannot be retracted, even if the judges unanimously consent to this."[38]

---

[37] *DC,* artt. 9 §2; 289 §§2-3.
[38] *DC,* art. 259.

Question 62:   I have Moved from one Diocese to Another. Will my Case be Sent to the Other Tribunal?

If the tribunal in which you were originally located has accepted and cited the respondent in the case, the same tribunal will continue with the adjudication of the case. Thus, a change of domicile from one diocese to another does not necessarily mean that the case will be transferred to the other diocese. "Once a cause is pending, a change of the domicile or quasi-domicile of the spouses does not remove or suspend the competence of the tribunal (cf. can. 1512, nn. 2, 5)."[39]

Question 63:   Can I Fix a Wedding Date with the Church While My Annulment Case is Pending at the Tribunal?

No plans for a future marriage should be made before the parties have received notification whether or not their previous marriage has been annulled or dissolved. There are no guarantees regarding when an annulment petition will be completed and whether the annulment will be granted. Even if granted, there are not guarantees that the respondent or the defender of the bond will not appeal the decision to a higher tribunal, which will further prolong the process.

---

[39] *DC*, art. 12.

CHAPTER 12: CURRENT MARRIAGES AND CHILDREN

Question 64:   Is My Current Marriage Invalid?

No! All marriages are presumed valid until the contrary is proven by the tribunal.[40] The fact that couples are going through difficult and rough times in their marital life does not mean their marriage may be invalid.

Question 65:   Does Annulment Make Children Illegitimate?

No! Annulment does not render children illegitimate. The legitimacy of children is determined by the civil government, and not by the Catholic Church. In fact, the Catholic Church teaches that children born of a valid or an invalid marriage are legitimate.[41] Furthermore, in countries in which there is separation of church and state, there are no civil effects to an ecclesiastical annulment of a marriage. Annulment does not affect the legitimacy of children and other civil law arrangements (e.g., child custody, visitation rights, etc.) imposed on the parties by the civil court magistrate pursuant to a divorce *a vinculo matrimonii*.

As already indicated above, the ecclesiastical annulment of a marriage is a declaration by the competent ecclesiastical tribunal that a particular marriage, which began in good faith, was in fact invalid from the moment of its inception as the Church defines and understands marriage. In most cases, the reasons people seek the annulment of their marriage from the Church are to bring peace to their conscience, to reconcile with the Church and return to the sacraments, to learn from their past mistakes, to heal wounds and hurts that resulted from the previous marital relationship, and to put a closure to that particular marriage.

---

[40] c. 1060.
[41] c. 1137.

Question 66: My Former Spouse Owes Spousal or Child Support. Can the Church Tell Him or Her To Pay the Money?

The civil effects of marriage and divorce such as spousal support or alimony and child support are matters that are within the jurisdiction of the civil courts in countries in which there is separation of church and state; thus, the Catholic Church in these countries does not usually interfere in such matters. However, if a marriage is declared invalid, the parties should always be reminded by the tribunal that the decision of the tribunal does not release either party from any natural, moral, or civil obligations toward the other spouse and any children born of the union.[42] Thus, the annulment of a marriage neither renders children illegitimate nor frees parents from their responsibilities toward their children. The annulment of a marriage also does not free one from any spousal support one party has toward the other party.

---

[42] cc. 1689; 1071, §1, 3°.

CHAPTER 13: THE RIGHTS AND OBLIGATIONS OF THE PARTIES

Question 67:   What are the Rights and Obligations of the Petitioner?

i.   To propose a petition for the nullity of his or her previous marriage to the Tribunal.

ii. To propose the claim on which the alleged nullity of the marriage is based.

iii. To propose witnesses and other forms of proofs (e.g., documents) in support of the claim.

iv. To answer questions put to him or her by the judge and to tell the whole truth.

v.   To be informed of the name of the judge and other tribunal officials assigned to the case.

vi. To know the canonical grounds on which the judge has decided to adjudicate the case.

vii. To be notified of any change of the grounds in the case.

viii. To review the information gathered in the case not already known to him or her.

ix. To respond, if he or she chooses, to the information reviewed in the case.

x.   To nominate a procurator who will represent him or her in the case and who will advise him or her.

xi. To be informed of the status of the case.

xii. To read the final decision of the judge.

xiii. To appeal the final decision of the tribunal, if dissatisfied by the decision.

xiv. To renounce the case, provided that the respondent does not object.

Question 68:   What are the Rights and Obligations of the Respondent?

i.   To be notified of the petition and of the claim of the petitioner.

ii. To agree or disagree with the claim on which the petitioner has alleged the marriage to be invalid.

iii. To participate in this case to the extent that he or she chooses.

iv. To answer questions put to him or her by the judge and to tell the whole truth.

v. To be informed of the name of the judge and other tribunal officials assigned to the case.

vi. To know the canonical grounds on which the case will be adjudicated by the judge.

vii. To propose other grounds or oppose the grounds proposed in the case.

viii. To be informed of any change of the grounds in the case.

ix. To propose witnesses and other forms of evidence (e.g., documents) to prove or disprove the claim of the petitioner.

x. To review at this or another tribunal the information gathered in the case not already known to the respondent.

xi. To respond, if he or she so chooses, to the information read in the case.

xii. To nominate a procurator or an advocate to represent him or her in the case as well as to advise him or her.

xiii. To be informed of the status of your case.

xiv. To read the decision of the judge.

xv. To appeal the decision if aggrieved by it.

CHAPTER 14: CATHOLIC ANNULMENTS AND NON-CATHOLICS

Question 69: Why Should I Petition for Annulment When I Am Not Catholic?

Question 70: Why Should I Petition for Annulment When I Was Not Catholic at the Time of My Previous Marriage?

Question 71: Why Should I Petition for Annulment When My Marriage Did Not Take Place in the Catholic Church?

All the above questions are related. First of all, the Catholic Church has the right to decide who can and who cannot marry in the Catholic Church. Second, the Church determines whether or not a marriage is valid as she understands the teachings of Jesus Christ concerning marriage and divorce. Third, the Catholic Church teaches that divorce or the breakdown of a marriage is not in itself proof of the invalidity of the marriage. The Church presumes that every marriage – whether or not it involves a Catholic– is valid until the contrary is proven. The canonical presumption of the validity of every marriage is not changed by the fact of a civil divorce.

Thus, if a Catholic invalidly contracts marriage outside the Catholic Church, the invalidity of the marriage must still be officially declared by the tribunal. If you were not Catholic at the time of the marriage or if you are not Catholic, that marriage still needs to be investigated by the Catholic Church in order to determine whether it is invalid in the eyes of the Catholic Church and in order for you to marry validly in the Catholic Church.

The same answer applies to a non-baptized person who was previously married. Inasmuch as the non-baptized person wishes to marry in the Catholic Church or wishes to marry a Catholic, it is law of the Church to determine whether the previous marriage of the non-baptized is valid according to the laws of God as understood and taught by the Catholic Church. The purpose of determining whether the non-baptized can marry in the Catholic Church is also to know whether he or she meets the requirements of the laws of the Church for the non-baptized person to contract validly in the Catholic Church.

In conclusion, for anyone validly to marry in the Catholic Church, it is the Church's right to decide, in accordance with it teachings and laws, whether or not the person is free to marry in the Church. Anyone, Catholics and non-Catholics alike, who have been previously married in or outside the Catholic Church, cannot marry in the Catholic Church, unless the previous marriage bond or bonds have been annulled or dissolved by the Catholic Church.

SELECT BIBLIOGRAPHY

1. Primary Sources

Apostolic Signatura. *Declaratio de recto modo procedendi in declaranda nullitate matrimoniorum successivorum initorum.*

Apostolic Tribunal of the Roman Rota. *"Subsidium* for the Application of the M.p. *Mitis Iudex Dominus Iesus."* Vatican City, January 2016.

Communicationes 19 (1987) 16-18.

Code of Canon Law: Latin-English Edition. Washington, D.C.: The Canon Law Society of America, 2012.

Congregation for the Doctrine of the Faith. 30 April 2001. *Norms on the Preparation of the Process for the Dissolution of the Marriage Bond in Favour of the Faith.*

    Available in: http://www.vatican.va/roman_curia/congregations/cfaith/documents/rc_con_cfaith_doc_20010430_favor-fidei_en.html. Accessed November 20, 2015.

Coram Boccafola. 12 March 1998. *Romanae Rotae Decisiones seu Sententiae* 90 (1998) 228-238. See also *Studia Canonica* 34 (2000) 518-528.

Coram Boccafola, 25 July 1989: *Rotae Romanae Tribunal Decreta VII*: 141-150. See also *The Jurist* (51) 1991: 203-217.

Coram Bottone, 20 January 2009. In *Studies in Church Law* 6 (2010) 383-387.

Coram De Filippi, 9 November 2000. In *Monitor Ecclesiasticus* 128 (2004) 338-359.

Coram Monier, November 23, 2000. *Studies in Church Law* 1 (2005) 447-461.

Pontifical Council for Legislative Texts. Instruction *Dignitas connubii*. January 25, 2005. Vatican City: Libreria Editrice Vaticana, 2005.

_____. "Letter Clarifying Some Unclear Points of the motu pro-prio *Mitis Iudex Dominus Iesus.*" October 1, 2015, Prot. N. 15138/2015.

_____. "Letter on the Consent of the Petitioner and the Respondent for the Use of the *Processus Brevior.*" October 1, 2015, Prot. N. 15139/2015.

_____. "Meaning of Senior Suffragan Bishop." October 13, 2015. Prot. N. 15155/2015.

Pope Francis. September 8, 2015. *Mitis Iudex Dominus Iesus.*

_____. September 8, 2015. *Mitis et Misericors Iesus.*

_____. September 8, 2015. *Ratio procedendi in causis ad matrimonii nullitatem declarandam.*

Sacred Congregation of the Sacraments. May 7, 1923. *Decree and Rules of Procedure for Cases on Non-consummation of Marriage. AAS* 15 (1923) 389-414.

_____. March 7, 1972. *Emended Procedure in Cases of Non-consummation of Marriage.* AAS 64-244.

_____. December 20, 1986. Prot. No. 1400/86. *The Process for the Dispensation from a Ratified and Non-consummated marriage. Communicationes* 20 (1988) 78-84.

2. Books

Akpoghiran, Peter O. *Proofs in Marriage Nullity Process.* Ugbugbu Heritage, Richmond, Virginia, 2011.

Canon Law Society of America. *The Tribunal Handbook: Procedures for Formal Matrimonial Cases.* Eds. Lawrence G. Price, Daniel A. Smilanic, and Victoria Vondenberger. Washington, D.C.: Canon Society of America, 2005.

Daniel, William L. Trans. and Ed. *Ministerium Iustitiae,* Jurisprudence of the Supreme Tribunal of the Apostolic Signatura. Woodridge, IL: Midwest Theological Forum, 2011.

_____. "An Analysis of Pope Francis' 2015 Reform of the General Legislation Governing Causes of Nullity of Marriage." In *The Jurist* 75 (2015) 429-466.

Kowal, Wojciech and Woestman, William H. *Special Marriage Cases and Procedures*. Ottawa, Canada: St. Paul University, 2008.

Lane, T. Loras. *Matrimonial Procedure in the Ordinary Courts of Second Instance*. The Catholic University of America Canon Law Studies, No. 253. Washington, D.C.: The Catholic University of America Press, 1947.

Lüdicke, Klaus and Jenkins, Ronny. *Dignitas Connubii: Norms and Commentary*. Washington, D.C.: Canon Law Society of America, 2006.

3. **Articles and Template Documents**

Akpoghiran, Peter O. "The Evaluation of Witness Testimony in Marriage Nullity Trials." In *The Jurist* 70 (2010) 163-185.

_____. "Proofs By Witnesses in Marriage Nullity Trials." *CLSA Proceedings* 76 (2014) 73-118.

Archdiocese of New Orleans, Louisiana. First Instance Template Documents.

Beal, John P. "Diriment Impediments in General." *New Commentary on the Code of Canon Law*. Eds. John P. Beal, James A. Coriden, and Thomas J. Green. New York/Mahwah, NJ: Paulist Press, 2000. 1272-1133.

_____. "Dissolution of the Bond." *New Commentary on the Code of Canon Law*. Eds. John P. Beal, James A. Coriden, and Thomas J. Green. New York/Mahwah, NJ: Paulist Press, 2000. 1359-1374.

_____. "Radical Sanation." *New Commentary on the Code of Canon Law*. Eds. John P. Beal, James A. Coriden, and Thomas J. Green. New York/Mahwah, NJ: Paulist Press, 2000. 1378-1392.

_____. "*Mitis Iudex* Canons 1671-1682, 1688-1691: A Commentary." *The Jurist* 75 (2015) 467-538.

_____. "The Canonical Nullity of the Marriage Process as the Search for the Truth." *Remaining in the Truth of Christ: Marriage and Communion in the Catholic Church.* Ed. Robert Dodaro. San Francisco: Ignatius Press, 2014. 210-241.

Daneels, Frans. "A First Approach to the Reform of the Process for the Declaration of Nullity of Marriage. *The Jurist* 76 (2016) 115-136.

Daniel, William L. "The Dissenting Conclusion of the Judge." *Studia Canonica* 44 (2010) 189-209.

_____. "Motives *In Decernendo* for Admitting a Cause of Marriage Nullity to an Ordinary Examination." *Studia Canonica* 45 (2011) 67-120.

_____. "Brief Notes on the Nature and Challenge of the Decree of Admission of the *Libellus. The Jurist* 73 (2013) 242-251.

_____. "The Abbreviated Matrimonial Process before the Bishop in Cases of 'Manifest Nullity' of Marriage." *The Jurist* 75 (2015) 539-591.

Diocese of Richmond, Virginia. "Determining the Correct Type of Marriage Cases." "Agreement of Understanding." "Radical Sanation Questions and Decree." "Pauline Privilege Questions and Decree." "*Ligamen*." Second Instance Decrees and Forms." "Vetitum and Monitum."

Gardiner, Vincent. "The Separation of the Spouses: Old Law, New Questions." *CLSA Proceedings* 81 (2019) 160-191.

Mendonça, Augustine. "Use of the 'Pauline Privilege.'" *Studies in Church Law* 2 (2006) 403-409.

_____. "Juridical and Pastoral Aspects of a Judicial *Vetitum. Studies in Church Law* 6 (2010) 269-334.

Robitaille, Lynda. "The *Vetitum* and *Monitum:* Consequences of Marriage Nullity or Pastoral Preparation for a New Marriage." *Studia Canonica* 38 (2004) 37-64.

St. Louis-Sanchez, Anthony. "Separation of Spouses *Propria Auctoritate* and the Nature of Ecclesiastical Intervention." *Studia Canonica* 48 (2014) 493-530.

Made in the USA
Las Vegas, NV
31 August 2022